access to history

The Changing Nature of Warfare

1792–1945 for OCR

NICHOLAS FELLOWS AND MIKE WELLS

SECOND EDITION

HODDER
EDUCATION
AN HACHETTE UK COMPANY

Photo credits: p6 Classic Image/Alamy Stock Photo; **p8** Classic Image/Alamy; **p16** Robert Gray; **p19** https://commons.wikimedia. org/wiki/File:Helmuth_Karl_Bernhard_von_Moltke_G%C3%BCnther_BNF_Gallica.jpg; **p24** Popperfoto/Getty Images; **p27** Heritage Image Partnership Ltd/Alamy; **p66** Library of Congress, LC-USZ62-39925; **p79t** Chronicle/Alamy, **b** Prisma Bildagentur AG/Alamy; **p86** Chronicle/Alamy; **p110** Library of Congress, 3c11781u; **p113** Library of Congress, 99447020; **p118** https://commons.wikimedia. org/wiki/File:Carl_von_Clausewitz.PNG; **p137** General Research Division, The New York Public Library. "France, 1795" *The New York Public Library Digital Collections.* http://digitalcollections.nypl.org/items/510d47df-b559-a3d9-e040-e00a18064a99; **p142** Library of Congress, LC-DIG-cwpb-03356; **p145** The Art Archive/Alamy; **p157** Artokoloro Quint Lox Limited/Alamy; **p161** Bundesarchiv, Bild 146-1968-101-20A/Heinrich Hoffmann/CC-BY-SA.

Acknowledgements: Aurum, *The Chief: Douglas Haig and the British Army* by Gary Sheffield, 2011. Cambridge University Press, *Douglas Haig and the First World War* by J.P. Harris, 2008. Cassell, *Warfare in the Eighteenth Century* by Jeremy Black, 1999. Eyre & Spottiswoode, *The Conduct of War 1789–1961* by J.F.C. Fuller, 1961. Houghton Mifflin, *The Enduring Vision: A History of the American People* by Paul Boyer *et al.*, 2008. Longman, *European Armies and the Conduct of War* by Hew Strachan, 1991. Lulu Publishing, *Winfield Scott's Vision for the Army* by Mark C. Vlahos, 2015. Oxford University Press, *A History of the Great War* by C.R.M.F. Crutwell, 1934. Sidgwick & Jackson, *The Smoke and the Fire* by John Terraine, 1980. Spartacus Educational, *First World War Encyclopedia* (http://spartacus-educational.com) by John Simkin, 2012. World War 2 , www.world-war-2.info/statistics/.

Every effort has been made to trace all copyright holders, but if any have been inadvertently overlooked the Publishers will be pleased to make the necessary arrangements at the first opportunity.

Although every effort has been made to ensure that website addresses are correct at time of going to press, Hodder Education cannot be held responsible for the content of any website mentioned in this book. It is sometimes possible to find a relocated web page by typing in the address of the home page for a website in the URL window of your browser.

Hachette UK's policy is to use papers that are natural, renewable and recyclable products and made from wood grown in sustainable forests. The logging and manufacturing processes are expected to conform to the environmental regulations of the country of origin.

Orders: please contact Bookpoint Ltd, 130 Milton Park, Abingdon, Oxon OX14 4SB. Telephone: +44 (0)1235 827720. Fax: +44 (0)1235 400454. Lines are open 9.00a.m.–5.00p.m., Monday to Saturday, with a 24-hour message answering service. Visit our website at www.hoddereducation.co.uk

© 2016 Nicholas Fellows and Mike Wells
Second edition © Nicholas Fellows and Mike Wells

First published in 2002 by
Hodder Education
An Hachette UK Company
Carmelite House, 50 Victoria Embankment
London EC4Y 0DZ

Impression number   10 9 8 7 6 5 4 3 2 1
Year   2020 2019 2018 2017 2016

Cover photo © Heritage Image Partnership Ltd/Alamy
Produced, illustrated and typeset in Palatino LT Std by Gray Publishing, Tunbridge Wells
Printed and bound by CPI Group (UK) Ltd, Croydon CR0 4YY

A catalogue record for this title is available from the British Library

ISBN 978 1471838446

Contents

Dedication

Keith Randell (1943–2002)

The *Access to History* series was conceived and developed by Keith, who created a series to 'cater for
students as they are, not as we might wish them to be'. He leaves a living legacy of a series that for over
20 years has provided a trusted, stimulating and well-loved accompaniment to post-16 study. Our aim
with these new editions is to continue to offer students the best possible support for their studies.

Introduction

This introduction will give you an overview of:

★ The OCR A level course
★ How you will be assessed on this unit
★ The different features of this book and how they will aid your learning
★ Background to warfare in the period 1792–1945

The OCR A level course

This study will form part of your overall History course for the OCR specification, of which there are three unit groups and a topic-based essay. The unit groups comprise:

- British period study and enquiry (unit group 1)
- Non-British period study (unit group 2)
- Thematic study and historical interpretations (unit group 3).

This book has been written to support your study of the thematic study and historical interpretations unit Y315, The Changing Nature of Warfare 1792–1945.

This unit considers the changes in the nature and methods of land warfare during a period of significant change. It analyses the importance of the factors that influenced the conduct of war. It will consider the impact of technological change on warfare. The impact of planning and preparation for war will be considered, both in terms of alliances and also the command structure and organisation of armies. The relationship between domestic factors and warfare is considered. There is also an in-depth analysis of the three interpretation depth studies:

- The French Revolutionary Wars 1792–1802
- The American Civil War 1861–5
- The Western Front and the First World War 1914–18.

How you will be assessed on this unit

Each of the three unit groups has an examination paper, whereas the topic-based essay is marked internally but externally moderated.

- Unit group 1: the British period study is assessed through two essays from which you answer one, and the enquiry is assessed through a source-based question. This counts for 25 per cent of your overall marks.
- Unit group 2: the non-British period study is assessed through a short essay and one longer essay. This counts for fifteen per cent of your overall marks.
- Unit group 3: the thematic and historical interpretations are assessed through two essays which cover at least 100 years, and one in-depth question based on two interpretations of a key event, individual or issue that forms a major part of the theme. This counts for 40 per cent of your overall marks.

For the topic-based essay you will complete a 3000–4000-word essay on a topic of your choice. This counts for twenty per cent of your overall marks.

Examination questions for unit group 3

You will have been entered for a specific unit for your A level, and your examination paper will contain only the questions relating to that unit. There will be two sections in the examination paper. Section A is the historical interpretations and Section B is the thematic essay.

In Section A there will be two interpretations about one element of one of the depth studies and one question. The question will be worth 30 marks.

In Section B there will be three thematic essay questions, each worth 25 marks, and you will have to answer two of them. As this is a thematic paper the questions may be drawn from more than one key topic.

Section A questions

Section A questions on the historical interpretations will be worded as follows:

Evaluate the interpretations in both of the passages and explain which you think is more convincing as an explanation of X. [30]

For example:

Assess the impact of developments in transport and communication on the conduct of war in the period from 1792 to 1945. [30]

Section B questions

Examples of questions using some of the more common command terms and specific requirements for each can be found at the end of each chapter.

The command terms are important and a key to success is understanding what these terms mean and what you have to do.

Command term	Description
Assess	Weigh up the relative importance of a range of themes and reach a supported judgement as to which is the most important across the whole period
To what extent/ how far	Consider the relative importance of the named issue or theme and weigh up its role by comparing it (comparative evaluation) with other issues or themes and reach a balanced judgement as to its relative importance across the whole period
How successful	Consider a range of issues or themes and make a judgement as to how successful each was before reaching an overall judgement about success by comparing each issue or theme

Answering the questions

The A level examination is two and a half hours long. Section A carries slightly more marks than each question in Section B and therefore, particularly as you will need time to read the interpretations, it would be sensible to spend about one hour on Section A and 45 minutes on each essay in Section B. Before you start any of the questions, make a brief plan. Advice on planning both the historical interpretations question and the thematic essay is given on pages 54–6 and 57–8.

The answers you write will be marked against the relevant mark scheme. It would be useful to familiarise yourself with the mark schemes before the examination so that you are aware of the criteria against which your work will be marked. Mark schemes offer guidance, but they cannot cover everything. If you write something that is relevant and accurate, but not in the mark scheme, you will gain credit for it. You will be rewarded for well-argued and supported responses that show evidence of synthesis across the period (see pages 94–7). Marks will not be deducted for information that is incorrect, but you should remember that incorrect knowledge may undermine your argument.

The different features of this book and how they will aid your learning

The book starts with a chronological overview of the major wars which will be explored throughout the main thematic chapters in the book. This is intended to act as a reference point that can be referred to throughout your study of the main themes.

Each main thematic chapter in the book covers one of the key topics listed in the OCR specification.

Each chapter also has a section on the three named depth studies and provides more detail and, where relevant, discussion of any historical debates about that study in relation to the theme of the chapter. The first chapter will look at the conduct of warfare and its impact on the history of modern warfare; the second will focus on the impact of technological change; the third will examine issues around the planning and preparation for war, and the final chapter will look at the relationship between domestic factors and warfare.

At the end of the book are suggestions for further reading.

The headings below outline the main features of each main thematic chapter.

Chapter overviews

Chapters start with a brief overview of the theme and a series of bullet points which list the main issues discussed. The structure of the chapter is outlined and a timeline lists the key dates for the events discussed in the chapter.

Chapter sections

The chapters are divided into sections, each addressing one of the bullet points listed in the overview. The section addresses a key question or questions, and is further broken down into a series of subheadings to help your understanding of the topic. By the end of each section you should be able to answer the key question.

Key terms

The key terms that you need to understand in order to grasp the important concepts and issues surrounding the topic are emboldened in the chapter the first time they are used in the book, and are defined in the margin and the glossary at the end of the book.

Key debates

Historians often disagree about the causes or significance of historical events and the role and impact of individuals. Key debates are listed at the start of the chapter and are discussed in the narrative of the chapter or, where appropriate, in the historical interpretations section at the end. Not only will this introduce you to some of the key historical debates about the period you are studying, but by using your historical knowledge and the information in the chapter you will be able to test the views of the historians, which will help you to prepare for the Section A question.

Chapter summaries

At the end of each chapter there will be a summary of the key points covered in the chapter, which will help with revision.

Refresher questions

There will be a series of refresher questions at the end of each chapter. These will not be examination-style questions, but will be designed to ensure that you have a clear understanding of the main points and issues raised in the chapter.

Study skills

Each chapter has a study skills section. In each section one part will develop the skills needed for the thematic essay and the other part will develop the skills needed for the historical interpretations question. There will often be examples of strong and weak paragraphs and the opportunity for you to practise the skills on relevant questions and interpretations.

Background to warfare in the period 1792–1945

The period from 1792 to 1945 saw warfare change considerably from that of the previous century. In the eighteenth century, war was rarely fought until one side or the other was reduced to total surrender or destruction. Political ideas played relatively little part in what has been called 'dynastic' or 'cabinet' war. The monarchs who fought the European wars of the eighteenth century had similar ideas about authority and did not mean to dethrone their rivals. The commanders were generally nobles who shared a similar outlook and culture with their rivals. The armies were composed partly of men who had been forced to serve, but also of professional soldiers who had little loyalty to a nation. In terms of technology, armies were fairly evenly matched. Battles were rarely decisive in the sense of destroying an enemy's military capacity. Successful campaigns often ended with treaties, negotiated in the common diplomatic language, French. These involved territorial gains and losses, but not wholesale occupation of other countries or what we might call 'regime change'.

Battles were often formal affairs and although there were brilliant tactics and perceptive strategy, the campaigns fell short of mobilising the whole nation. The wars of the eighteenth century have been described as 'limited', but there were exceptions. The war of the **American Revolution** between the American colonists and Britain, which France and Spain joined to take advantage of British distraction, did have a significant 'regime change' and was fought, at least on the American side, for a cause.

The emergence of the new nation of the United States and the ideological element in the war, together with some of the features of the fighting – the use of irregular forces, for example – does not fit this pattern. Neither were all commanders formal and limited in their approach. **John Churchill**, Duke of Marlborough, fought a brilliant campaign of rapid movement leading to

 **KEY TERM**

American Revolution
(American War of Independence.) Britain had colonised the eastern coastal areas of North America since the seventeenth century. By the 1770s, disputes had arisen between the colonists and Britain which led to a declaration of independence. Britain failed to maintain control of the colonies in a war from 1776 to 1783. The rebels received help from Britain's European enemies and set up the United States of America.

 **KEY FIGURE**

John Churchill (1650–1722)
Served William III and Queen Anne, winning a brilliant victory against France in 1704 and important battles in Flanders in 1706 and 1708. He was given Blenheim Palace in Oxfordshire as a reward and his descendant Sir Winston Churchill wrote his biography.

Frederick II ('The Great') of Prussia (1712–86)

Ruled between 1740 and 1786. A gifted musician and a cultured ruler, he was also a skilled commander who fought campaigns against Austria and Russia throughout his reign and gained Silesia and part of Poland. He transformed the way armies moved and fought on the battlefield.

the French defeat at Blenheim in 1704 (although this did not end the war, which lasted until 1714) and **Frederick the Great of Prussia** brought tactical manoeuvring to a new level in his campaigns. However, once again, few conflicts were decisive.

New ideas on military organisation were thrown up in the eighteenth century, although military technology did not develop once the musket with bayonet had been established as the key weapon for infantry at the end of the seventeenth century.

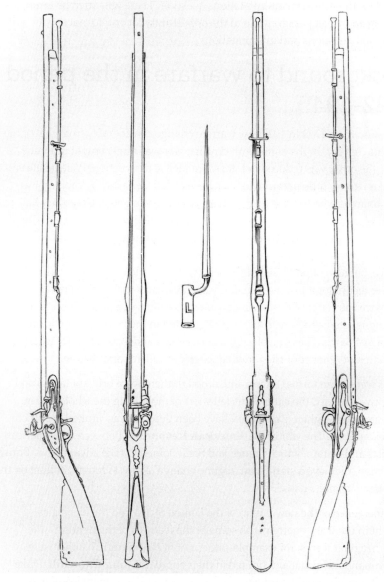

Figure 0.1 A British eighteenth-century musket nicknamed 'Brown Bess' with a socket bayonet.

The Revolutionary and Napoleonic Wars

The **French Revolution** was the signal for a new type of warfare. The overthrow of the French monarchy in 1792 pitted a radical republic against conservative monarchies. The Revolutionary War took on the character of the American War of Independence and led to a new concept – the nation in arms (see page 30).

The French developed mass volunteer forces, commanded by new types of general and supported by the bulk of the population in a nation organised for war. The Revolutionary War 1792–1802 shaded into the Napoleonic Wars (1803–15) as war brought military dictatorship in France, led by Napoleon Bonaparte who declared himself emperor in 1804. No longer were armies more similar than different in aims and outlook. The French aimed to carry the Revolution into Europe and to change forever the old world of kings, princes and priests. From the conquest of border areas in the Revolutionary Wars, Napoleonic forces moved to take over much of central Europe. Not since ancient times had a single commander had such an impact on Europe.

The Napoleonic experiments came to grief as France overextended its lines of communication and supply in the extremities of Europe – Spain and Russia – and could not take command of the seas from Britain. However, at his peak, Napoleon showed a quality of generalship that has led to his being considered more a genius than a general. That concept has been challenged but his record to 1807 is one of the most impressive in all military history.

After 1792, warfare could not easily return to the limited aims of the eighteenth century. However, the sheer costs of the wars from 1792 to 1815 made the European powers anxious not to repeat what was virtually a world war. What had emerged was:

- very large armies
- the need for armies to be supported by the whole economy and society of belligerent nations
- wars fought for great causes
- troops being motivated by inspirational leaders and not merely being expected to be professional 'cannon fodder'
- a mass of military theory based on the analysis of the Napoleonic campaigns.

What was new from 1815 was the development of technology and industry. The wars of Napoleon had been fought by men who had marched into battle in the same way as ancient, medieval, early modern and eighteenth-century armies. Given Europe's poor roads, fast manoeuvres were difficult. The battles were fought in a mass of smoke, and the muskets of the day depended on a concentration of fire and relatively close range. The most famous battle of the war, the **Battle of Waterloo**, became a slogging match and battle of wills.

 **KEY TERMS**

French Revolution Forced by financial problems to call the equivalent of a parliament in 1789, the French King Louis XVI faced increasing challenges to his authority. These led to the overthrow of the monarchy in 1792 and his execution in 1793. The revolutionary governments fought wars with other European states from 1792. The Revolution culminated in a successful general Napoleon Bonaparte taking power in 1799 and declaring himself emperor in 1804.

Battle of Waterloo After defeat by his enemies, Emperor Napoleon had been exiled to the small Mediterranean island of Elba in 1814. In 1815 he returned, gathered support, overthrew the French King Louis XVIII and invaded Belgium, where he was defeated in a hard-fought battle in June 1815 in which the British, under the Duke of Wellington, held off French forces until their Prussian allies arrived. Napoleon was then exiled to the Atlantic island of St Helena, where he died in 1821.

Machine gun A rapid-firing gun – modern weapons can fire 1800 rounds a minute. It was first developed in its modern form in 1861 by an inventor called Richard Gatling but a faster model was developed by Hiram Maxim in 1884. It gave defenders huge advantages and made modern war very deadly and destructive for attacking forces.

First War of Independence Sometimes known as the Indian Mutiny. Grievances of Indian troops ('sepoys') were linked to opposition among some Indian princes to British rule and a general dislike of British interference with Indian customs and religion. After initial successes, superior British military power led to the suppression of opposition.

Isandlwana On 22 January 1879, a British invasion of the independent Zulu kingdom in South Africa from British-held territory was decisively defeated by a Zulu force. The news shocked Britain and Europe as it had been assumed that European military strength would always be too powerful for native peoples. The Zulu leader Cetawayo was a highly skilled commander but could not hold out against superior firepower brought to bear by Britain in 1880.

War of Italian independence After 1815, Austria dominated Italy, which was divided into a number of states. Central Italy was ruled by the pope and the south by the King of Naples. The Italian state of Piedmont led a movement for greater unity and obtained French *(cont'd)*

However, there were changes:

- Transport changed dramatically after 1815. Better roads and then railways carried troops to the front more rapidly without the soldiers having to exhaust themselves from forced marches.
- Whole departments of armies were given to planning and training.
- In advanced industrial countries, bigger, more powerful and efficient weapons emerged.
- By the later part of the eighteenth and nineteenth centuries, battlefields were not obscured by smoke, and men were killed by large-scale precision artillery, repeating rifles and handguns, and by rapid-firing **machine guns**.
- A communications revolution meant that nations were mobilised for national causes and long struggles could be sustained by rallying the whole nation behind its leaders.
- Greater populations could sustain very much larger armies.

The impact of these developments fell on peoples outside Europe very heavily. China and Japan, for instance, could not compete with heavy weapons, more powerful ships and European troops fighting for 'civilisation'. Indian attempts to regain independence in the so-called mutiny of Indian troops in the **First War of Independence** of 1857 had little chance of success in 1857–8 and the

Figure 0.2 A Maxim automatic machine gun.

'mutineers' were symbolically tied to the muzzles of the British Empire's great guns and blown to pieces.

In Africa and Asia, Western military skills and technology swept all before them – with some occasional disasters brought about by overconfidence, such as the defeat by superior Zulu tactics at **Isandlwana** in 1879. However, heavy weapons brought retribution, and military developments underpinned imperial expansion in Europe and the United States.

Warfare also determined big changes in Europe in the wars of the mid-nineteenth century. In the **War of Italian Independence**, relatively short military campaigns in northern Italy by France ended the Austrian hold on Lombardy in 1859, and a whirlwind military campaign in the south by the patriot Garibaldi led to the formation of a new Kingdom of Italy in 1861. War also brought about **German Unification**.

In Germany, the planning and technological skill of the Prussian armies led to rapid defeats of Denmark (1864), Austria (1866) and France (1870–1) to create a new German Empire. These short and decisive campaigns were fought against relatively weak and inefficient enemy forces. What was to be more typical was the **American Civil War** (1861–5), where the forces were more evenly matched until the sheer scale of Northern resources shifted the balance.

Losses were considerably higher than in the European wars, and there were features that came to be common to the later wars of the period up to 1945; in particular:

- War of attrition, which depended for its outcome on the wearing down and destruction of the whole economic capacity of the enemy.
- War where ideology and the fear of losses being in vain prevented any compromise peace.
- Considerable civilian suffering and heavy casualties.
- A degeneration of conflict into brutal frontal attacks from entrenched positions.
- War where the control of transport systems was important and where Napoleonic-style manoeuvres proved increasingly ineffective in the light of more accurate weapons used defensively.
- War where the long-term consequences of defeat were considerable, and the nation did not just 'get back to normal'.

It was a tragedy that military planners assumed that future wars would be as short and decisive as the conflicts in Italy and Germany, rather than seeing the American Civil War as the likely model for the future.

The technological developments of the later nineteenth and early twentieth centuries confirmed that future wars would be highly costly and dangerous. The second industrial revolution from the 1860s had increased the use of steel. Chemical advances had allowed the development of high explosives, and

KEY TERMS

support, leading to French armies fighting Austria in northern Italy in 1859. Fuller unity came when a volunteer force under Garibaldi invaded the south and linked up with Piedmontese forces, leading to the formation of a new Kingdom of Italy in 1861.

German Unification Germany after 1815 was divided and dominated by Austria. The German state of Prussia, led by the statesman Otto von Bismarck, built up its armies and industries and challenged Austria. A joint Prusso-Austrian War against Denmark led to disputes between the victors, and Prussian armies went on to defeat Austria in 1866. France was resentful about loss of influence, and a subsequent war between France and Prussia led to complete Prussian victory and the establishment of a new Prussian-led German Empire in 1871.

American Civil War Differences had appeared between the Southern states, which maintained slavery, and the North, which no longer used slave labour. There were disputes about whether slavery should be extended to new lands in the West. Compromises failed and eventually, when a president opposed to the extension of slavery, Abraham Lincoln, was elected in 1860, most of the South broke away to form its own country – the Confederacy. Lincoln saw this as rebellion against the American Union and fought to force the South back. A long war with heavy casualties on both sides resulted.

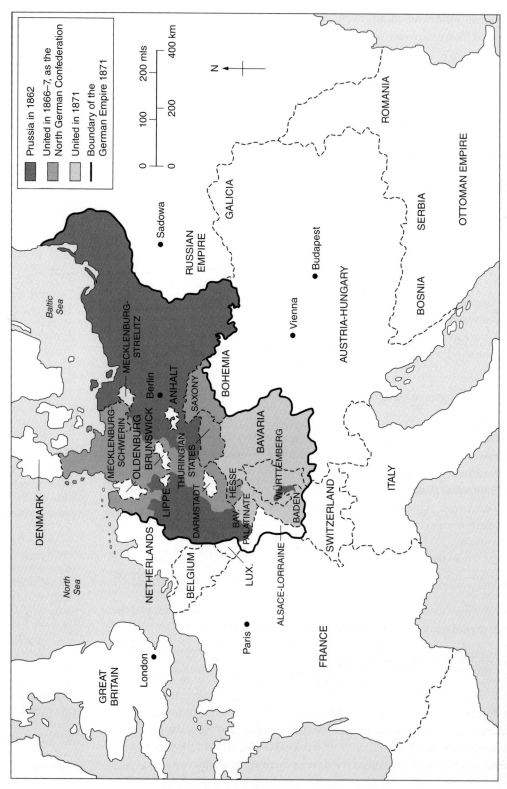

Figure 0.3 The German Empire in 1871.

engineering had enabled the precision weaponry that could produce machine guns, grenades and **magazine rifles**. The battlefield became smokeless, so highly dangerous. Yet, short wars fostered the illusion that warfare could be decisive. Japan defeated China in 1896 and Russia in 1905 using modern weapons coupled with a very high degree of personal bravery and aggression. The Balkan Wars of 1912–13 were short and quite decisive: first of all Turkey was defeated by a coalition of independent Balkan states, which then defeated Bulgaria. The wars led to important territorial changes and the end of most Turkish rule over European lands.

Despite the evidence of the American Civil War and the obvious dangers from very heavy artillery, magazine rifles, machine guns and a lack of cover from smoke, the general belief was that the next war would be short and decisive. This was because:

- The great powers, Britain apart, had developed sophisticated plans with great detail that gave the generals and politicians confidence in early victory.
- There was a strong belief in national morale in all countries by 1914 and that sheer willpower and belief in the national or imperial cause would bring victory.
- The widespread use of quite similar military technology meant that no one nation had an advantage, so the playing field, as it were, was level.

The result was a conflict greater than any previous war. It failed to produce a final decisive battle, and ended with the major protagonist, Germany, having no foreign forces on its soil. No great final campaign ended the war by a Waterloo-type victory. Even though Russia had signed a separate peace, the balance of resources had swung decisively towards the Allies – France, Britain, Italy and the USA. The entry of the USA into the war in 1917 had not brought much in purely military terms, but the potential economic power and supply of fresh troops outweighed the loss of Russia, given that Germany's allies had collapsed.

The war had become one of brutal and costly attrition along the lines of the conflict in the USA in 1864 and 1865. Victory would go not to any brilliant individual campaign such as Napoleon's in 1805–7 but to the side with the greater resources.

The message was not lost on Germany, and when the war resumed after a twenty-year truce, the aim was to act quickly to gain the resources to maintain the struggle. Instead of getting bogged down in trenches, the German forces moved quickly first into Poland (1939) and then into Norway, Denmark, the Netherlands, Belgium and France (1940). German rearmament lacked the depth to sustain a long conflict on the lines of 1914–18 or the American Civil War. It was based on short intense periods of movement which would paralyse the numerically stronger but military weaker enemies. To that extent, it was modelled on Napoleon. German forces also took their ideology to war: just as

 **KEY TERM**

Magazine rifle A rifle is a musket with a groove in the barrel which allows the emerging bullet to spin and to travel further with greater accuracy. Rifles initially remained, like muskets, one-shot weapons requiring reloading each time they were fired. The first breech-loading rifle dates from 1836 – the Dreyse needle gun. Better developed and engineered repeating rifles were the French Chassepot of 1866 and the Colt from 1855. The later part of the nineteenth century saw rapid developments.

French soldiers of the Revolutionary and Napoleonic Wars were motivated by the ideology of the French Revolution, so many German troops were motivated by the ideology of Nazism.

In the end, though, the war of movement had its limitations, and when Germany invaded the USSR in 1941 the sheer distances and numbers of the enemy, together with the problems of fighting in severe winter weather, ended hopes of rapid victory. Once more, a war of attrition set in by 1942.

Military success depended on careful planning and managing resources, and also in co-ordinating air, sea and land resources.

The most brilliant masterstrokes of the war were German, but they did not secure victory. That went to the side with the greatest industrial resources and the most developed scientific and technological capacity. Japan's campaigns in 1941–2 were outstandingly good in purely military terms. German strategy and tactics in the invasion of France were brilliant. The generalship of **Rommel in north Africa** was a feat of arms worthy of Napoleon. The German Ardennes offensive of 1944 was an imaginative and well-executed assault, which was one of the best in the war. By contrast, Allied campaigns were often poorly executed and badly followed up, for example the victory at El Alamein. The idea of invading Germany by means of a long struggle through Italy was strategically flawed.

Russian offensives were pursued with a relentless lack of concern for casualties and relied on an underequipped enemy. However, victory did not go to brilliance, but to organisation and sheer resources. Eventually, the whole history of warfare was transformed by the Allied development of the **atomic bomb** – a symbol of US technical power.

KEY TERMS

Rommel in north Africa
The German General Erwin Rommel (1891–1944) led a special army in North Africa. His aim was to drive Britain out of Egypt, secure the oil of the Middle East and link with the German attacks in Russia. From 1941 to 1942 Rommel showed Napoleonic flair and drove the British back, but shortage of fuel and supplies led to his defeat at El Alamein in October 1942 and he was forced out of Africa. He plotted against Hitler in 1944 and was made to take his own life.

Atomic bomb This was developed in a US-funded project and was based on scientific research into releasing extraordinary power by splitting uranium atoms. Two bombs were dropped on Hiroshima and Nagasaki in Japan in August 1945. It is the only use of atomic weapons to date and it brought the Second World War to an end, initiating a new phase in the history of warfare.

CHAPTER 1

The impact of factors on the conduct of war 1792–1945

This chapter is concerned with military factors, particularly the importance of leadership and how the demands changed over the period. Also considered are the changing nature of armies and the impact of mass conscription. New technology, new types of army and changing leadership led to the development of new tactics. Both tactics and strategy were influenced by military theorists. As warfare changed, so did the demands that states made on their people to wage war. The total war which resulted, in turn, had an effect on the way that war was conducted, and this will be considered.

This chapter analyses these developments under the following headings:

★ The impact of generalship on warfare
★ The impact of the quality of soldiers, both professional and volunteers
★ The development of strategy (aims and outcomes)
★ The development of tactics (shock tactics and the cult of the offensive)
★ The work of military theorists and its impact on the conduct of war
★ The development of the idea and practice of total war (civilian involvement and casualties)

It also considers the debates surrounding three in-depth topics:

★ Did Napoleon's successes in the period 1793–1802 depend largely on his own abilities as a general?
★ How important was the quality of leadership in the American Civil War?
★ How far was the indecisive warfare which characterised the war on the Western Front and the heavy casualties it involved the result of inept military leadership?

Key dates

1792	Beginning of Revolutionary War	1916	Battle of the Somme
1796–7	Napoleon's Italian campaign		Battle of Verdun
1805–7	War of the Third Coalition	1937–45	War between China and Japan
1808	Peninsular War	1939	War between Germany, France and Britain
1812	Napoleon's invasion of Russia		
1815	Battle of Waterloo	1940	Germany defeated France
1859	War of Italian Independence	1941	Germany invaded Russia
1861–5	American Civil War		Japan attacked Pearl Harbor. War between Japan and Britain and the USA. Hitler declared war on the USA
1866	Prussian War against Austria		
1870–1	Franco-Prussian War		
1899–1902	Second Boer War	1942	British victory at El Alamein
1904–5	Russo-Japanese War	1943	Germany defeated at Stalingrad
1912–13	Balkan Wars	1945	End of Second World War
1914–18	First World War		

1 The impact of generalship on warfare

▶ *How did the role of generalship change between 1792 and 1945, and what impact did this have on the conduct of warfare?*

The period between 1792 and 1945 saw considerable changes in the role of generalship. The first and most significant change was probably in the size of armies. Eighteenth-century armies had been relatively small. Large forces could not be easily sustained by the administrative apparatus available. Mass armies could not carry out the precise manoeuvres necessary for the battles of the period. There was also not the will to mobilise the whole population. The French Revolution gave rise to much larger armies. The Revolutionary Wars saw the French Republic organise a mass conscription programme called the *levée en masse*. Citizen armies had to be led in a different way from the professional armies. Enthusiasm for a cause became a vital element in victory and generals had to embody the cause and be seen as inspirational figures. This was apparent in some of the revolutionary generals but reached its high point in the career of Napoleon Bonaparte.

8 May 1796 → led bayonet charge in Lodi

The campaign in Italy, which ended with the surrender of Austria and the general making his own peace at Campo Formio in 1797 and state building in northern Italy, was a major turning point. In 1798, Napoleon invaded Egypt and achieved spectacular tactical victories by deploying his men in modern formations and destroying the Turkish–Egyptian forces in a way which anticipated European colonial campaigns of the next century.

Toulon 1793: - after N was made Brigadier General + commander of Army of Italy

By the time Napoleon returned to France and took power, the main elements of his military leadership style had been established. They were applied on a much larger scale in Italy again in 1800 but more spectacularly in the War of the Third Coalition in 1805. The campaign from 1805 to 1807 against three major European powers – Austria, Prussia and Russia – represents the highest level of achievement and commanders ever since have tried to analyse and emulate it.

In terms of generalship, it can be reduced to some key points:

- Napoleon moved his forces rapidly
- he broke his armies down into self-sustaining corps, moving separately but combining to fight
- he was able to defeat the Austrians at Ulm in September 1805 more by sheer manoeuvre than by large-scale fighting
- he defeated a numerically superior force at Austerlitz in December 1805 by keeping his right flank deliberately weak, luring the Russian forces towards it and then advancing into the centre of the Russian army

- his tactics involved the concept of the advance, the fighting and the pursuit being a single military action; this has been called the idea of the 'strategic battle'
- it meant that the Russian and Austrian forces were decisively defeated by a rapid advance, a brilliantly conceived battle plan and a savage follow-up which prevented the enemy regrouping.

The victory at the **Battle of Austerlitz** in December 1805 led to the rapid withdrawal of Austria from the war. Napoleon marched rapidly and decisively to fight Prussia. His forces were divided but in self-contained units. As soon as the Prussian army was found, the armies concentrated their forces. Napoleon achieved a decisive victory at Jena in October 1806 only to find that he had miscalculated and had engaged with only half of the Prussian army. The other half was tackled by one of the French corps under **Louis Nicolas Davout**, heavily outnumbered.

However, Davout followed his emperor's instructions and his 'mini' army defeated the larger and less flexible Prussian force. The Russians were finally defeated at Friedland in June 1807. This battle was noticeable for decisive leadership from Napoleon. In particular:

- he acted quickly before the Russian army could establish a better defensive position or reach the heavily fortified town of Königsberg
- he launched a heavy attack on the right flank of the Russian position but held back reserves to deal with a Russian counterattack
- a dogged defence of well-positioned French troops prevented a counterattack on the French right.

The Battle of Friedland was fought by 35,000 French troops and 45,000 Russian troops. French casualties were 10,000 and Russian casualties 20,000. The battle was not won without cost and the Russians were not, this time, followed up in retreat, but it was decisive enough to bring the tsar to negotiation and for him to agree to divide the world between Russia and France.

In terms of his personal command of relatively small forces, Napoleon had proved a remarkably successful general, but there were limits to the role of generalship.

At Wagram in 1809, against a resurgent Austria, a victory cost 39,000 French casualties to 40,000 Austrians. There had been key elements of generalship such as a well-planned initial manoeuvre involving the crossing of the Danube, skilfully executed, and a well-judged deployment of reserves to support a key assault. However, the costs were rising.

The later campaigns saw improved enemy forces, larger numbers, heavier casualties, greater understanding of Napoleon's possible tactics by his enemies and much heavier casualties. When Napoleon invaded Russia with unprecedentedly large forces of over 500,000, the nature of his generalship had changed.

KEY TERM

Battle of Austerlitz Fought in December 1805 in what is now the Czech Republic. Facing the larger Russian army on higher ground, Napoleon left his right flank weak to tempt the Russians to attack. He then struck at the Russian centre with the bulk of his forces and was also able to assault the Russians from the rear. This classic action achieved the most complete of all Napoleon's victories. The war of 1805–7 was the high point of Napoleon's success as a general.

KEY FIGURE

Louis Nicolas Davout (1771–1823)
A professional cavalry officer who joined the Revolutionary army in 1792. He was a stern leader who held the right flank against Russia at Austerlitz. The youngest of Napoleon's marshals, he won the Battle of Auerstädt against Prussia and led the rearguard during the retreat from Moscow. He tried to defend Paris for Napoleon after the defeat at Waterloo and lost his title, but was restored to favour by Louis XVIII in 1819.

Napoleon Bonaparte

1769	Born in Corsica
1784	Entered military academy in France
1793	Took part in the breaking of the siege of Toulon
1796–7	Italian campaign made his reputation
1798	Egyptian expedition
1799	Coup of Brumaire, became First Consul
1800	Victory at Marengo
1802	Became Consul for Life
1804	Declared himself emperor
1805–7	War of the Third Coalition
1808	Peninsular War began
1812	Invaded Russia
1813	Battle of Leipzig
1814	Abdicated
1815	Hundred Days and defeat at Waterloo
1821	Died

Early career

Napoleone Buonaparte (he only later changed his name to Napoleon Bonaparte) was born in Corsica. He served as an artillery officer and took a leading part in breaking the British siege of Toulon in 1793 and was promoted to head French forces in Italy. The campaign of 1796–7 was highly successful and Napoleon ensured that his deeds were well publicised. In 1798, he led an expedition to Egypt where he defeated the forces of the local rulers, but the British Admiral Nelson destroyed most of his ships.

Napoleon at his height 1799–1807

In 1799, a coup made him First Consul and he then became Consul for Life in 1802. In 1804, he declared himself emperor. He fought a highly successful campaign against his enemies in Europe from 1805 to 1807, but suffered a major defeat at the hands of Nelson at Trafalgar in October 1805. By 1807, he was master of much of Europe but could not prevent opposition growing. Determined to cut Britain off from trading with Europe in the so-called **Continental System**, he was driven to invade Spain and Portugal, which involved him in war with the British on land (the Peninsular War) and guerrilla war by the Spanish people.

The Russian Campaign and failure

In 1812, Napoleon invaded Russia, whose ruler Alexander I rejected the Continental System and Napoleon's domination. This campaign involved a vast army of over 500,000 men, most of whom were lost. After a costly battle at Borodino in September he went on to Moscow only to find it deserted. He was forced into a costly retreat in the depths of winter. Austria and Prussia were able to turn against him. Napoleon raised more large armies and fought costly battles in Germany before retreating to France. He could not win against Prussia, Austria, Spain, Russia and Britain, and abdicated in 1814. Sent to Elba, an island off Italy, in exile, he escaped in 1815 and returned to France but was defeated finally in an invasion of Belgium, exiled to the remote Atlantic island of St Helena under permanent guard from Britain and died of cancer in 1821.

Napoleon's campaign in Italy in 1796 and 1797 established the legend and the qualities he showed throughout his career:

- he issued heroic and dramatic appeals to his under paid and poorly equipped forces
- he moved his forces more quickly than his Austrian opponents expected
- he had the gift of 'an eye for the battlefield' deploying his troops effectively and outmanoeuvring slower enemy forces
- he knew how to make the most of his successes against weaker opponents through bulletins and reports showing his brilliance
- he developed the style of knowing his men, tweaking the cheeks of hardened veterans, being known as 'le petit caporal' ('the little corporal')
- above all, he knew his trade and deployed his light artillery to maximum effect and had the quality that he looked for most in his subordinates – luck.

KEY TERM

Continental System
A remarkable attempt at economic warfare to counter the traditional British tactic of a naval blockade to prevent trading with France. Napoleon cut off Europe from British trade in the hope of causing unemployment and unrest in Britain. It led to unrest in Europe and despite causing hardship in Britain, it did not lead to Britain withdrawing from the war.

'cult of the offensive'
= attacker will be
victorious regardless of
circumstance

Rapid movement and brilliant deployment did not feature in a march into Russia which depended on logistics and supply more than outflanking and tactical skills. The Battle of Borodino (September 1812) was fought by brutal frontal assault. With 33,000 French casualties and 40,000 Russian casualties it was, like Wagram in 1809, costly. The Russian forces were not destroyed, and Napoleon's entry into Moscow had little strategic significance.

The retreat from Moscow cost Napoleon the bulk of his huge army. The larger forces of the later stages of the Napoleonic Wars were not handled with the same dexterity. At Leipzig in a three-day battle in October 1813, Napoleon lost 72,000 men to the Allies' 54,000. The campaigns of 1812 and 1813 had resulted in casualties amounting to 500,000 a year.

Napoleon never replicated the stunning successes of 1805–7. His final defeat at the Battle of Waterloo in 1815 can be attributed to very determined defensive tactics by his opponent Wellington, who had owed his successes to utilising defensive strategy, and the failure of Napoleon's commanders to prevent Prussian reinforcements. The cream of Napoleon's army was wasted on unimaginative frontal assaults.

Generalship with substantial, but not overwhelming, forces had been a key element and was a feature of the Napoleonic Wars which was seized on. Napoleon distinguished himself by personal military leadership. Thus, the Napoleonic Wars were studied by military theorists and historians largely in terms of the importance of this type of personal leadership. The key elements were seen as:

- Napoleon's brilliant organisation of his forces into corps.
- Napoleon's grand tactics. A small advanced guard would find and engage the enemy. This would be joined by the nearest French corps. The enemy would be attracted. Then more forces would engage the enemy on another flank. Enemy reserves would move in to deal with this new threat. At a vital movement, judged by Napoleon, further reserves including heavy cannon and cavalry would be thrown in to turn the enemy flank. The retreating enemy would be vigorously pursued. Judgements about where and when to start the battle and when and where to commit the reserves were key decisions of generalship.
- The conduct of this sort of warfare needed independent and flexible commanders and highly committed troops. The initial onslaught of enemy forces needed to be vigorously defended. The individual corps had to function semi-independently.
- Trust in the leader and the image of invincibility, which he created, were major motivating elements.

Gerhard von Scharnhorst (1755–1813) and August von Gneisenau (1760–1821)

Prussian officers who introduced vital army reforms after Prussia's defeat in 1806, introducing a new short-service army based on conscription, a reserve army, reduction of savage punishments, promotion on merit and more staff planning. They laid the basis for German military successes in the mid-nineteenth century.

Robert E. Lee (1807–70)

Initially Lee fought brilliant campaigns to defend the Southern capital of Richmond. However, his attempts to invade the North were less successful and he lost the key battle of Gettysburg in 1863.

- When Napoleon's enemy generals were able, like **Gerhard von Scharnhorst** and **August von Gneisenau** in Prussia, to reorganise and restructure forces, it became harder for Napoleon to win so decisively.
- When Napoleon's own tactics were used against him and when his actions were anticipated, then again he was less successful.
- When armies became too big for one person to make these decisions and when sheer weight of numbers was seen as sufficient for victory, then generalship as such became less important.

Napoleon's generalship was a product of a particular period and depended for its success on a number of conditions:

- the lack of effective aerial reconnaissance meant that his divided forces could surprise the enemy
- fighting against much less flexible and much more concentrated forces gave him an advantage
- fighting against poorly co-ordinated coalitions gave his unified command a considerable advantage, especially as he was head of state and commander in the field
- relatively small forces of largely French origin and reliable subordinate commanders gave him a big advantage.

By 1812–13, these advantages had began to decline. Napoleon's larger forces could not really be hidden and in the spaces of Russia could not easily be divided to achieve surprise. Also, his tactics no longer offered much surprise. By 1812, he headed a multinational force not unlike, although on a much larger scale than, the professional armies of the eighteenth century. That intimacy and 'personal touch' had been lost.

The Waterloo campaign was not typical of the way that war had developed in 1812–14. Generalship had become more reliant on large-scale organisation and efficient movement. Its nature had changed considerably by the mid-nineteenth century from the 'wonder years' of 1795–1807.

Wars of the mid-nineteenth century

In terms of the organisation and movement of troops and weapons, Prussia led the way and, in some ways, its generals were similar to Napoleon in seeing the key to success as lying in flexible corps. However, with the advent of the railway, the speed with which troops could be moved was much greater and led to generals being much more absorbed by planning and logistics than was the case with Napoleon. Helmut von Moltke achieved victories over Austria (1866) and France (1870–1) which might be seen as Napoleonic in decisiveness and rapidity.

The American Civil War (1861–5) did see elements of Napoleonic leadership. This was more apparent in terms of high command, in the generalship of **Robert E. Lee**, the most important commander of the Confederate forces.

Helmut von Moltke

1800	Born into a Prussian military family
1830s	Became an expert in maps and planning
1857	Head of Prussian general staff
1859	Weak mobilisation of Prussian forces
1862	Army reforms
1864	Led war against Denmark
1866	Defeated Austria at Battle of Sadowa
1870–1	Franco-Prussian War
1891	Died

Early life

Moltke came from a military family and was interested in planning. He was made head of the general staff in 1857 and introduced reforms to the Prussian army in terms of map work, planning for war and understanding transport and supply needs. He was ordered to mobilise his forces in 1859 when it seemed that Prussia might go to war against Austria, and the weaknesses and inefficiency shown moved him to speed up his reforms.

Key victories

By the time that Prussia did go to war against Austria in 1866, Moltke put well-supplied and well-trained forces into battle very quickly using railways. This was a key element in his victory at Sadowa, which brought the war to a rapid conclusion. He developed planning and boosted the army's supply of artillery. His organisation ensured that in the war against France in 1870, Prussian forces were deployed on the battlefield well before those of France. His tactical skills exceeded those of the French commanders, and the French emperor Napoleon III was captured after a decisive defeat at Sedan in 1870.

Importance

Moltke's genius was essentially that of an organiser, but he was a key figure in the development of warfare. Moltke was not a revolutionary but a solid staff officer, specialising in maps and surveying. His experience of battle was limited to a brief secondment to Turkish forces in a war against Russia in 1839. He was more interested in railways and rifled weapons. Longer-range weapons allowed him to draw his enemy into a central position and rapid deployment allowed for encirclement by the flanks. However, subordinate to daring on-the-spot decisions was the longer-term deployment of forces by railways and the equipping of his troops with the new rifled breech-loading 'needle gun'. Moltke was not an inspirer, a bold and daring battlefield leader; he was an organiser and a technocrat. He took some key ideas from Napoleon, particularly the importance of movement and an independent corps system, but the demands of generalship had changed quite rapidly by 1864.

Like Napoleon, Lee found himself with smaller forces. He too forged a strong personal bond with his men, who saw him in the early years of the war as invincible. His defence of the South from the invasions launched by the North showed a mastery of the battlefield. Lee's strategy of defending Richmond while sending fast-moving forces into the Shenandoah Valley was effective in preventing the North from using superior numbers to take Richmond. At the second Battle of Bull Run in 1862, a Northern attack was met with a rapid and unexpected counterattack from reserves brought quickly into the battle. A daring attack into Northern territory in 1863 distracted the North from its attacks and, although there was heavy fighting at Antietam, Lee was able to withdraw in good order and escape Union attempts to cut his forces off from the South. It showed that the South was capable of attack and able to withstand a heavy Union attack and still outmanoeuvre the North. Lee's defensive action around Chancellorsville in 1863 to prevent a heavy Union invasion was also brilliantly conducted.

Lee, like Napoleon, had an eye for the battlefield; he divided his forces effectively and inspired confidence by some bold strategic and tactical decisions. In other ways he was more similar to Wellington because of his effective defensive leadership. Like Napoleon, though, he found that frontal assaults on well-established positions and the continuing loss of manpower against enemies with greater human resources eroded his reputation.

The Battle of Gettysburg was his greatest failure. He had been unable to secure the necessary high ground and against well-dug-in defensive forces his troops were defeated. With his impressive military bearing and his honest and direct manner when talking to his troops, Lee's image as a military gentleman was in its own way as impressive as that of Napoleon or Wellington. However, it did not win the war. Wars of manoeuvre in the 22 campaigns fought between Washington and Richmond gave way to a war of greater strategic imagination fought on the Union side by **Ulysses S. Grant**.

Grant aimed for railway junctions and for the key fortress of Vicksburg on the Mississippi, whose capture using gunboats as well as army units split the Southern states. He was not a charismatic presence, often accused of drunkenness. He persisted with two strategies which seem more modern. The first was a relentless attack on Confederate defences, which involved costly frontal assaults and bombardments and which drained the South of manpower. This was accompanied by an attack on the homelands of the South, pursued by Grant's ally William Tecumseh Sherman in his 'march to the sea', waging brutal economic warfare and destroying key supplies of food and cotton. In addition, Grant was willing to use African Americans in the Union forces. This was seen as a radical move and deeply shocked the slave-owning Southerners, who often killed any black soldiers they captured. Lee was the Napoleonic tactician, but Grant's way of warfare pointed forward to future conflicts. Both were important but in different ways. Grant and Moltke each showed how the tasks and priorities of generals had changed.

The mid- to late-nineteenth century did not, however, quite see the ascendancy of the organiser over the traditional leader. The **Crimean War** (1854–6), fought between France, Britain and the Ottoman Empire on one side and Russia on the other, did show the importance of leadership skills.

The importance of leadership tended to be demonstrated when leadership was weak. The absence of effective leadership on the British side resulted in a poorly fought war with one memorable incident: the Charge of the Light Brigade. Relations between an elderly and indecisive British commander, Lord Raglan, and his haughty and uncommunicative commander, the Earl of Cardigan, impeded the British war effort. A poorly worded order which Cardigan had not the patience to clarify led to a suicidal British cavalry charge on a major Russian artillery position and not, as Raglan intended, on a retreating smaller Russian battery. The Charge of the Light Brigade has passed into history as an example of poor leadership.

KEY FIGURE

Ulysses S. Grant (1822–85)

A dogged and successful Union commander, he took the key fort of Vicksburg in 1863 and divided the South. Lincoln made him overall commander in 1864 and he persisted in wearing down the Southern forces. He was later president of the USA.

KEY TERM

Crimean War In 1853, Russia went to war with the Ottoman Empire. A rapid Russian advance into the Balkans worried Britain and France, who sent forces to help the Turks. An invasion was made of the Crimean Peninsula to destroy the Russian naval base of Sebastopol and keep Russia from the eastern Mediterranean. The allied forces were poorly organised and led, and the neglect of casualties led Florence Nightingale to take nurses to Constantinople to look after the wounded. Sebastopol was eventually taken but the peace terms of 1856 were overturned in 1871.

The other major war of the mid-nineteenth century was characterised by heavy casualties and indifferent leadership on both sides. The Italian War fought by France against Austria in 1859 was famous for the two costly battles of Magenta and Solferino. The French emperor was horrified by the casualties and brought the fighting to an end.

Wars of the later nineteenth century

The slaughter of a British force in South Africa by Zulu warriors executing a well-staged military manoeuvre in 1879 showed both the importance of military leadership in having 'an eye for the battle' on the Zulu side and the importance of poor British leadership. This was demonstrated again in South Africa by the **Second Boer War of 1899–1902** when superior mobile tactics by the Boer generals de Wet and Smuts led to British defeats. The generalship of Lord Roberts, who replaced his inefficient predecessors, was in the Grant mode by attacking the homelands of the Boers and imprisoning their families in concentration camps.

The wars that Japan fought against China and Russia were conducted by their generals with a disregard for casualties and a reliance on frontal assaults. Modern weapons led to very heavy losses in the Russo-Japanese War and pointed the way to the First World War. However, as both wars were short, the lesson was taken that costly attacks could bring decisive results.

The First World War 1914–18

By 1914, Europe was divided by two systems of alliances and agreements. Germany and Austria-Hungary were allied. France and Russia were allied. Britain had colonial agreements with France and Russia. In 1914, the heir to the Austrian throne was killed by a terrorist based in Serbia, a neighbouring country hostile to Austria but linked to Russia. Austria declared war on Serbia. Russia protested and mobilised its forces. Austria and Germany declared war on Russia. France was an ally of Russia and mobilised, causing Germany to declare war on France. To defeat France, Germany invaded Belgium, with whom Britain was allied, and so Britain declared war on Germany. Italy joined France and Britain in 1915 and Turkey joined Germany in November 1914. The USA joined France and Britain in 1917.

By the time of the First World War, nearly all major countries had developed large general staffs and planning units, and had equipped their forces with weapons of greater power and range than those available to Napoleon. Napoleonic tactics had been possible in the mid-nineteenth-century wars because of the relatively small scale of the armies involved, so there was some link to the past.

However, one feature of the later nineteenth century was the considerable growth in the size of armies (Britain excepted, as it kept only a small professional army). Large-scale conscription had led to swollen forces with large

---

KEY TERM

Second Boer War of 1899–1902 The original European settlers in South Africa were Dutch colonists. Britain gained the Cape of Good Hope after the Napoleonic Wars. When the British abolished slavery, the Dutch (the Boers or farmers) went inland and set up their own states. The discovery of gold, however, in the Boer state of the Transvaal led to British settlers going inland too. As a result of clashes, a war broke out between the Boers and the British in 1899 and lasted until 1902. Initially, British forces suffered defeats. The Boer troops did not fight in the same way as the more formal British forces, relying on hastily improvised troops of cavalry (commandos), often seen as 'irregular' soldiers akin to guerrilla warriors, and were difficult to defeat. In the end, the British resorted to putting the Boers' families in concentration camps and cutting the fighters off from their homelands.

reserves. Generalship now had much to do with managing large forces and moving them rapidly and efficiently. The railway timetable was a major weapon of war and leaders were hardly seen by their forces. The German commander von Moltke ('the younger'), the nephew of the great general of the 1860s, was essentially a prisoner of an extensive and detailed plan; he did not have freedom of manoeuvre as he felt obliged to follow the war plans developed since 1898. The French military leaders were gripped by the 'doctrine of the offensive', which required hazardous frontal assaults, rather than Napoleonic brilliance. Similarly, Russian planning involved a rapid advance into eastern Germany with few real strategic objectives, while Austrian plans involved concentrating on the invasion of Serbia.

The scope for Napoleonic generalship was limited at the start, and became even more limited when the various attacks petered out and the war became static and dominated by trenches. These had been seen before – usually in sieges such as that of Sebastopol in the Crimea and in the later battles of the American Civil War. However, trenches dominated the battlefields in the west from November 1914 and in Russia in 1915. Not even the most brilliant tactics of a Napoleon, a Lee or a Moltke the elder could have done much in this highly defensive warfare, especially when a huge array of heavy artillery and machine guns were brought in to defend the trench lines. Generalship changed from Napoleonic rapid manoeuvres to the narrower problems of breaking through heavily defended lines. Leaders like Sir **Douglas Haig** may have dreamed of cavalry campaigns but were intent on using technology to break the lines.

Plans were more based on techniques for greater accuracy of artillery bombardment, the use of poison gas, or mining under the enemy and planting huge amounts of high explosives. In the tradition more of Grant than Napoleon, the German commander Falkenhayn talked of 'bleeding the French dry' by inflicting casualties in attacks on the highly defended fortresses of Verdun in 1916.

Imaginative leadership, where it was shown, was more in terms of tactics such as using techniques like stormtroops to break through lines, as adopted by the German commander Ludendorff in 1918. Inspirational Napoleonic flourishes were made by the French General Nivelle before disastrous frontal attacks in 1917. However, more typical of inspirational military leadership was Marshal **Henri Philippe Petain**'s dogged resistance at Verdun in 1916, with his famous phrase *'Ils ne passeront pas!'* ('They shall not pass!'), and Haig's call for defence to the end during the German breakthrough of 1918 'with our backs to the wall and believing in the rightness of our cause'.

The final months of the war did produce more effective cooperation between the Allied leaders and more imaginative combinations of infantry, armoured vehicles and air power. However, leadership had involved the deployment of very large forces and their use in mass attacks in a way that was more reminiscent of the *levée en masse* attacks of the Revolutionary War than some of the skilled manoeuvrings of Napoleon.

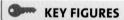

KEY FIGURES

Douglas Haig (1861–1928)

A career officer who had studied at Oxford and had experience of warfare in the Sudan and South Africa. He took part in army modernisation after the defeats in South Africa showed weaknesses. He was a friend of the king and owed high connections to his appointment as commander-in-chief of the Western Front forces in 1915. He fought costly battles in 1916 and 1917 but led the British army to victory in 1918.

Henri Philippe Pétain (1856–1951)

A farmer's son who joined the French army in 1876 and trained as an officer in 1884. He served in north Africa and then as a commander on the Western Front in 1915. He led the defence of the fortresses of Verdun against the Germans in 1916 and dealt with the mutiny of the French army in 1917 with some humanity. He led the French regime that collaborated with Hitler after the French defeat of 1940. He died in prison in 1951.

The First World War generals have been seen as remote, uncaring, 'butchers and bunglers'. However, the number of generals who were actually killed in battle suggests that the commonly held view that generals were remote from the battlefield and sat in luxurious headquarters while their men fought on their behalf is something of a misconception. With large forces, personal contacts were bound to be limited. Haig's proud bearing and confident manner may well have been an inspiration, and he was a respected figure with ex-servicemen whose cause he championed after the war in the British Legion. However, it was not his role, in comparison with the Napoleonic leaders or those of the Crimean and the American Civil War, to take actual battlefield command. The type of leadership model offered by the elder Moltke was more the model followed by leaders of very large forces.

When it came to the **Second World War** (1939–45), the opportunities for brilliant strategic and tactical strokes, as well as the need for macro-managing huge forces and economic resources both increased.

Generalship was something of a mixture of all previous wars. Exploiting resources, planning and ensuring that forces could have as much advantage as possible from better equipment were key elements of generalship. The US General Marshall was essentially a corporate manager rather than an inspirational battlefield figure, as was his British equivalent Sir Alan Brooke, the chief of the Imperial General Staff. Such figures had been important before, like Napoleon's chief organiser Berthier, but now they were the overall military leaders. General Eisenhower, the supreme US military commander in Europe, too, had little actual combat experience, but was an effective organiser and manager.

German initial successes depended greatly on previous planning and on generals like Heinz Guderian who had perfected the planned use of rapid motorised forces supported by air power. In turn, the invasion of Europe by Allied forces depended heavily on detailed planning, secrecy and the accumulation of enough forces to gain local superiority on the beachheads of Normandy. Again, as in the later stages of the First World War, combined operations or cooperation between armies, air forces and navies were key elements in achieving victory.

At the other end of the spectrum, there were leaders with grand designs, none more so than Hitler, who was cautious about the invasion of France, but enthusiastic in his grand strategy to invade and conquer Russia. The three-pronged massive advance into the USSR was one of the boldest ideas in the history of warfare. Napoleonic daring was shown too by the Japanese commander Yamashita, who advanced into Malaya and Singapore in 1941–2, overcoming superior numbers by rapid movement and daring assaults. The German general Rommel taking personal command of forces in north Africa waged a brilliant campaign until shortages of fuel and men ended his run of victories which had threatened the British position in Egypt. The daring use

 **KEY TERM**

Second World War A war that started in Europe over Germany's revision of the Treaty of Versailles, which had ended the 1914–18 war. Germany had broken the terms of the treaty by invading Poland in 1939, leading to a declaration of war by Britain and France. In Asia, war between Japan and China began in 1937 and was extended by Japanese attacks on US and European colonies to secure raw materials from December 1941, starting with the Japanese bombardment of the US fleet at Pearl Harbor, Hawaii. Germany declared war on the USA after this attack. Hitler had invaded the USSR in June 1941. Thus, the Grand Alliance led by Britain, the USA and the USSR (the 'Allies') fought the so-called 'Axis' powers, Germany, Italy and Japan.

of paratroops by German leaders in Crete in 1941 produced a major victory over Britain. The attempt to send paratroops ahead of a rapid thrust into the Netherlands in 1944 in the Arnhem campaign by British general Sir Bernard Montgomery, hoping for a Napoleonic coup, suffered a fate comparable to Lee's invasion of Pennsylvania in 1863, which ended at defeat at Gettysburg. The last great brilliant attack of the war was the last-ditch assaults by Germany on weaker US units in the Ardennes forest. This Napoleonic stroke again failed because of a lack of resources and the ability of US commanders to bring up reinforcements.

Thus, generalship was a mixture of continuity and change in the period. The example of Napoleon's successes was so strong that many military leaders wanted to emulate it. The plan that the German Field Marshal Von Schlieffen devised, and the younger Moltke attempted to carry out, had echoes of the bold Napoleonic campaigns of the War of the Third Coalition of 1805–7, coupled with the management skills of the German campaigns of 1866 and 1870 which defeated Austria and France so quickly. The stalemates of the First World War, so like the later stages of the American Civil War, showed the importance of managing large forces and weapons, as well as economic strength. But they also led to frustration and a determination by leaders like Hitler to return to the days of decisive and imaginative military leadership. This was also shown by Montgomery and, to an extent, the US General Patton developing striking personal styles. 'Monty' took pains to talk directly to his troops and to appear in a variety of distinctive headgear; Patton was famous for his pearl-handled revolver and his tough, gruff manner. This cult of personality was popular with troops and characterful and distinctive, along the lines of Napoleon. It was very different from the grey, managerial style of Moltke, Schlieffen, Falkenhayn and Haig.

Figure 1.1 Monty (right) talks to war correspondents in 1944 dressed in his characteristic beret, jumper and baggy trousers. Haig never appeared except in immaculate formal uniform and never gave press conferences.

The impact of the quality of soldiers, both professional and volunteers

▶ *What impact did the quality of soldiers have on the way war was fought from 1792 to 1945?*

Armies of the age of dynastic warfare

The armies of the eighteenth century reflected the social structure of the period and the aims of the monarchs. They were led by aristocrats, and their aim was to serve not the nation, but the dynasty. They were not intended to destroy rival dynasties, but to gain disputed territories, establish colonies, suppress internal revolts and reflect the power and glory of the ruler. Because of the costs involved, and the problems of maintaining large forces, armies were relatively small. A typical eighteenth-century army might be 40,000–50,000 strong. Armies were based in barracks and fortresses away from the civilian population. They moved relatively leisurely and with slow-moving supply trains. They were rarely more than five days' march from supply depots.

The deployments of eighteenth-century battles placed heavy emphasis on drills and discipline. Armies marched as great units. When they encountered their enemies they usually marched into three lines. They fired single shots from long, smooth-bore muskets. To achieve a sustained fire, precise and fast-loading drills were needed. Thus, the parade ground marching and the practising of loading and firing aimed really to achieve a 'walking musket'. Soldiers were not expected to think for themselves or to seek cover and shelter in a battle. Firing was only possible from a standing position and effective range was only 100 yards. Advance was effective with bayonets fixed to the long muskets in a measured pace with the troops maintaining a strong line. Iron discipline was necessary to maintain the formal lines within the danger zone of 100 yards and the recruits were ferociously trained by seasoned **non-commissioned officers**.

Marching and arms drill were practised incessantly. Uniforms were bright and colourful partly because in the masses of smoke which the guns created, it was vital to pick out one's own side. But more than that, the armies reflected the glory of the monarch. The armies had little room for the promotion of talented but less well-born officers, and did not look for a belief in the national cause. Loyalty was to the regiment or to individual leaders and to one's comrades.

Armies could be international in nature. The Russian officer corps particularly attracted professional soldiers from a range of nations and Prussia's armies depended on recruitment from other nations. The armies which Napoleon took into Russia had many different nationalities and the overcrowded districts of northern Italy led Italians to seek military employment throughout Europe.

 KEY TERM

Non-commissioned officers Smaller units (platoons) were commanded by a junior officer equivalent to the rank of lieutenant; but within the unit there were senior soldiers equivalent to the modern ranks of corporals and sergeants who maintained discipline and could take over if the officer was killed or wounded.

The major change in the nature of armies came with the French Revolution and with the subsequent rise of nationalism. After 1792, the French Republic faced major threats from the professional armies of the European monarchs. France had been a great military power in the eighteenth century, but many officers had refused to serve the Revolution and the new regime could rely on only a core of the previous royal army and navy.

The growth of the armies

France had been the greatest military power in the late-seventeenth century, with a permanent army of around 130,000. In the eighteenth century, the peacetime standing army was between 140,000 and 160,000. In time of war this rose. Louis XIV could raise 390,000 men and in the Seven Years' War (1756–63) France had 330,000 men. The massive recruiting effort of the Revolutionary Republic produced, on paper, 1 million men in 1794. In practice, the peak which could actually serve was around 390,000, while the peak of the Napoleonic armies was 650,000.

The French peacetime forces fell to 75,000 in 1816 but the norm was higher at around 300,000 in the period 1818–54. France raised 590,000 troops for the Crimean War and 650,000 for the war in Italy in 1859, although not all were used. France, aiming to raise a million men for the war of 1870, actually raised 567,000, fewer than Prussia. After 1870, the aim was for a conscripted standing army of 5 million and in 1914, France had 730,000 men in the peacetime force but mobilised 3.58 million men by the late summer. In 1940, France was able to mobilise an astonishing 4 million, some 110 divisions.

Russia had an eighteenth-century army of 200,000 and fought Napoleon in 1812 with 410,000. In theory, Russia's army at the time of the Crimea was 850,000 strong. It mobilised more men in 1914 than either France or Germany. Prussia's standing army under Frederick the Great in the late eighteenth century was 162,000 strong. It raised 335,000 men to fight Austria in 1866 but 1.2 million to fight France in 1870. Its peacetime forces had reached 750,000 in 1913 and it mobilised 3.8 million in 1914. Eighteen million soldiers served in the Second World War, even though the Treaty of Versailles had reduced the army to 100,000.

The Continental army formed by the American colonists to fight for independence from Britain never exceeded 17,000 men, while the largest British troop numbers in America during the war, including mercenaries, never exceeded 39,000. The American Civil War involved 1.5 million Union soldiers of whom six per cent were conscripted and 750,000 Confederate soldiers of whom twelve per cent were conscripted. From 1941 to 1945, 4 million served in the US forces.

The **conscription** of larger forces involved considerable changes in the nature of warfare.

The French Revolution swept away aristocratic privilege and allowed for the promotion of commanders on the basis of talent and success. The hastily-recruited armies involved changes in tactics because the years of intensive training in drill and musket technique could not be crammed into basic training. Thus, the lines gave way to a mixture of lines and dense columns of men used almost like a battering ram against enemy lines, as shown in Figure 1.2. The enthusiasm for the Revolution and *Patrie* (fatherland) summed up in the marching song *La Marseillaise*, together with the vestiges of professional armies, showed that the Revolutionary armies could withstand the trained professionals. Victories at Valmy, Wattignies and Jemappes had a profound effect on the morale of the French and the anxieties of their enemies. The Revolution also allowed the theories of the eighteenth century to be put into action, for example, a more flexible use of artillery advocated by the theorist Gribeauval (see page 40). Similarly, the use of the self-contained corps advocated by writers like de Bourcet and de Broglie allowed faster movement and freed forces from contact with supply depots.

The smaller units of up to 10,000 men were protected by cavalry and artillery, needed fewer supply wagons and where possible lived off the land. The commanders needed to be able to take key decisions, and the troops needed to be able to show initiative at company and platoon level. The rigid line formation gave way to a mixture of column and line. The revolutionary and Napoleonic armies became much less well-drilled 'walking muskets' and more committed and cooperative members of national forces.

KEY TERM

Conscription The calling up by the state of men to fight in the armed forces. Universal conscription spread after 1792 so that every man had a legal obligation for service.

Figure 1.2 French columns and lines at the Battle of Eylau 1807.

With the growth of much larger armies after 1807 and with the introduction of more flexible tactics by the armies opposing Napoleon, the distinction between them and the revolutionary forces created by the war minister Carnot and developed by Bonaparte lessened. Wellington's successes depended on flexible defensive tactics employed in Spain and by well-motivated men sustaining heavy casualties. The Battle of Waterloo was won by a heroic defence of a farm, La Haye Sainte, and by the ability of professional troops to endure bombardment of defensive squares, not by formal lines. Larger forces needed management and the reforms of the Prussian army after 1806 put more emphasis on organisation and less on rigid and mindless discipline. The French had suffered from the well-motivated irregular warfare waged by the Spanish **guerrillas** in the Peninsular War in Spain (1808–13). They also faced intense opposition motivated by devotion shown to the Russian motherland by both the regular Russian army and irregular fighters and peasants during the 1812 campaign.

The armies of the post-Napoleon world became once more smaller and professional. However, the changes of the revolutionary period did not disappear. Although the mid-nineteenth-century wars in Europe were fought by professional armies, the element of national enthusiasm was important. The most impressive results of highly motivated nationalists were seen in the 1860 invasion of Sicily and southern Italy by the 'thousand' volunteers led by the dynamic patriot **Giuseppe Garibaldi**.

The professional French forces, aided by Piedmont, had driven Austrian forces out of northern Italy, but the expedition to the south, which gained popular support, defeated the much larger Bourbon forces of the King of Naples. The expedition resulted in a much larger Italy than originally intended and showed the power of national enthusiasm as much as the French victories of 1792 and 1793. The national motivation was strong on both sides in the Franco-Prussian War. Heroic attacks by German reservists in the face of the efficient French **Chassepot rifles** and the large forces of civilian resistance in the so-called *Francs-tireurs* after the defeat of France's armies, may show the inspring influence of nationalism. However, the wars were essentially decided not by motivation as by much as superior organisation.

The American Civil War had much more similarity to the *levée en masse* and the popular enthusiasm of the Revolutionary War and looks forward to the mass volunteer armies of 1914. The armed forces of the USA had been small before 1861, largely deployed in protecting western migrant routes and in the defeat of Mexico in 1848.

Both sides needed to raise citizen armies and to sustain morale in the face of the casualties resulting from the greater destructiveness of weapons. A strong sense of loyalty to causes was a major feature in sustaining the war, and both sides were willing to sustain heavy casualties without resorting to a compromise peace.

KEY TERMS

Guerrillas Fighters not in uniform or in a regular army who attack enemy forces, often behind their lines. The word comes from the Spanish for 'warriors' or fighters.

Chassepot rifle Adopted by the French army after 1866, the Chassepot rifle was a single-shot bolt-action breech-loading weapon which replaced old-fashioned muzzle-loading rifles. It was efficient and fired more rounds more quickly than the older weapons.

KEY FIGURE

Giuseppe Garibaldi (1807–82)

A passionate supporter of Italian unification. He led a major movement in 1848 for independence. In 1860, he led 1000 volunteers who invaded Sicily and then the Kingdom of Naples to bring the south of Italy to join the new Italian kingdom. He was a hero of the so-called *Risorgimento* (Resurgence) of Italian nationalism.

One of the key features of warfare after the eighteenth century was this inability to end wars by settlement. Most eighteenth-century wars ended with relatively modest territorial changes. Even the Revolutionary War saw an attempt at a compromise peace in 1801, even if it did not last. Total determination to destroy regimes or to bring about a massive change emerged more in the nineteenth century. Even after the French invasion of Russia of 1812, and the loss of hundreds of thousands of men, it was not impossible for a compromise peace to have been reached in 1812, even if by 1814 and 1815 this was not possible. The Wars of Italian Unification (1859–60) led to a massive change in Italy with the emergence of a new nation. Similarly, the wars from 1862 to 1866 saw the total reorganisation of central Europe. The American Civil War ended with the end of slavery in the USA, a virtual military occupation of the Southern states and the imposition of considerable social change.

The engagement of so much enthusiasm made it harder to end wars or to avoid wars having major and irreversible consequences because citizen or national armies invested so much more into the fighting than did the professional forces. The Crimean War was possibly the last of the 'cabinet' wars, and the terms of the Peace of Paris were more like the treaties of the eighteenth century and were changed fairly quickly.

Wars of the twentieth century

By the twentieth century, wars had much greater consequences. The Russo-Japanese War led to a major revolution in Russia and to the Japanese, who were victorious, expanding significantly into China. The huge national pride which led to suicidal charges by Japanese forces at Mukden in 1905 meant that so much 'spirit' was invested into the area that Japan was led to a full-scale attempt to dominate the whole of China in the 1930s and 1940s.

The First World War was the culmination of the national enthusiasm of the Revolutionary Wars and the mass nationalism of the century after 1815. The initial campaigns were accompanied by brutal and discriminatory actions against people of different nationalities, which indicted that this was to be a war where compromise was impossible.

The swollen armies of the late nineteenth century, rather in the same way as the French in 1792, could not easily deploy in small and effective units but were used as battering rams. Technology got the troops to the battlefields but once there the emphasis was on sheer weight of numbers. The terrible casualties, for example, suffered by the French attacks in Alsace and Lorraine in the autumn of 1914 could only be endured by armies committed to the national cause. The limited numbers of mutinies in a war which consumed millions of lives shows that the real forerunner of future warfare was the American Civil War. Conscription had increased in Europe since 1870 but volunteers created the largest British army ever raised. The virtual extinction of the old professional armies in the fighting of 1914 and 1915 left European powers heavily reliant on volunteers and new recruits. With the backing of most of the populations, and fed by patriotic propaganda, these troops sustained a long war. Only in Russia did this result in internal disturbance strong enough to topple the regime. Even after the tsar's abdication in March 1917, the new government felt obliged to continue the war. The poor terms gained by the new Bolshevik regime were a major reason for the civil war in Russia.

If the First World War showed that with mass armies, the nation in arms and intense national feeling a return to the limited warfare of the eighteenth century was impossible, this was more than confirmed by the Second World War.

A lethal mix was a strong military professionalism in Germany, with high-level training stressing the importance of even non-commissioned officers being able to take leadership roles, and a new type of ideological nationalism which was strongly represented in the large armies raised by Hitler's Third Reich. Even more so than the First World War and the American Civil War, this was a war between peoples and not just armies. The guerrilla warfare which was seen in the Peninsular War, the American Civil War and the Franco-Prussian War was a major element in the Second World War, with irregular forces in Yugoslavia, Russia, China and occupied France being met with savage reprisals. Bombing and racial extermination brought war to civilian populations. Citizen armies endured even more horrific casualties – especially on the Eastern Front – and the cities of the belligerent countries became the front line.

During the period as a whole, the advent of the **citizen army** changed the nature of warfare. The citizens had to be engaged with the national cause and not simply be the means of dynastic expansion or glory. This meant that wars became much more difficult to end, short of total and unconditional surrender on the part of the enemy.

It was significant that Grant's nickname was 'Unconditional Surrender' and that it was a stated war aim in the Second World War by the Allied side. The nature of the citizen army affected **tactics and strategy**. Mass citizen armies could not perform complex manoeuvres and so there was a reliance on mass frontal assaults from the days of the Revolutionary War through to the American Civil War, to the deadly assaults of the First World War (for example at the Somme and Passchendaele) and the Russian mass assaults in the campaigns on the Eastern Front.

However, a more educated and knowledgeable body of soldiers, many of whom were willing volunteers allied to increasing reliance on technology, did mean that the citizen armies had to learn quickly more skills than their eighteenth-century and Napoleonic ancestors. By the closing stages of the Second World War, Allied forces were fighting in small units within the larger armies. They were expected to know their objectives and to be adept at handling modern weapons. The complex arrangements of the many Allied seaborne invasions

KEY TERMS

Citizen army Used to distinguish between volunteers and recruits who serve for a short time and then return to their normal lives and long-term professional soldiers who are dedicated to a military life.

Tactics and strategy Tactics relate to how a battle is fought, the arrangement of forces, the timing and nature of attacks, and how defence is organised. Strategy is the wider conduct, organisation and planning of campaigns or even whole wars.

depended on a high level of individual responsibility. The campaigns waged against the Japanese in the Far East in Burma in 1944 and 1945 were very far from the mass charges of the Somme in terms of what was expected at platoon level. The development of night attacks, complex creeping barrages, the use of stormtroop units and the co-ordination of air power, infantry and tanks in the First World War showed that mass armies could fight with a great deal of professional skill and personal bravery.

Despite the changes in European armies, certain qualities remained constant throughout the period.

3 The development of strategy (aims and outcomes)

> ▶ How did the aims and desired outcomes of warfare impact on the strategy for warfare in the period from 1792 to 1945?

The major changes of the period from 1792 to 1945 discussed so far have dealt with the quality and impact of leadership and the size, nature and skills of soldiers. The aims of war changed, as we have seen, from dynastic and limited conflict to more ambitious aims involving the making of new states, the ending of supposed evils, the desire to destroy forever threats to the existence of nations and the wish to impose ideological systems on other peoples. The campaigns of the Revolutionary Wars were markedly different from the wars of the eighteenth century because of the spread of new revolutionary ideas, which accompanied the expansion of French power and influence. The mid-nineteenth-century wars had nationalist aims and created a new Italy and a new Germany, changing the balance of power in central Europe. The American Civil War was motivated by the desire to end the evil of slavery in some parts, and in other parts to preserve the unity of the US union, while the South fought against what it saw as the tyranny of those who would not respect the rights of the American states.

By the time of the First World War, national survival itself was seen to be at stake. Austria feared that an enlarged Serbia would threaten the existence of its empire. Germany feared that it was encircled by hostile powers, France, Russia and Britain. Britain feared that national security was being threatened by militarism, German trade rivalry and a large German fleet. Russia felt that its national status would be fatally undermined if Austria crushed Serbia, the fellow Slav nation that looked to it for protection. France feared that without the alliance with Russia it would never be safe from Germany or able to fulfil its ambitions to recover the lost borderlands of Alsace Lorraine. Higher-level aims thus predominated.

embargo = an official ban on trade with a particular country

… time of the Second World War, these aims had gone beyond security. … Germany had geopolitical ambitions to create a 1000-year Reich, free from … reats of Communism and the economic insecurities of capitalism and … on racial purity. France and Britain looked to free themselves from the … ng insecurities caused by German aggression. After the shock of initial invasion, the USSR saw itself in a position to regain lands lost to Russia and possibly to spread the Communist ideology through Europe. Japan wanted to create an East Asian empire which would make it economically independent from the West and to fulfil its destiny as the dominant Asiatic power. The USA's motives for war were less clear cut, but it set out very clear war aims: the **Atlantic Charter** called for a world based on the principles of freedom and democracy, and implicit in that was the liberal capitalism which underpinned it.

Given the ever-more complex and ambitious aims, the strategies followed to achieve them changed. The eighteenth-century wars of isolated battles and lengthy sieges gave way to much more ambitious co-ordinated plans and overall concepts. Despite the generally held truth expressed by Moltke the elder that no plan survives the first encounter with the enemy, the trend was to devise strategies.

The Grand Strategy

The origin of **Grand Strategy** in the period may be seen as the Continental System of Napoleon. This system was based on the assumption that military defeats could bring Napoleon's continental enemies to the conference table, but British naval power would allow Britain to go on opposing France indefinitely. With the naval defeat at Trafalgar in October 1805, there was no way that a naval strategy could defeat Britain, so the emperor turned to economic warfare postulated on forcing or persuading his European empire and his allies to cooperate to put an embargo on British exports to Europe, to hit Britain's economy and the means of subsidising allies. It was a deliberate counter to the British strategy of relying on naval power, blockading France, using British wealth to subsidise allied armies in coalitions and avoiding large-scale commitment of 'boots on the ground' in central Europe.

Neither strategy was without flaws. Napoleon's led him into overextension in trying to enforce the ban on British trade by occupying Spain and Portugal and then invading Russia. It caused unrest among his allies and within his empire, and did not achieve its objective because of the problems of enforcing a trade ban. The British strategy was highly costly and the coalitions which Britain financed had limited successes for many years. The blockade of France involved conflicts with other European powers and with the USA, and was less effective when France had so much economic control over large areas of central Europe after 1806.

The Union General Winfield Scott proposed a remarkable overall strategic plan at the start of the American Civil War. This depended on a Union naval blockade

1807-14 (S+P)
→ 70,000 troops
→ enforce C.S.
→ poor road network
→ S used guerilla tactics

1812 (R)
→ outnumbered
→ victory @ Borodino + siezed Moscow
→ scorched earth
→ 120,000 survivors

32

·only stopped ⅓ of ships
→couldn't stop British

of the Southern ports and coastline to prevent cotton exports and food imports. The North would use its superior numbers to go on the defensive to prevent any attacks on Washington while at the same time launching an attack using naval and military forces to secure the Mississippi, cutting off the south-east from the south-west.

Boxing in of the South and relying on constricting its economy and supplies would be a long-term strategy for ending the war without heavy casualties. A drawn-out war with heavy fighting might be politically dangerous as there were many in the North who had little sympathy for a long and costly war against slavery. It recognised the value of superior Union resources and naval power. This so-called Anaconda Plan was rejected and Scott's subordinate **George Brinton McClellan** went back to a Napoleonic-type tactical solution of advancing into the South to capture Richmond and bringing the South to battle.

The Anaconda Plan re-emerged in the later stages of the war after Grant took Vicksburg in 1863. However, the Union blockade was not effective enough and two strands were added to the original plan: heavy attacks to wear the South down and a march through the Southern homelands to directly destroy the South's morale and economic capacity. Only possible after bitter fighting had inured the North to death and destruction, this more brutal plan was effective in purely military terms.

Moltke's successes

The rapid victories of Moltke led to a great increase in strategy – even though Prussian victories were based more on tactical elements coupled with a belief in rapid movement. The victories led to a resentful France, which eventually allied with a suspicious Russia. Thus, the threat that German forces faced was of an attack on two fronts over a great area of central Europe, which lacked effective natural defences. The tactical use of railways led to an overall strategic conception that aimed at defeating Germany's enemies rapidly and decisively. Had it worked in 1914, Germany would have been as dominant in Europe as Napoleon had been after his great 1805–7 campaign. Its concept was for a short aggressive war against France using railways to transport a million men for a rapid assault which would encircle Paris and drive the French on to their own defensive positions. Railways would then transport troops to the east. Here, lighter forces would take advantage of Russia's slower mobilisation to defend the homeland until the victorious reinforcements arrived. Superior German tactical skill, weaponry and morale would then defeat Russia, leaving Germany dominant in Europe, with Britain, even if it had decided to join in, without allies. It would lay open the possibility of economic domination of eastern Europe and colonial expansion. However, most of all, it would end the perils of encirclement.

Most countries had military plans, but this Grand Strategy was unique to Germany, and perhaps unique in European history to date, in its ambitions and its colossal imperfections and fallacies. The timetables were disrupted by

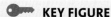

KEY FIGURE

George Brinton McClellan (1826–85)

A professional soldier who was in charge of the key Union army of the Potomac in the Civil War which aimed to take Richmond. McClellan believed in manoeuvring his forces into a favourable position in the manner of Napoleon, whose campaigns he had studied, and achieved little in the way of a decisive battle. He was removed by Lincoln and later stood against him as a presidential candidate.

unforeseen events, and the Germans were left fighting a long war on two fronts which they had very little chance of winning.

Grand Strategy was at the heart of the Second World War because of the nature of the struggle. The rapid and unexpected fall of France in 1940 opened up the chance for the vision of a 1000-year Reich dominating the east to become reality. The flaw in the German strategy to conquer eastern Europe and take its forces to the Urals, and perhaps beyond, was that for it to be successful, Germany would need to have concentrated all its resources, and not to have to be fighting Britain and have the prospect of a war against the USA.

Nevertheless, the scale of **Operation Barbarossa** in June 1941 was impressive, and victory would have brought off the grandest strategic objectives. The three huge attacks against Leningrad, Moscow and the oilfields of southern Russia, if they had worked, would have seen the conquest of the USSR and would surely have brought about the surrender of Britain, and the focus of the USA on its Pacific problems with Japan without war in Europe. Its failure determined the whole outcome of the war. The Grand Strategy gave Britain an ally in the east which absorbed millions of German troops and huge amounts of resources. It made it possible for Britain and the USA to have their own Grand Strategy, which depended heavily on the USSR taking the bulk of the casualties.

The Grand Alliance of nations opposed to Hitler and his allies, Italy and Japan, pursued an unusual overall strategy. With German forces fighting a desperate war in Russia after their initial advance had been halted, the logical move for Britain and the USA would have been to open a second front in western Europe by an invasion in France in 1942. Failing that, the logical position would have been for the USA to recover its possessions taken by Japan in 1942 and defeat Japan, which had directly threatened its interests, before attacking Germany, which had not.

Instead, the Allies opted for a Mediterranean strategy. US and British air power would destroy German fighting capacity by bombings. The Russians would be supplied and encouraged to maintain very costly warfare in Europe. The USA would prioritise the war in Europe, which would be fought in the Mediterranean, first by defending British Egypt and the Suez Canal and then by driving German forces out of north Africa and invading Italy. Only in 1944 did this Grand Strategy involve an invasion of northern France and a steady driving of German forces eastwards. Only then, too, was there a concentrated effort to use massively superior US naval and military power to drive Japanese forces out of South-East Asia. The invasion of Japan planned for 1946 was facilitated by the Japanese surrender after the dropping of two atomic bombs. This was not part of the Grand Strategy.

The trend was for strategies to become more ambitious, to involve more complex planning and to lack realism and coherence. They often overstressed the impact of economic warfare. Napoleon's continental blockade and the British naval

KEY TERM

Operation Barbarossa
The name given to the invasion of the USSR by Germany in 1941. It was the greatest military operation in history, involving 4 million men, 600,000 vehicles and 700,000 horses over a front of 2900 kilometres. Initially successful, its three main thrusts did not achieve their key objectives by the time winter conditions prevented further advance, and neither Moscow nor Leningrad fell.

blockade were not decisive and neither could Scott's Anaconda Plan by itself have ended the war. Ambitious military invasion plans were no more successful in 1941 than they had been in 1914 and it was difficult to predict changing circumstances, such as the rapid invasion by Russia of East Prussia in 1914 and the unexpected resistance by Belgium, which slowed the German timetable. The delays caused by having to send troops into Greece and Yugoslavia to rescue failed Italian campaigns in 1941 meant that heavy winter conditions hit the German advance before they could achieve key objectives in 1941. Similarly, British desire to avoid too much commitment of troops to warfare in the heart of Europe was a feature which may have prolonged war both in the Revolutionary and Napoleonic Wars and in the Second World War.

4 The development of tactics (shock tactics and the cult of the offensive)

▶ *How effective were tactics in the period from 1792 to 1945, and how did they evolve?*

The tactical limitations of many of the battles of the eighteenth century gave way to the more dramatic tactics of the Revolutionary and Napoleonic periods. Already, more rapid movement was affecting tactics, and tactics were resulting in more decisive battles. Having said that, Napoleon found it difficult to permanently suppress his enemies. After brilliant victories against Russia and Austria, for instance, those countries re-emerged as enemies. Also, even after the terrible losses of the Russian retreat in 1812, Napoleon was able to raise further large armies and fight large-scale campaigns in 1813–14 and come back to wage another major campaign in 1815.

The rapid deployment of forces to the battlefield and the existence of much more powerful long-range weapons changed the nature of tactics by the mid-nineteenth century. Napoleon often tried to gain, as at Austerlitz, a central position by breaking the enemy line. Lee attempted this unsuccessfully at Gettysburg in 1863. Moltke used his rapid deployment to lure his enemies into a central position and then surround them. With relatively small armies, outflanking was still of major importance, as for example in Lee's defensive campaigns in 1862. However, traditional tactical manoeuvring was becoming more difficult as the century went on and had become almost impossible by the time of the First World War. This was because the offensive which most tactical skills rely on was giving way to the supremacy of the defensive. However brilliant the manoeuvring, the offensive must carry the day and destroy the enemy. With heavy artillery, magazine rifles and rapid-firing machine guns operating at a much longer range, the offensive became more difficult. Eighteenth-century advances were conducted through a smoke-filled battlefield and defensive volleys from muskets, which were not very effective at a range of 100–150 yards. As weapons technology, despite some innovations, did not change dramatically in the Revolutionary and Napoleonic Wars, effective offensive actions could often follow successful tactical moves, as at Austerlitz, where a rapid advance was able to take the central high ground.

By the mid-nineteenth century, the heavier weaponry had begun to favour the defence more. The Prussian successes of the 1864–70 period owed a lot to the superior firepower of the new rifles. However, more powerful Austrian artillery was a considerable challenge even in a successful battle like Sadowa in 1866. The French artillery and the Chassepots inflicted heavy casualties in battles in the Franco-Prussian Wars. Attacks in the battles in Italy in 1859 led to heavy losses at Solferino and Magenta. The most famous repulse of an offensive was at Gettysburg in 1863, which ended Lee's invasions of the North and any real hope of victory. However, Union losses in frontal assaults such as Petersburg and the Wilderness were very heavy.

There were examples of successful advances with limited losses, such as Garibaldi's campaigns in southern Italy. However, attacks were increasingly costly even if the outcomes were successful. Often the offensives were successful because of enemy weaknesses in organisation or the ability of effective transport to move forces to the front quickly, where they could enjoy a temporary advantage in numbers.

However, tactics were increasingly based on a belief in the offensive, despite the fact that much success in war in the nineteenth century had been essentially defensive, for example Wellington's defence at Waterloo and his brilliant defensive campaigns in Spain and Portugal, when he repeatedly withdrew to heavily defended positions at Torres Vedras outside Lisbon. Lee's greatest achievements were in defensive battles.

Offensives

A number of late-nineteenth-century developments points to the hazardous nature of offensives. There were great technical advantages in steel-based artillery, explosives and fuse technology and the magazine rifle, and the development of powerful and longer-range machine guns. The battlefields became smokeless and the only protection was to dig in. There had been extensive trench fortifications in the American Civil War and in the Russo-Japanese War of 1904–5 but tactics did not deal with the defensive as much as going on the attack. For example, the Schlieffen Plan (see page 114) depended on rapid and decisive advances. Similarly, French plans dealt with advances, as did those of Russia. Austria too focused on a rapid Balkan offensive. The conclusions drawn from recent wars in Manchuria in 1904–5 and the Balkans was that rapid attacks would be decisive and that morale – or, as the French put it, *élan* – would be the decisive element. In military planning and theory there was a cult of the tactical offensive.

Offensive tactics for most of the First World War fell foul of well-established fortifications, barbed wire, heavy artillery, machine guns and ineffective preliminary bombardments. A new feature was air reconnaissance, which eliminated much of the element of surprise. Tactics of manoeuvre gave way to tactics of gaining local advantage and trying to establish a 'breakthrough' by 'a big push'. Both sides seemed to think that once a war of movement restarted then tactics of the offensive could be resumed and success would follow. However, even when successes were achieved, the rapid deployment of heavy artillery and reinforcements for use in counterattacks meant that breakthroughs could not be sustained.

By and large, most of the battles on the **Western Front** brought more casualties to the attackers, but the cost of defence could also be high given the huge bombardments (8 million shells were fired before the Battle of the Somme in 1916) and the costs of counterattacks. Successful tactics did emerge, but little could be done to stop very high casualty rates and any successes achieved tended to be temporary. For example, extensive tunnelling under the German lines and the use of high explosives were effective at Vimy Ridge in 1917, but did not result in overall success. The use of small groups of attackers who bypassed strong points, found weaknesses in the opposing line and opened the way for reinforcements was very effective in the German attacks in March 1918, but the outcome of innovation was to create bulges in the line that were dangerous to defend.

Co-ordinated attacks

The most effective tactical innovation was the co-ordinated attacks by infantry, the newly developed tanks and aircraft in the counterattacks on the Western Front under a united command and an overall *generalissimo,* the French commander Ferdinand Foch. However, this was against a weakened enemy whose allies were on the verge of collapse and who faced the prospect of a large US force arriving in France after the USA had joined the war in 1917. The Allied attacks were more skilful, but the costs remained high and no German territory had been invaded when the First World War ended.

The co-ordinated attacks were deeply studied and formed the basis of the most famous of the tactical advances of the Second World War, the so-called *Blitzkrieg* or lightning war. This had its origins in Napoleonic campaigns of movement and Moltke's brilliant staff work in 1866 and 1870 in the Prussian campaigns against Austria and France.

 **KEY TERM**

Western Front The name given to fighting along the defensive lines drawn up from November 1914 from the Belgian coast to the Swiss border. The fighting on this front in Belgium and France continued until 1918.

In the invasion of France in 1940, rapid military advancement by motorised units supported by air power took the French by surprise. There was no attempt to repeat the mass movement of the Schlieffen Plan, although the routes taken were similar. Motorised units prevented the slow advance that had resulted in stagnation in 1914. Pitched battles were avoided and rapid encirclement of French and British forces was successful. Air attacks ensured that vital communications were impeded by columns of French and Belgian refugees. The front was not allowed to be established, and the French were not given the chance to 'dig in'.

Even so, with more steadfast resistance or more skilful use of reserves, the campaign might not have been decisive; but the French commanders were convinced of the superiority of the defence and that attacks would come to grief against strong defensive lines. In the event, these did not extend to the Belgian frontier and the Germans merely outflanked them. Rapid tactical movement, as in 1805 in the War of the Third Coalition by Napoleon and 1866 by Prussia in the war against Austria, seemed to have ensured victory. It was the basis of other successful campaigns in the Balkans and rapid and effective deployment was at the heart of German victories in north Africa in 1941 and 1942.

However, tactics based on rapid victory were not sustainable in the much greater distances of Russia. When the initial victories of the Russian campaign did not end in the taking of key objectives, the long lines of communications and the absence of back-up in terms of winter equipment were signs that tactics needed to be adapted for a different war. Tactics needed to be much more akin to the attritional fighting of the First World War or the later campaigns of Napoleon and the fighting in the USA. Without the resources needed for this type of warfare, the Germans found tactical brilliance as limited as the occasional breakthroughs on the Western Front.

Commanders on the Allied side preferred to rely on the accumulation of numerical superiority and the use of the huge US resources. The most important British victory of the war in 1942, when Montgomery defeated the German Afrika Korps under Rommel and was able to go on to the offensive for the first time since 1940, was not won by tactical brilliance. 'Monty' relied on having more men and more tanks and guns. His initial plan involving an advance along too narrow a corridor was failing, and only a rapid rethink and the availability of enough heavy armour to make it work saved the day. Had Rommel had more resources, the outcome might have been very different.

The accumulation of massive resources characterised the Allied war effort in 1943–5. Heavy bombing raids on Germany affected its industrial capacity, although probably not decisively. The Soviet production of tanks meant that Germany could not rely on its large tank forces and was defeated at the world's greatest tank battle at Kursk. The extensive planning and heavy deployment of resources allowed the Allies to gain their foothold in Europe, aided by air and naval supremacy. The nature of the war after 1944 was essentially one in which tactics were of less significance than the organisation of resources and the destruction of the infrastructure of the enemy. The breakout from the **Normandy beachheads** was slow and difficult, while the invasion of Germany by both the British and Americans and the Russians depended on wearing down dogged German resistance.

Tactical brilliance

Tactical brilliance was more evident in the German Battle of the Bulge, a daring and well-executed attack in the winter of 1944, than on the Allied side, where a cautious overall US commander Eisenhower relied on steady advancement on a broad front using superiority of manpower and war supplies. Hitler's attack could not overcome the underlying realities of limited German resources. What is remarkable is the persistent determination to resist, coupled with highly effective local resistance. This shows the power of the decentralised German command model, with small units managing effective resistance and making the Allies fight for every inch.

In this context, tactical strokes had limited use. An attempt to shorten the war by using paratroopers to secure the bridge at Arnhem in 1944, and then forcing through mechanised troops to join them and sweeping into the Ruhr from the Netherlands, was a failure because of the unexpected German resistance and the problems of relying on one roadway into Arnhem.

The German tactical successes of 1940 depended very much on weak enemies. By 1944–5, even facing defeat, this was not the case with a deeply militarised and politicised German army fighting for the homeland. Perhaps the greatest tactical success of the war – the successful landings of D-Day in Normandy in 1944 – was a triumph of planning and accumulating men and material. But even this owed a lot to German decisions not to rely on holding the beaches but rather to deploy mobile defences inland; also to German assumptions that the landings would be in the Pas de Calais region and to the massive distractions that Russian attacks made to the German war effort as a whole.

Brilliant tactics on their own were often not enough to secure victory. Napoleon depended on the weaknesses and divisions of his enemies and their poor command decisions, especially at Austerlitz where the Russian emperor, Alexander I, did not see the trap of a weak French left wing. Tactical brilliance could fall foul of determined troops with effective defensive weapons or be rendered impossible by circumstances such as trench warfare, which precluded manoeuvring, outflanking and much of the element of surprise.

 **KEY TERM**

Normandy beachheads
Britain and USA launched the biggest amphibious invasion in history on 6 June 1944 to invade German-occupied France at Normandy. Their forces secured the beaches but found it more difficult to break from these positions into open country and to thrust towards Germany.

Table 1.1 Some military theorists and their theories

Theorist	Main ideas
Comte de Guibert, *General Essay on Tactics*, 1772	Advocated a citizen army whose love of country would motivate the soldiers rather than being merely professionals. He urged concentration of firepower and skirmishers to weaken the enemy line, and a mixture of lines and columns with troops switching from one to the other as needed
Maréchal de Saxe (1732)	Advocated flexible and fast-moving forces made up of column formations with gaps for attacks by cavalry and protected by skirmishers
Jena Baptiste de Gribeauval, *French Artillery Regulations*, 1776	Advocated lighter artillery with standardised parts, concentrating artillery for major effect
Chevalier du Teil, 'A new use of artillery in field warfare', 1778	Advocated greater use of artillery; deployment of light, mobile artillery against infantry
Pierre de Bourcet, *Principles of Mountain Warfare*, 1764–71	Urged the division of armies when advancing to battle and then concentration at the battle itself
Antoine Jomini, *Treatise on Major Military Operations*, 1804–11 and *Summary of the Art of War*, 1838	Stressed the role of the commander in deciding the theatre of war and manoeuvring forces to attack the enemy at the most favourable point. The key elements were the strategic movement of troops, threatening enemy communications and forcing the enemy to fight at a point most favourable to the attacker. Well-trained and well-prepared small professional armies were more effective than larger citizen armies, and the organisation and staff work were crucial
E.B. Hamley, *The Operations of War*, 1866	Argued that the objects of war should be achievable in a short campaign. Strength should be applied to the enemy's weakest point. Economic strength and the provision of supplies were crucial factors
Carl von Clausewitz, *On War*, 1832	For von Clausewitz, war was an instrument of politics, a means of achieving political objectives. It can have limited political aims or render an opponent politically and militarily helpless. Wars fought by nations with stronger emotional and political motivation are likely to be more successful. Modern warfare favours the defender. Within war – hazardous, uncertain and dangerous – the main aim is to bring the enemy to battle and to apply maximum force to destroy him
Charles de Gaulle, *Towards a Professional Army*, 1934	Urged the creation of a regular mechanised army capable of limited war by rapid offensive strikes rather than a defence-based total war
Basil Liddell Hart, *Strategy: The Indirect Approach*, 1929	Thought the concentration of mass forces old fashioned and destructive. Future wars would be won by manoeuvre, cooperation between different elements and surprise. Mobile mechanised warfare was the key. Initial deep penetration by rapid movement using tanks and mechanised vehicles and well-motivated forces supported by air power would avoid the need for mass attacks. This was the origin of *Blitzkrieg*
Giulio Douhet, *The Command of the Air*, 1921	Argued that there was no effective defence against the bomber and civilian morale would be shattered by extensive air raids. Air power would be crucial and ensure that future wars would be shorter

The work of military theorists and its impact on the conduct of war

▶ *How did the ideas of prominent military theories impact on the way wars were fought in the period from 1792 to 1945?*

Throughout the period, military theorists were influential on the conduct of the war. A brief summary of key ideas is given in Table 1.1 (page 40).

Revolutionary and Napoleonic Wars

Much of the work of the military theorists after 1789 was a result of study of the campaigns of the Revolutionary and Napoleonic Wars. The French Revolution allowed the ideas of Enlightenment theorists such as Du Teil and Gribeauval to be put into practice. Napoleon, as a trained artillery officer, was receptive to ideas about the concentration and standardisation of artillery. Perhaps the greatest impact was in the ideas on the rapid movement and manoeuvring of armies. Much was made by the Swiss theorist Jomini and the theorists who were influenced by him of Napoleon's use of the corps system and his flexibility of manoeuvre. This emerged not only from his consideration of military theory, but also from the practical necessity of having to move quickly to achieve numerical superiority when faced with larger but more static enemy forces. The development of general staffs and war academies reflected the importance of manoeuvre and in turn commanders attempted to emulate Napoleon's flexible tactics.

Wars of the mid-nineteenth century onwards

The wars of the mid-nineteenth century reflect the theories of keeping forces mobile and attempting the concentration of force. However, the increasing size of armies and the growing nationalism of the later nineteenth century made Clausewitz a more compelling model than Jomini. War had indeed been used as an extension of political aims in the wars of unification in Germany. The national enthusiasm confirmed his view that emotional and political motivation were key elements. The army came, in France and Germany, to symbolise the nation. War was associated by 1914 with the achievement of political aims and was intended to reduce enemies to political and military helplessness. However, what was not taken from Clausewitz by military leaders who studied his theories was his perception that war would favour the defence. Clausewitz believed in the key importance of the decisive battle – something the First World War generals tried to implement – and after that he believed that defence was the key. However, the massive emotions and enthusiasm for victory which the 'nation in arms' demanded were not compatible with a largely defensive war.

The American Civil War received less attention from theorists and the lessons drawn were largely from the later stages. The First World War was studied intensely by theorists, just as Jomini and Clausewitz had studied the Napoleonic Wars. In terms of practical application, the ideas of Liddell Hart developed by the German General Guderian may have had the greatest impact. The German *Blitzkrieg* attacks of 1940 followed the key ideas. Dive-bombers provided the form of mobile artillery barrage. Fast-moving mechanised units manned by troops with very high levels of training and motivation broke through and carried on, regardless of infantry support or supply lines, to disorientate the enemy. Manoeuvre and speed rather than depth of support and concentration of mass at decisive points were all. Technology and tactics meant that defence and mass citizen armies did not, as Clausewitz had suggested, have the advantage. However, his view of war as an extension of policy – of national and ideological expansion – was confirmed.

What impact did theories have on warfare?

The dangers of reliance on theories based on previous experiences, however, were constantly shown throughout the period. *Blitzkrieg* did not work in Russia and here the supremacy of the defence and the ability of the Soviets to concentrate their forces proved more important. The flexible formations of the eighteenth-century theorists de Saxe and de Bourcet could not work with the mass forces that Napoleon took into Russia. Jomini's elegant theories of manoeuvre being more important than battle did not survive the trench warfare of the First World War. Douhet's emphasis on heavy bombing and the collapse of civilian morale did not prove accurate, neither did his view that the terror brought by bombing would make for short wars.

As staff colleges were created to study war, the theorists obviously did have a major impact on its conduct. The Union General McClellan aimed to emulate Napoleon, as analysed in the work of the theorist Jomini, by his complex manoeuvres with his army of the Potomac, but achieved little. The strength of a nation fighting together – the nation in arms – was an important concept after 1870. It was thought that a united national army would have great morale and thus would fight so bravely and in such a determined way that victory would be inevitable. However, it led to needless sacrifice by mass attacks in the First World War. The *Blitzkrieg* theorists did help with initial victories by Germany, but their ideas, like earlier theories that stressed rapid manoeuvre, were less applicable to vast armies in Russia fighting on an extended front. In the end, Clausewitz probably voiced the greatest truth: that nothing can be predicted in the 'fog of war'.

The development of the idea and practice of total war (civilian involvement and casualties)

▶ How did the idea and practice of total war evolve from 1792 to 1945?

The classic text for the development of total war comes from the decree of the French Revolutionary Convention in 1793.

On 23 August 1793 the Convention decreed:

> *Every Frenchman is permanently requisitioned for the needs of the army. The young men will go to the front: the married men will forge arms, and carry food: the women will make tents and clothing and work in hospitals: the children will turn old linen into bandages: the old men will be carried into the squares to rouse the courage of the combatants, and to teach hatred of the kings and the unity of the Republic.*
>
> *(From Hew Strachan,* European Armies and the Conduct of War, *Longman, 1991, p. 39.)*

Faced with internal opposition and dangers from the British Navy, and the highly trained professional armies of Austria, Prussia and Russia, the French revolutionaries of the period after 1792 looked to the heroism of the Roman Republic of the ancient world. Among these notions of heroism were the ideas that war would be won by the nation with the greatest 'virtue' and by the strength and unity of 'the people', and that nothing could resist the moral force of the nation in arms. These were not just ideas but were used to justify their actions in warfare too. The revolutionaries argued that the *Patrie* or revolutionary homeland had the right to take all resources, end the distinction between civilian and soldier, enforce a military-style discipline on all citizens, punish profiteering, defeatism and political opposition, and conscript any citizen. The total resources of the nation would be employed to defend the Revolution and win the war. The ideology of the Revolution would be confirmed by victory and spread to lands conquered by the Republic.

These concepts were at considerable variance with previous wars and did not really re-emerge in Europe until the twentieth century, but they were of major importance in the development of warfare after 1792, as Clausewitz saw.

- *Involvement of civilians in warfare.* Civilians had always suffered from war, from the ravages of armies passing through their land, from enforced military service, from the loss of family and loved ones. However, there was a distinction between civilians and military. Exceptions were guerrilla warfare, which brought savage reprisals as in Spain in 1808–14 and in the

Franco-Prussian War. In the First World War the distinctions became blurred as nations pressed their populations and resources into a total war effort. Occupied areas like Belgium were treated badly by Germany, their citizens placed under military rule and deported. Austrian forces committed atrocities and were repressive to civilian areas under their control, as in Serbia. Russian forces in Germany in 1914 did not respect civilian rights. Bombing raids and long-range bombardments involved deliberate civilian casualties. By the time of the Second World War, which involved more occupation of civilians and greater bombing, there was even less distinction. The tradition of the nation in arms was such that every citizen could be seen as a legitimate target. The British perfected firebombing techniques to inflict the maximum damage to homes and civilian loss of life as much as the German bombing raids and reprisals in occupied territories. The war also included assaults on whole civilian populations and races. One historian has seen the Holocaust and the death of 6 million Jews as 'the War against the Jews'. Russian policy was to evacuate whole populations considered as likely or actual collaborators with the Germans.

- *The control of resources.* Monarchs had taxed their subjects and requisitioned materials, but the size of armies restricted the scope for economic controls and costs. The growth in army size and the greater costs resulting from technological changes meant increasing control of resources by the state for total war. Napoleon's forces had lived off the land and Sherman and Grant had made economic destruction a weapon of war. The French Revolution had set the precedent for state control of prices, but the First World War carried militarisation much further into everyday life as states controlled transport, livestock and prices, and introduced rationing in the face of economic warfare. The Second World War involved much greater controls because the administrative experience of the First World War facilitated the growth of government controls. Germany and the USSR were already totalitarian states, but even their control over resources increased as war became more desperate and costly.

The German propaganda minister Goebbels' speech in 1943 has many echoes of the Convention of 1792.

We are all children of our people, forged together by this most critical hour of our national history. We promise you, we promise the front, we promise the Führer, that we will mould together the homeland into a force on which the Führer and his fighting soldiers can rely on absolutely and blindly. We pledge to do all in our life and work that is necessary for victory. We will fill our hearts with the political passion, with the ever-burning fire that blazed during the great struggles of the party and the state. Never during this war will we fall prey to the false and hypocritical objectivism that has brought the German nation so much misfortune over its history.

Chapter summary

The nature of generalship changed quite radically from 1792 to 1945 in some respects. Large-scale planning, the management of resources, the use of technology and the grasp of logistics became more important than merely brilliance on the battlefield by the later stages of the Second World War. The increase in the sheer size of armies, the need to maintain alliances and the political aspects of military leadership loomed larger in the twentieth century than they had in the Revolutionary and Napoleonic Wars. The importance in the early period, however, of 'an eye for the battlefield', of maintaining morale and radiating confidence and of taking key tactical decisions became less significant. However, leadership skills in many ways remained constant through the period.

The development of mass citizen armies was a major change of the period and they had to be led and managed, organised and supplied in a different way from the smaller forces of the eighteenth century. As well as the sheer size of forces, the nature of war and its objectives changed. Strategies had to be devised which would lead to total and complete victory, given the increasing difficulties of a compromise peace after 1801–3. Tactics had to change too, given the increasing problems of large armies operating in secret or remaining unobserved. The Napoleonic Wars gave rise to considerable military analysis, and military theory had a far greater effect on the conduct of war as training and planning assumed much greater importance. Vast armies, detailed planning, the obvious importance of economic strength and technological development, together with the rise of nationalism and great political ideologies, saw an inexorable development towards total war.

With the entire population vital for the war effort, less and less difference was observed between combatants and non-combatants. The destruction of cities, hospitals, factories and homes eroded the will of the enemy to continue and so became a legitimate means of waging war. At the start of the period, the British novelist Jane Austen was writing in a time of war but there is little direct reference to its events. By the end of the period, it is difficult to see how such a level of detachment would have been possible as civilian and military lives were so merged.

Refresher questions

Use these questions to remind yourself of the key material covered in this chapter.

1 What were the key features of dynastic warfare before 1792?

2 How did the Revolutionary War change warfare?

3 What were the key features of Napoleon's military generalship?

4 What contribution did Moltke make to military generalship?

5 What was the difference between Lee's and Grant's generalships?

6 What characterised military leadership during the First World War?

7 By the time of the Second World War how had the requirements of military leadership changed?

8 What was so important about universal conscription in the conduct of war?

9 What changes in the quality of troops took place between 1792 and 1945?

10 What is the difference between strategy and tactics?

11 Which of the military theorists in this chapter do you think was most important in changing the nature of warfare?

12 Why did twentieth-century wars have more impact than earlier wars on the civilian populations?

13 What is meant by total war?

14 Why was warfare so much more total in the Second World War than in previous wars?

In-depth studies and key debates

The examination requires you to study three topics in depth and for this unit they are:

- The French Revolutionary Wars 1792–1802
- The American Civil War 1861–5
- The Western Front and the First World War 1914–18.

This section will go into more detail about these periods and introduce you to some of the key debates about changes in the conduct of warfare so that you will have enough depth of knowledge to be able to evaluate passages that are set on any of these topics.

Key debate 1: did Napoleon's successes in the period 1793–1802 depend largely on his own abilities as a general?

There has been much debate about the importance of military leadership. Discussion has centred on whether dynamic leaders like Napoleon were the key factor in the development of warfare. The alternatives to consider are whether technological developments such as the use of more flexible artillery were more important and whether the organisation of armies had more significance than individual decisions about tactics and strategy. For example:

- the sheer size of armies grew
- the 'nation in arms' meant that new tactics had to be adopted
- the citizen armies had greater motivation.

The Revolution brought about new opportunities for talented commanders like Bonaparte to rise. It also enabled key military ideas that had been discussed in French military academies and among the high command to be put into practice. Commanders like Bonaparte and Augereau were not innovative thinkers and they did not inaugurate key changes, particularly in the development of artillery. The fact that they were not from the privileged aristocracy of France did not in itself mean that they would be open to new ideas. The idea of self-contained divisions came from the Marshal de Saxe, a member of one of France's aristocratic families. The armies which the new French leaders commanded were larger than those of their opponents in some cases. The initial threat to the Revolution by Prussian invasion was met by the raising of very large French forces organised by Carnot (see Chapter 4, page 138) and supplied by rigorous confiscation of military supplies and appropriation of resources, workshops and factories.

The difference between mercenary forces and a 'nation in arms' was that soldiers fighting for a cause gave the new leaders an enthusiastic and committed body of troops. It also allowed them to trust their forces far more than had been the case in the wars of the kings of the eighteenth century. Tighter discipline was needed to prevent desertion, and armies moved in a unitary fashion with slow-moving supply trains and the need for depots of supplies. The new armies could be more easily broken up into self-contained corps and could move much more rapidly. The failure of their opponents to develop new organisation was also crucial. This became less important during the Napoleonic Wars, but the aristocratic generals of Austria and Prussia found it difficult to deal with fast-moving forces of committed armies.

The case against Napoleon's leadership

Thus, it could be argued that context was all and that individual leadership, such as that of Bonaparte at Toulon (1793) and during the Italian campaign (1796–7), was not important. For some historians, the Italian campaign was not the glittering success for Bonaparte that he claimed:

- Bonaparte inherited a strong force of 41,000 effective well-trained troops hardened by two years of mountain warfare. Its enemies were divided between 25,000 men of the Piedmontese army and 38,000 Austrians.
- He was lucky in that an initial assault on the fortress of Ceva had failed but the Austrians withdrew in order to link up with the Piedmontese; he was then lucky because the Piedmontese, without having been defeated, made a peace with France.
- He broke conventional rules by marching through the neutral territory of Parma and fought a costly and unnecessary battle at Lodi, which passed into legend. The long and unsuccessful siege of the Austrian stronghold at Mantua does not appear in the legend, however.
- Napoleon's unscrupulous plunder of the Italian territory he captured provoked violent unrest. An Austrian counterattack was fought off in July 1796 and this owed much to Bonaparte's troops. The Austrian peasants were outfought by the aggressive soldiers of the Italian army.
- Austrian attacks caught Bonaparte's forces both dispersed and unprepared. In November 1796 he was in despair. His victory over the Austrian General Alvinzi at Arcola owed much to an unnecessary retreat by the Austrians.
- At the crucial battle of Rivoli in January 1797, French troops were outmanoeuvred but the Austrian forces were beaten in a violent slogging match.
- The triumph that many see exacted at the peace which followed, left Austria with the great prize of Venice at the expense of surrendering indefensible Belgium. The French abandoned their claim to the Rhine frontier, to Austria's advantage, and in return were given Lombardy, which had no direct land frontier with mainland France. Warfare had not brought a much more decisive result than the cabinet wars of the previous century.

The case for Napoleon's leadership

Against this unfavourable view, other military studies see leadership as the most significant element. Some see Bonaparte as the key:

- It was he who regrouped the army of Italy to constitute an offensive mass.
- He inspired his men by leading a storming column across the Adda bridge at Lodi.
- He repulsed counterattacks, making full use of interior lines of communication.
- He concentrated his forces against separate Austrian counterattacks and it was he who shattered Austrian morale.
- To his historical admirers, Napoleon was the leader who took over a neglected, ill-disciplined and largely demoralised force and had a clear strategy to lead it to victory.
- He used the 'strategy of the central position' by concentrating on the centre of widely deployed enemy forces. The Italian campaign meant, in the words of one admirer, 'Bonaparte's apprenticeship was over. The Eagle had found wings, beak and talons.'

How important was Napoleon's reliance on earlier theorists and developments?

Even those who regard Napoleon Bonaparte as the major figure see him as being influenced by preceding theorists like Guibert; but it was not the inheritance or the weakness of his enemies that brought victory, but the qualities of what one historian called, 'a young Corsican devil who does not respect the classic principles of war, who takes scandalous risks and who is everywhere at the same time.'

More technical military studies attribute Napoleon's victory at Arcola to the sophistication of the 'mixed order', positioning skirmishing troops ahead of the line and mixing columns of men with lines. Cavalry, artillery, columns of infantry and lines of infantry were combined. This achieved more flexibility and was a result of previous experience, military theory and having available troops who were trained and flexible enough to move from column to line. Napoleon was in ultimate charge and must take credit for the deployment, but the tools he had to hand had been formed by the experience of war since 1792.

Key debate 2: how important was the quality of leadership in the American Civil War?

Explanations which attribute high importance to the quality of leadership as determining the outcome of the American Civil War tend to contrast the strengths of Grant and Sherman with the more limited military abilities of McClellan in the earlier part of the war. It was this weakness, together with the superior military skills of Lee, that allowed the war to last for so long and to give the North the greater advantage of resources.

Leadership and resources

However, resources alone were not the key. Only when Lee failed and when Grant was able to use resources effectively was the war ended. Thus, military leadership can be seen as the dominant factor.

Strategy

The strategy of Grant, in particular, has been seen by some military historians as decisive. Some of these historians have argued that Grant brought a new vision to warfare. Others have seen him driven by Clausewitzian principles of total war, as opposed to earlier Union commanders like McClellan and Halleck and his Southern opponents like Lee and Johnson, who were thinking along the lines of the theorist Jomini and sought victory by a war of movement and manoeuvre.

Instead of looking for the decisive battle on Napoleonic lines, Grant saw the need for a strategy to deal with the particular nature and character of this war. Manoeuvring and seeking a decisive result on the battlefield had not brought the North victory by March 1864. In addition, the seventeen separate Union commands had proved ineffective. What was needed was a joint strategy followed by both army and navy. This should involve bringing Lee's forces, depleted after the failure of Gettysburg, but still intact and dangerous, to 'continuous battle', not dependent on one encounter. While the main Confederate forces were being engaged, Sherman should attack towards Atlanta, relying on fast movement and bring the war into the South's homeland by a march to the sea involving economic destruction of key elements, such as railways. In addition, there should be a joint naval and military assault on Mobile.

Attrition: Grant's successful concept

However, what counted was relentless pressure on the South and, rather than a single knockout blow, the attrition of the South's forces and the support from its largely untouched homeland. Grant wrote in his memoirs that after the Battle of Shiloh, 'I gave up the idea of saving the Union except by complete conquest.' This involved a dogged pursuit of victory and the use of co-ordinated tactics. The cooperation with naval forces allowed him to take the key fortress of Vicksburg in 1863 after repeated failures and so dominate the Mississippi and cut the South in two. His campaign in Virginia ignored casualties. It did not matter if at the Battle of the Wilderness he lost 17,000 men to Lee's 7500 because Grant pursued his forces in a series of battles, culminating in a costly siege at Petersburg, which did indeed wear down Confederate resistance. Meanwhile, Sherman avoided large-scale battles after initial failures and concentrated on cutting the Confederacy in two and hitting its economic and communication resources. Lee's more effective tactical abilities led him into an ill-judged invasion of Pennsylvania, resulting in defeat at Gettysburg in 1863. He was able to defend in a way that has been seen as brilliant, but it was Grant's strategic grasp and ability to see the war as a whole that was decisive.

A critical assessment of Grant's leadership

The view has been challenged by critical studies of Grant, which see him as an unreliable commander, often drunk, who led his forces to endure heavy and unnecessary casualties by mindless frontal assaults. Without the numerical superiority and greater arms provided to him by Lincoln's administration, this type of warfare would have been costly and ineffective. Many studies place Grant firmly within the context of the inevitability of Northern victory because of the undoubtedly greater resources that the North had. They argue that for all Lee's tactical skill, his generalship alone could not be decisive, and for all Grant's brutal realism and his overall grasp of Clausewitzian principles, his generalship alone was insufficient to be seen as the decisive element.

An overall assessment

Grant's brutal realism was the decisive element in the Northern victory. However, without the superior resources of the North it would not have been such an option. Lee defended the South with far fewer resources but did not appreciate that in a modern war, that type of warfare could not be decisive. As neither side could accept a compromise peace, the war would only be won when it was impossible for one side or the other to continue. For that to be the case, the resources of one side had to be worn down regardless of cost. It was to be a tragic forerunner of the world wars of the twentieth century.

Key debate 3: how far was the indecisive warfare which characterised the war on the Western Front and the heavy casualties it involved the result of inept military leadership?

In the aftermath of the First World War, when writers reflected on the losses, there came the view, not held much during the actual war, that the leaders had been incompetent and that the loss of life had been in vain, the result of unimaginative and foolish tactics. The view passed into many novels, textbooks and films, and famously on television with *Blackadder Goes Forth*.

The arguments may be summarised as follows:

- The military leaders did not understand that modem warfare meant that frontal assaults were likely to be unsuccessful and lead to heavy casualties.
- They ignored the lessons of key conflicts such as the American Civil War and preferred to look at shorter and more decisive conflicts, such as the wars of the mid-nineteenth century in Italy and central Europe; the Sino-Japanese and Russo-Japanese Wars and the recent Balkan Wars (1912–13).
- There was a belief that sheer morale and willpower could overcome heavy artillery, machine guns and magazine rifles capable of sustained firing.
- Commanders did not anticipate trench warfare, even though it had featured heavily in the later stages of the American Civil War.

- They pursued 'breakthroughs', even though it was repeatedly shown that attempts to break through would lead only to heavy losses and bulges in the line (salients) which would be hard to defend.
- Military leaders clung to a belief in the eventual use of cavalry, even though modern warfare with warplanes and heavy artillery made this type of warfare unlikely.

The key criticisms of the military leaders

Underestimating the power of modern weapons

Military leaders have been accused both of underestimating new technology in the form of machine guns and overestimating it in the form of assuming mistakenly that heavy artillery bombardments and high explosives could make frontal assaults possible. They have also been accused of relying on mass attacks by relatively untrained troops.

Failure to learn from experience

Probably the greatest charge levelled against the leaders is a failure to learn. Similar tactics failed for similar reasons with similarly tragic consequences for over three years. The 'standard method' is often said to be the accumulation of large forces in a relatively small battlefield area. Their attack was prepared by a large-scale artillery bombardment intended to clear the way for a frontal infantry assault. In practice, this merely threw up obstacles of barbed wire over 'no-man's land' and channelled attackers through gaps in the wire where they were easy targets for the defenders. The barrage, although highly terrifying and destructive, ended any chance of surprise and the time gap between the end of the barrage and the start of the attack gave the defenders who had survived the chance to fire on the attackers. Troops from the rear were quickly brought up to plug any gaps in the defences and exhausted attackers faced rapid counterattacks. In Flanders, the situation was made worse by boggy ground, the muddy conditions making attacks even more difficult.

More of the same

Although some changes were made, essentially the terrible attacks at Passchendaele in 1917 were not much different from earlier unsuccessful attacks on the Somme in 1916 and in Flanders in 1915. Similarly, the French attacks in 1917 were not much different from the attacks in 1915 and 1916. Only the Germans in their attacks of March 1918 showed any significant large-scale adaptation of these tactics, but the policy of 1916 of 'bleeding the French white' by deliberately attacking their strongpoint of Verdun was the crassest strategy of attrition of the war. In any case, this attack was not properly followed up, as after initial successes the German leaders were tempted to put in more and more men to try and achieve the ever-elusive breakthrough.

Advocates of mobile warfare saw the war in terms of static and costly war and incompetence and some influential critical studies followed that tradition.

Historians with military experience were often critically arguing that it was strange that the generals so slowly fathomed the crucial difficulty of trench warfare, and that they failed to understand that with more and more artillery, the more the surface of the ground would be damaged and from a normal battlefield it would become a crater area. By the time this ground had been repaired and roads built to get men and supplies to the front, the enemy would have re-entrenched, so another attack would be needed.

A defence of the military leaders

Given the very large numbers of casualties on the Western Front and the harrowing personal accounts of hardship and loss, it was difficult to reject these criticisms. However, different views were taken by revisionist historians who took a fresh look at Haig, and there have been an increasing number of studies which have attempted to rehabilitate the commanders:

- It is a myth that generals merely ordered attack involving mass death from comfortable headquarters. A surprising number were killed in action.
- It is a myth that no one understood the conditions. Careful reconstructions of the attack area were made so that troops should know what lay ahead.
- It is also untrue that there was no development of tactics. British artillery was innovative in laying down creeping barrages. Night attacks became more common. Individual units were given more initiative. Use was made of surprise tactics, such as the attack at Vimy Ridge, which involved extensive tunnelling under enemy lines.
- German tactics evolved dramatically before the last great German offensive of the war in March 1918, based on experience of smaller units of stormtroops in the east, with limited initial bombardment, rapid advances which avoided strong points and found weaknesses in the enemy line, and independent action by well-trained smaller groups. Initially, these tactics, which opened the way for advances by reserves held at the rear, were highly successful.
- The British and French also innovated by combined arms operations using aircraft and importantly tanks with the avoidance of heavily fortified points and the use of air reconnaissance in the attacks of 1918.

The revisionists' view

Defenders of Haig see him being prepared to learn, and to use new technology and tactics. The heavy casualties were common to the war as a whole and featured once again when large forces were committed during the Second World War. They were inseparable from modern warfare. Haig, like Grant, understood modern warfare and knew that victory would only come by wearing down the enemy's army and breaking its morale. He relied on a belief that 'the mobile battlefield would reassert itself' and that his army should be ready for that. When the front did move again in 1918, Haig had the necessary resources, including cavalry, to take advantage of that and bring Britain to victory. He maintained the trust of his army, and his subordinate leaders were able and committed. Even costly battles were vital in weakening the enemy and he supported new technology such as poison gas and tanks. The view of the generals as remote Victorian figures is belied by Haig's interest in equipping his men with machine guns and by his reorganisation of the British army's transport system in France in 1916 and 1917. His German counterparts took an acute interest in securing the resources for war. Russian leaders aimed to ensure supplies and also to modify tactics. The stereotype of the 'butcher and bungler' is inaccurate and reflects more a hatred of war itself.

An overall assessment

The issue of leadership is so emotional that judgement is bound to be clouded. It seems unrealistic, however, to see every military leader of the war as blinkered and incompetent. Leaders were often held in the highest esteem by ex-soldiers. Haig was a much-respected head of the British Legion for ex-servicemen. Foch had streets in France named after him. Hindenburg became the German president. Up to a point they did learn, they did try to use new methods and new weapons. Modern warfare cannot avoid heavy casualties by its very nature. However, the persistence of very futile and unsuccessful attacks is not easy to explain away. The lessons of the Somme were not really applied to the dreadful and wasteful Battle of Passchendaele, and the failure to accumulate enough reserves doomed the great German attacks of 1918. The US General Pershing ordered his men into punishing frontal attacks in 1918, despite all the experience of his allies in the previous three years. In the end, generalship involves responsibility. The leaders shouldered that, but cannot escape the consequences of their failures.

Study skills: thematic essay question

How to plan the essay

The title of the unit, 'Thematic study', makes it clear that the essay section should be approached thematically rather than chronologically, particularly if you want to reach the higher mark range. In answering essay questions, you are required to make connections, comparisons and links between different elements of the period and aspects of the topic. In the opening paragraph you should try and establish a hypothesis based on the question; this should be tested in the main body of the essay before reaching an overall judgement. This is much easier to do if you approach the essay through a thematic structure. In your answer you will need to cover the whole period, and answers should look to establish patterns of change and continuity and similarity and difference.

Given the large amount of material that you will have to handle, it is very important that you spend time planning your answer. As the essay should adopt a thematic structure, it makes sense if the plan follows the same format and is therefore not chronological or just a list of dates.

In developing your skills to answer essay questions for units 1 and 2, you will have considered the wording of a question. Although you will also have looked at planning an answer, the requirements for these types of question are, as was suggested above, somewhat different, as you will need to establish the themes you will consider.

Consider the question below:

'The ability to inspire troops was the key aspect of generalship.' How far do you agree with this view of generalship in the period from 1792 to 1945?

In this essay you would need to consider how you would deal with the key elements of leadership and comparing this element with other factors. To meet the demands of 'How far … ?', this is better than trying to make a list of military leaders and dealing with them in turn.

Consider the example below:

Key elements of military leadership

- **Inspiration of troops:** important at the start of the period, for example, Napoleon in Italy. Remained important, for example, Lee and Grant both popular figures; Haig very well respected; Montgomery and Rommel offered personal inspiration, but as war grew in scale less personal contact.
- **Tactics:** management of the battlefield still important during Revolutionary and Napoleonic Wars. Tactical organisation significant in American Civil War until later stages and in outcomes of wars of 1866 and 1870–1. However, leadership became more focused on strategy after mid-century.
- **Strategy:** overall approach to war, for example, Grant; Haig; Hitler; joint military planners in Second World War. Much more important with longer wars and more professional planning staff and when war is more total.
- **Management of resources:** war became more dependent on resources, for example, with railways, needle gun and heavy artillery mid-century, less on battlefield improvisation like Napoleon. Big operations like Schlieffen Plan required careful resource management. Intensive planning for the big push necessary for commanders to know about. By Second World War, commanders like Eisenhower managed huge resources (for example, for D-Day).
- **Understanding of politics and public opinion:** this may be a constant. Napoleon and bulletins and projection of heroic image; Napoleon III and support of liberty and nationalism in Italy; conscious need for rapid victories to appease public demand for short victorious war in 1914; need for military leaders to work with political leadership.

- **Conclusion:** despite circumstances bringing about a change in the role of leaders and their direct influence on tactics as opposed to strategy, some elements remained constant, notably the management of men and resources and the need to inspire confidence among the troops and the nation as a whole.

The plan does not simply list the individuals, but offers a comment about their importance in different aspects of leadership, and the conclusion offers a clear line of argument, which has been supported in the previous paragraphs. Planning an answer will help you to focus on the actual question and marshal the large amount of knowledge you have, in this case about different elements of generalship and war. This should stop you writing about each war in turn, which will not score highly or show your ability to deal with thematic questions.

How to write the opening paragraph

Having planned your answer, you are in a position to write the crucial opening paragraph in which you should set out your line of argument – establish your thesis – and briefly refer to the issues you are going to cover in the main body of the essay. This will help you to remain focused on the actual question. In establishing your thesis, it might be helpful to consider the following questions:

- What was the situation at the start of the period?
- What was the situation at the end of the period?
- Were there any parts of the period where there was considerable change or does the pattern remain the same throughout the period?

These questions will help you to remain focused on the key elements being tested in this unit: continuity and change.

The following is an example of a good opening paragraph to the question:

How important was the quality of generalship to the conduct of war in the period from 1792 to 1945?

Response

The quality of leadership remained the most important factor in the conduct of war but the qualities required by generals changed. As well as the generalship, there were other factors that were important. The period saw a considerable increase in the power of weapons; the size of armies grew; the way that states organised themselves for war was transformed. All these factors changed war, but only in as far as skilful and imaginative leadership took advantage of them. There was a constant interaction between these factors and the developing art of military leadership; but resources alone did not win wars. They had to be used. Successful commanders adapted their leadership style, their tactics and their strategy in the light of other changes but it was their personal qualities, from the leaders of the French Revolutionary armies through to the Second World War, that was of the greatest importance in the conduct of war.

Analysis of response

- The opening offers a clear view about the importance of the key element in the question.
- It outlines some of the other factors that will be considered and offers a view as to their relative importance.
- It reaches a judgement as to the most important factor and offers a thesis which can be followed through in the essay, showing a sense of change over time.

The focus of this section has been on planning and writing a good opening paragraph. Use the information in this chapter to plan answers and write the opening paragraph to the questions below.

Essay questions

1 To what extent was generalship less important in the conduct of war after 1914 than it was before?
2 Assess the view that total war was the most significant development in warfare in the period from 1792 to 1914.
3 'Conscription was the most important development in the conduct of warfare.' How far do you agree with this view of warfare in the period from 1792 to 1945?
4 The Napoleonic period saw the greatest transformation in the role of military leadership.' How far do you agree with this view of warfare in the period from 1792 to 1945?

Study skills: depth study interpretations question

How to plan the essay

The specification identifies the three topics from which the interpretations question will be drawn. In answering this question, you have to assess and evaluate the arguments in the passages by applying your own knowledge of the events to reach a supported judgement as to which is the stronger interpretation.

The question will require you to assess the strengths and limitations of two interpretations of an issue related to one of the specified depth studies. You should be able to place the interpretation within the context of the wider historical debate on the key topic. However, you will not be required to know the names of individual historians associated with the debate or to have studied the specific books of any historians, and it may even be counterproductive to be aware of particular historians' wider historical debate on the key topic, as this may lead to your simply describing their view, rather than analysing the given interpretation.

How should the question be approached?

Using the question and the two passages below on the generalship of Haig, it might be helpful for you to think of a four-paragraph structure to your answer:

- In the first paragraph, explain the interpretations in the two passages and place them in the wider debate about leadership on the Western Front.
- In the second paragraph, apply your own knowledge of the Western Front to Interpretation A to evaluate the validity of its view about leadership. What knowledge do you have of the effectiveness of Haig as a military commander that either supports or challenges the view of Passage A?
- Repeat the second point, but for Interpretation B. What knowledge do you have of the effectiveness of Haig as a military commander that either supports or challenges the view of Passage B?
- In the final paragraph, reach a supported and balanced judgement as to which passage you think is more convincing as evidence for the effectiveness of Haig as a military commander.

Evaluate the interpretations in both of the passages and explain which you think is more convincing as an assessment of Haig as a military commander. [30]

PASSAGE A

Adapted from Gary Sheffield, *The Chief: Douglas Haig and the British Army*, Aurum, 2011, pp. 377–80.

Haig's strategy, like those of other Great War generals, implicitly accepted that there would be very heavy losses among his own troops. To the casualty-intolerant twenty-first century, this is callous disregard for human life. Haig was not a modern man, and he should not be judged as if he was. The man needs to be placed in the historical context. His mistakes were outweighed by his achievements. First, he took a leading part in reforming the army and preparing it for a major war. Second, he played a major part in transforming the British army into a war-winning army. Third, Haig's generalship was a vital component in the Allied victory. Haig's battles in 1916–17 – the Somme, Arras, Third Ypres – played a vital role in destroying the enemy and in 1918 the British forces led the way in defeating the Imperial German army in the field. Transforming the British army on the Western Front was one of his greatest achievements.

PASSAGE B

From J.P. Harris, *Douglas Haig and the First World War*, Cambridge University Press, 2008, pp. 544–5.

It seems impossible to make a case for Haig as one of history's great generals. In relation to most of the war it is difficult to see him as a good general. The Western Front was a time and place that tended to make nearly all generals look inadequate. However that is not to say that the British army could not have waged war more efficiently than it actually did and achieved equally good, or better, results at a lower cost. The systematic application of step-by-step methods backed by massive firepower would have been the best approach in 1915–17. The biggest obstacle was Haig who remained obsessed with decisive breakthrough. It seems amazing that Haig survived as commander-in-chief. Even more remarkable is the continuous run of great and cumulatively decisive victories won by his armies between August and November 1918. Haig did play a vital role in this Hundred Days but after spending years predicting the imminent collapse of German morale, when it was actually happening in November 1918, he failed to perceive it.

Using this model, a developed plan to the same question might look something like this:

1 The two passages agree that Haig had achievements. Passage A offers a more favourable view of Haig's development of the army, but does not ignore casualties, whereas Passage B places more emphasis on costly battles fought to gain an impossible objective.
2 Passage A suggests that preparation and development of the armies put Haig on the road to final victory and that the battles prior to 1918 should be seen as preparing the way for that victory.
3 Passage B thinks that Haig's previous poor performance made the final victories surprising, and that Haig himself did not understand the collapse of German morale that made them possible.
4 Both passages acknowledge a degree of success and a degree of failure but Passage B is considerably less favourable. Passage A offers an unconvincing view of casualties and the early battles. Passage B is balanced enough to acknowledge Haig's achievement in 1918 but it may not be entirely convincing to allow this to influence a view of his earlier, less successful actions.

How to write the opening paragraph

Now look at this possible opening paragraph to the question on page 58.

Response

These two passages both acknowledge that Haig was important in the final campaigns that led to victory on the Western Front in 1918. They also agree that Haig's leadership resulted in casualties. However, the tone and content of both suggest considerable differences in their view of his leadership overall. Passage A is focused on the way that Haig prepared for the final victory. The reforms of the army and the way that his leadership transformed the British Expeditionary Force into a war-winning army are seen as the major achievements. This is not the focus of Passage B, which sees Haig not as an instrument of victory throughout the war but as a barrier to a more efficient way of fighting the war by his insistence on decisive attempts to break through instead of more realistic step-by-step actions in which the superior British artillery might have supported smaller attacks, more likely to have been successful. Also, Haig is not seen as a master planner but as someone taken by surprise by the German collapse. Both take into account the historical context and Passage B accepts that the Western Front was hard for all generals while Passage A argues that the acceptance of casualties was part of the context in which Haig worked.

The implication in Passage B is that Haig's ability to understand situations was limited, whereas he seems much more in control in Passage A. Thus, the two passages are significantly different in their view.

Analysis of response

- The student acknowledges that both interpretations are aware of the context and recognise Haig's achievements in 1918.
- The student is aware that the two interpretations put forward different views of the key elements of his leadership. The response identifies the key differences.
- The student analyses the different approach taken to the preparation for victory and there is some good analysis of the implications of the passages.

CHAPTER 2

The impact of technological change

The prevailing state of technology in both the military and non-military fields was important in determining both the nature and the outcome of wars. Throughout the period, nations were concerned to gain and develop the most effective or destructive weapons. The type of weapons available determined the strategy and tactics adopted and, therefore, played an important role in shaping the nature of wars. Just as important were developments in non-military technology, which could be adapted for the war effort, most notably in transport, communication and detection, even if they were not invented for military purposes. This chapter analyses the significance of technological changes under the following headings:

★ Industrialisation and technology

★ Developments in weaponry

★ Developments in communications and transport

It also considers the debates surrounding three in-depth topics:

★ How important were developments in weaponry in the outcome of the French Revolutionary Wars?

★ How significant were developments in transport in the American Civil War?

★ How important were developments in weaponry in the First World War?

Key dates

1841		Prussians accepted Dreyse breech-loading needle gun for service	1916		First use of tanks at Battle of the Somme
1845		Breech-loading artillery gun invented	1917	Nov.	Large-scale use of tanks at Battle of Cambrai
1849		Invention of the Minié bullet			
1915	April	First use of poison gas at second Battle of Ypres	1945	Aug.	Two atomic bombs dropped on Japan

Industrialisation and technology

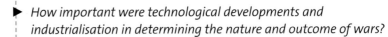

▶ *How important were technological developments and industrialisation in determining the nature and outcome of wars?*

It could be argued that nations, or in the case of the American Civil War, opposing forces, with the most advanced industries and economies were ultimately successful in warfare. This certainly appears to be the case in nineteenth-century wars with the British against Napoleon, Britain and France against Russia in the Crimean War, Prussia in the Wars of Unification and the Northern states in the American Civil War.

However, in the twentieth century the picture is less clear. Japan was less developed economically than Russia, but was still victorious in the Russo-Japanese War, while in both the First and Second World Wars it was the length of the wars that saw the side with the greatest industrial strength and productive capacity, rather than the most technologically advanced industries and economy, emerge triumphant. For example, Germany produced far better tanks than the Allies, but could not make enough of them.

Industrialisation produced a succession of developments that revolutionised the conduct of warfare and also allowed the greater organisation of resources, both economic and human. However, industrialisation also changed the nature of warfare, particularly in the twentieth century as the greater development of weapons such as gas, heavy **artillery**, machine guns and tanks together with air warfare dehumanised warfare and made it industrial.

Although the period witnessed tremendous technological advances, and industrial developments allowed the mass manufacture of weapons, it must be remembered that technology only creates possibilities. The development of new weaponry does not mean that it will necessarily be used effectively. This was seen in the early years of the First World War with the tank owing to a misunderstanding of its actual potential, although, by 1918, there was evidence of greater co-ordinated use of tanks by both Britain and France. However, technological and industrial developments have meant that each war has had the potential to be more destructive than the previous and to bring about far more deaths.

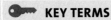

The Revolutionary and Napoleonic Wars

Both the Revolutionary and Napoleonic Wars have many features of modern warfare, with mass armies fighting over large areas and the mobilisation of whole populations, but industrial developments played only a very limited role in both the nature and outcome of the wars. Technology had not brought about significant improvements in the weapons available since the dynastic wars of the

---

KEY TERMS

Industrialisation The development of large-scale and developed industries which used machines to increase production levels and therefore relied on people working in factories or other large-scale enterprises, rather than at home.

Artillery Heavy guns which are capable of firing large shells, usually over long distances.

earlier eighteenth century, and industrial developments had yet not resulted in the large-scale production of weapons that could bring about mass destruction. The major changes in warfare associated with both the Revolutionary and Napoleonic Wars were more associated with socio-political and organisational developments (see Chapter 3). Technology, therefore, played a minor role in determining the outcome of the Revolutionary and Napoleonic Wars, although the French workshops of St Etienne were much more productive than those of the *ancien régime*, producing 97,000 handguns by 1809, compared with a maximum of 26,000 a year in the past. This improvement certainly helped to support Napoleon's large armies. However, the technological changes and industrial developments after 1815, and particularly from the middle part of the century, would play a significant role in warfare.

The developments in military technology after the Napoleonic Wars were closely allied to the developments of the **Industrial Revolution**, particularly steam power. Mass production through the growth of factories in the period from the 1850s onwards further increased the production of weapons. The Industrial Revolution had a particular impact on land warfare in three areas:

- the development of the steam engine
- the electric telegraph
- the mass-produced rifle musket.

The first two of these developments had a great impact on strategy, as they allowed men to be moved quickly and organised more effectively, which had an impact on planning, while the rifle musket had more of an impact on tactics. The range and rate of fire were dramatically increased, as was the scale of destruction. However, at least initially, these developments did not mean that the weapons were effectively used, and they did not see a move away from the concept of the **cult of the offensive**.

The technological developments meant that the size and scale of the war zone increased, but this did not have an initial impact on the belief in either cavalry or infantry attacks. Technological developments meant that heavy weaponry equalised armies and some military strategists therefore argued that, in order to avoid stalemate, an offensive spirit was needed. It would only be towards the end of the nineteenth century that there would be a change in approach, and that was adopted only very slowly.

So then, despite developments in technology, the French army still believed in the 'offensive spirit', as would be seen in their charges across no man's land at the start of the First World War, with General **Joseph Joffre** commenting that 'The French army, returning to its traditions, no longer knows any other law than that of the attack.' It was this approach that led to the high casualty rates in the early months of the First World War.

However, it was not just in the French army that industrial developments were slow to have an impact on armies and the tactics they adopted. As late as 1907,

KEY TERMS

Ancien régime The 'old regime'. Refers to the monarchical and aristocratic political and social system that was established in France from the fifteenth century until the French Revolution in 1789.

Industrial Revolution Economic developments which started initially in Britain in the eighteenth century but eventually spread across Europe, whereby factories and mass production came to replace small-scale production of goods, often carried out in small workshops.

Cult of the offensive The belief among military strategists that the advantages of attack so outweigh those of defence that the defender would stand no chance of repelling an attack.

KEY FIGURE

Joseph Joffre (1852–1931) A French general and commander-in-chief of French forces on the Western Front 1914–16.

the British cavalry training manual still stated that 'It must be accepted as a principle that the rifle, effective as it is, cannot replace the effect produced by the speed of the horse, the magnetism of the charge, and the terror of cold steel [the bayonet].' Haig even brought back the lance in 1909!

The Crimean War

In contrast to the Revolutionary and Napoleonic Wars, technology and industrial developments were important in determining the nature and outcome of the Crimean War. The British and French had a massive technological lead over Russia and as a result possessed better artillery and rifles as they had the latest equipment (see page 82), whereas the Russians relied on **smoothbore muskets**, which were less accurate and could fire over much shorter distances. However, although the British and French had a technological lead, factors such as leadership and organisation, particularly with the British as seen in the ill-fated Charge of the Light Brigade, meant that they were unable to overwhelm Russia. However, it must also be remembered that it was only an expeditionary force which was fighting a long way from home and was nevertheless able to take Sebastopol and force Russia to make terms.

However, British forces were also fortunate in that they were faced with a more incompetent enemy. Russian industrial backwardness and non-existent quality controls also impacted on the levels of production, with the result that despite having overwhelming numbers – an army of over 1 million men – they were unable to get their forces to the war zone quickly enough as they lacked railways.

The war clearly showed that industrialisation, particularly the development and use of steam power, be it in ships or railways, had a massive impact on the balance of military power and that Russia simply did not have the technological ability in terms of railways to take advantage of their numbers and geography. The Crimean War therefore represented a change as traditional military power was replaced or superseded by the power given by industrialisation.

The American Civil War

Industrialisation played a significant role in the outcome of the American Civil War. It was the more industrialised North that eventually won. As the historian Alan Farmer argued in *The American Civil War 1861–1865* (1996), the civil war reflected the impact of industrial growth. It was the first war where outproducing the enemy was just as important as outfighting them. As a consequence, many historians have seen the American Civil War as the first modern war, more like the First World War than the Revolutionary Wars of the late eighteenth century. There is certainly much evidence to support such a view. Railways moved troops and supplies; strategy and tactics reflected the effectiveness of the rifle-musket, which became commonplace after 1863, and resulted in an advantage for defenders. Steam-driven ships also played an important role as an ordinary steamboat could carry, in one trip, enough

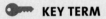

KEY TERM

Smoothbore musket
The inside of the barrels of smoothbore muskets, as the name suggests, was smooth and this limited their range. They were fired from the shoulder while standing. Muskets would later be replaced by rifles.

supplies to support 40,000 men and 18,000 horses for two days. However, despite these developments, no battle saw armies of over 100,000 men, and horses were still used as a means of transport, and cavalry remained a major feature of some campaigns. This suggests that despite industrial changes, the wars still had some characteristics of earlier wars and perhaps should be seen as a half-way house between the old and modern forms of warfare.

As the war became a long, drawn-out affair, it was the industrial capacity of the North that had an impact on the ultimate outcome. The North in 1860 produced some 97 per cent of US firearms, 94 per cent of its pig iron and 90 per cent of its boots. It had also had twice as much railway track as the South, which allowed it to move troops and supplies more easily, while it also possessed many more engineers and skilled workers who were able to maintain the rail network. Overall, the North had six times more factories than the South and ten times its productive capacity. Given these considerable economic advantages, it might be argued that what was most surprising was that the war lasted as long as it did, suggesting that economic power on its own was not enough to secure victory and that strategy, tactics and the ability of commanders were still important factors in determining the outcome of a war.

The Wars of Unification

In the War of Unification of the mid-nineteenth century, economic factors played a more significant role in both the nature and final outcome. Austria's lack of economic development was an important factor in its defeats to both France in 1859 and Prussia in 1866, while Prussia's economic dominance enabled it to defeat both Austria and France. Prussia's economic superiority ensured that the wars were short as not only was it able to move its troops by rail more quickly to the areas of conflict, but its industrial dominance allowed it to supply and equip its forces with modern weaponry, such as the **Dreyse needle gun**, which was far superior to that of the Austrians, reflecting Bismarck's comment that Germany would be unified not by 'Blood and Iron' but by 'Coal and Iron'. However, although their economic power and weapons gave the Prussians advantages, it was not just these which brought about victories but their organisational skills and the limitations of their enemies (see Chapter 3) and tactics. The French actually had an advantage with their breech-loading rifle, the Chassepot, but Prussian artillery, particularly the rifled steel cannon, was far superior to the French artillery and was one of the major factors in deciding the outcome of the two major battles at Metz and Sedan.

The Russo-Japanese War

Economically, neither Russia nor Japan was developed. Russia had made some progress since the Crimean War, but it still lagged a long way behind its European counterparts, while Japan was only starting to emerge as a modern power at the end of the nineteenth century. Despite being considerably

KEY TERM

Dreyse needle gun
A breech-loading rifle, the name comes from the needle-like firing pin. It was also the first rifle to use the bolt action. Its rate of fire was ten to twelve rounds a minute.

Otto von Bismarck

1815	Born the son of a Prussian Junker
1836	Entered civil service
1847	Became a member of the Prussian Diet (assembly); he was a conservative
1851–9	Prussian delegate at the Bundestag (Parliament)
1859	Appointed Prussian ambassador to Russia
1862	Appointed minister-president
1864	War against Denmark
1866	War against Austria
1870–1	War against France
1871	German Empire declared
1871–90	Chancellor of the German Empire
1898	Died

Early life

The son of a Prussian landowner, or *junker*, he was brought up on the family estates. His background gave him a strong sense of duty and service, but it also made him very conservative in his political outlook. On his mother's death in 1839, he helped to run the estates but by 1847 he had become involved in Prussian politics.

Political career 1847–62

During the revolutions of 1848, he was active in helping to put them down and was seen as anti-liberal. In 1850, he spoke in defence of the Prussian surrender to Austria at Olmütz, arguing that fighting was not in Prussia's interest. As a result, he was appointed Prussian envoy to the Bundestag, where he remained until 1859, with his prime concern being to oppose Austria and becoming increasingly anti-Austrian. This convinced him that war between the two was likely, resulting in a divided Germany. By 1858, he was arguing that Prussia should seek support among German nationalists and by 1859 that Austria should be driven out of the German Confederation.

Minister-president

Initially, his aims were for Prussia to dominate north Germany, being a Prussian patriot, rather than a nationalist. However, he soon realised that nationalism might be manipulated in Prussia's interest. He was also determined to make Prussia as strong as possible both economically and militarily. Although he hoped to avoid war, and remove Austria from the Confederation by diplomacy, this failed and it was through the three wars of the 1860s and 1870 that unification was achieved.

Chancellor

Having driven Austria out, Bismarck then set out to consolidate German power and avoid entanglements through a series of alliances with Austria and Russia, which would keep France isolated and prevent it from seeking revenge for 1870. This was maintained until his fall from power in 1890, which was soon followed by a rapprochement between France and Russia, which would lead ultimately to the First World War.

🔑 **KEY TERM**

Battle of Tsushima Bay
The major naval encounter of the Russo-Japanese War. The Russian fleet had sailed 18,000 miles from the Baltic but because of its poor condition and lack of speed it was quickly defeated, with nearly the whole Russian fleet lost.

outnumbered, Japan was able to move its armed forces to the theatre of conflict by sea, whereas although the Russian army was much larger it was dependent on a 5000-mile single-track rail line, the Trans-Siberian railway, to move both troops and supplies to the area around Port Arthur. Similarly, although the Russians had a far larger navy, being the third largest in the world, Japan's large warships had been built in Europe to British designs and were of a superior quality. Thus, Russia's economic backwardness gave the Japanese local superiority in both land and sea forces at the start of the conflict but was particularly important in securing Japanese naval victories, such as at the **Battle of Tsushima Bay**. However, in the Battle of Mukden, fought for control of a key rail centre, it was Japan's ability to sustain heavy losses that ultimately resulted in victory and left southern Manchuria securely in its hands.

The First World War

The period after 1870 saw a dramatic increase in industrialisation throughout much of Europe, but particularly in Germany. This had a dramatic impact on the levels of steel production, which rose from 3.16 million tons in 1890 to 13.15 million tons by 1910, surpassing that of Britain. However, just as important were developments in the chemical industry, where Germany had a substantial lead over all other European powers. These developments would provide the materials needed for the armaments industries and ensure that the First World War was the first truly modern war, with weapons dependent on industrial and technological developments.

Industrialisation not only ensured that unprecedently large armies could be supplied with weapons, but also ensured that the war was destructive. The mass production of machine guns gave the advantage to the defender, and meant that a small number of soldiers could hold territory and inflict large-scale casualties, giving the advantage to the defenders and destroying the concept of numerical advantage. At the same time, the production of large artillery weapons and the ability to supply millions of shells meant that much of the bombardment of enemy troops took place from miles behind the front line. Not only did these developments ensure that, unlike the Wars of Unification, which were over in a matter of a few weeks, the war lasted much longer and was more costly. Some even argue that commanders continued to resist the adoption of the new weapons as they believed that they undermined courage and the morale and discipline of the forces, which even at the start of the war they believed was more important than the advances in mass-produced technology.

The Second World War

The Second World War witnessed a technological arms race to develop the most sophisticated and destructive weapons possible. At first, there was little change, just improvements, in the weapons produced at the time of the First World War. This was seen in many areas such as tanks and armoured vehicles, as well as aircraft such as the **Stuka**, Spitfire and Hurricane, all of which were considerable developments on the First World War. However, the Allies had made some technological advances before the outbreak of the war, such as the development of radar, which played a crucial role in the Battle of Britain. The British would also develop the digital computer, which allowed them to crack German codes and anticipate German attacks and troop movements.

However, as the war progressed, attempts were made to use technological advances to develop weapons that could shorten and win the war. This was particularly true in Germany with the development of the jet engine and the **V-1 and V-2 rockets**. The Allies also developed their technology, culminating in the development of the most destructive weapon of the period, the atomic bomb. It was the development of the atomic bomb which played the most

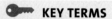 **KEY TERMS**

Stuka Also known as the Junkers Ju87, this was a German dive-bomber and ground-attack aircraft, which played a significant role in the early *Blitzkrieg* attacks.

V-1 and V-2 rockets German weapons used towards the end of the war. They had a terrifying impact on London, with the V-1 delivering 1 ton of high explosives. However, it could be shot down by anti-aircraft guns. The V-2 was more devastating as it flew at over 2000 miles per hour and could not be seen, and thus spread considerable fear. They were mostly used against civilian targets.

 **KEY TERM**

Manhattan Project
The research and development project in the USA to develop the atomic bomb. There were concerns about the German production of such a weapon and there was a race to beat them.

significant role in changing the war. Its deployment against Japan in August 1945 brought the war in the Far East to a rapid conclusion, although it could also be argued that Japan was already defeated, so that the dropping of bombs on Hiroshima and Nagasaki simply brought it to an end more quickly. However, there can be little doubt that both the Allies and Axis powers considered technological advances to be crucial to the outcome. The Americans invested large amounts of money in the **Manhattan Project** to develop the atomic bomb, worried that Germany would get there first. Meanwhile, Germany developed a number of weapons that would not be fully utilised in the war, largely because of political interference, which resulted in too many projects being pursued and its resources being spread too thinly, particularly after defeat in Russia.

Developments in weaponry

▶ *In what ways did developments in weaponry change the nature of warfare?*

The type of weaponry available has had an impact on both the nature and outcome of warfare. Superiority in weapons has been at least a contributory factor in the outcome of wars, as was seen in both the Austro-Prussian War of 1866 and the Franco-Prussian War of 1870, while weapons have also had a considerable impact on the nature of warfare, with the most obvious example being the First World War where the machine gun resulted in a largely defensive, static war on the Western Front. However, it must also be remembered that weapons may be developed, but they are not always used effectively or to their full potential, as was seen with the tank in the First World War.

The Revolutionary and Napoleonic Wars

During the course of the eighteenth century there had been slow but significant improvements in the development of weapons technology, but warfare was dominated by two main weapons:

- the musket-bayonet
- artillery.

It was these weapons that the French Revolutionary armies and those of Napoleon and his enemies would rely on at the end of the eighteenth and the start of the nineteenth centuries. As with transport and communications, there was therefore little change in the weapons available in this period from the previous period of dynastic warfare, although the development of lighter artillery may have had an impact on the Revolutionary and Napoleonic Wars.

The Crimean War

The first significant change in weapons that impacted on the nature of warfare was improvements to the rifle. The most notable were the developments of the percussion cap, introduced about 1820, and the Minié bullet, developed in the late 1840s.

Percussion cap ignition

This development replaced the previous flintlock musket, which had a misfire rate of some twenty per cent due to either damp or gusts of wind. Fulminate of mercury, an explosive which detonated once struck, replaced the old flintlock, and this helped to increase the firepower of the infantry. Along with the Minié bullet (see below) and the development of the **cap and ball rifle**, it meant that the infantry had an accurate range of fire of some 600 yards, which was five times further than the old rifles and also reduced the rate of misfire to virtually zero.

 **KEY TERM**

Cap and ball rifle The cap replaced the old flintlock firing mechanism which meant that it was more reliable, particularly in damp weather, and was faster to reload.

The Minié bullet

The Minié bullet was an expandable, cylindro-conoidal shaped bullet. This made the loading of a musket as quick as a smoothbore. The bullet could be easily dropped down the barrel of a rifle, but expanded when fired to fit the rifle grooves. This was a dramatic improvement on the musket ball, which was difficult to push down the barrel of a gun and therefore took a long time as it had to be forced against the rifle grooves. The speeding up of the loading process meant firing was more rapid and, alongside the development of the percussion cap, gave the tactical advantage to the defensive side. The defensive forces could pile up earthworks to protect themselves and, at the same time, fire at a much more rapid rate into the mass formations of the enemy armies, which still dominated the battlefield, with a high success rate, which would account for some 90 per cent of victims during the American Civil War.

In contrast, developments in artillery were much slower and had little impact on the nature of warfare, and it would not be until the 1860s that there were significant developments. In 1845, a breech-loading, rifled artillery gun had been invented, but developments were held back, at least in part by costs, as countries were unwilling to re-equip their whole army. The British did convert some of their cannon, and the results were dramatic, showing far greater accuracy and range in the bombardment of Sebastopol, which encouraged subsequent developments by other states.

However, in most instances the role of the artillery was limited because of the rifle developments. If armies attempted to move their artillery into close enough range to engage with the enemy they were likely to be gunned down by enemy rifles which benefited from the improvement in range. Yet, if the artillery was not moved close enough and stayed out of the range of enemy rifle fire they were unable to inflict any damage and could not support attacking troops.

The American Civil War

Improvements in military technology and weaponry changed the nature of the war. In previous conflicts, the main weapon had been the smoothbore musket. This had an effective range of no more than 100 yards and therefore armies had relied on the **massed volley**. This had required armies to advance in close-order formation, making them an easy target for enemy fire. However, in some instances, the inaccuracy of the fire from defenders, as in the **Mexican War** of 1846–8, had allowed the attackers to overwhelm the defenders.

The major change that impacted on the American Civil War was the development by 1855 of the rifle-musket. The adoption of the Minié bullet, an inch-long projectile which expanded in the barrel's rifled groove, meant that it could be loaded and fired just as quickly as the smoothbore. The big advantages of this were that the rifle-musket was more accurate and had a far greater range, being able to kill up to 1000 yards and accurate up to 600 yards, and would therefore have a great impact on the battlefield. However, it was not until 1863 that the rifle-musket became readily available; at the start of the war the smoothbore was the norm, with troops attacking in mass formations and the defender returning volleys of fire.

The development of the rifle-musket changed the nature of the war as tactics favoured the defending force and ensured that the casualty rates in the war were high, with some 90 per cent of wounds caused by bullets. Given the speed at which the rifle-musket could be reloaded, the defending forces were able to fire several rounds at the attackers and therefore kill large numbers before they could use their bayonets, with the result that less than one per cent of wounds were caused by bayonets. However, it should be remembered that the spade became just as important a weapon in this and future wars as the rifle, as soldiers now 'dug themselves in' to protect themselves from the increased firepower they encountered. This had a further impact on tactics as generals could no longer undertake massive frontal attacks because of the casualty rates and so attempted turning movements. The defenders ensured that their flanks were protected, and this forced commanders back to frontal assaults if there was to be any movement. As a result, the battles of the Civil War were not only bloody affairs, with high casualty rates and large numbers of bullets fired – some 19 million were fired in May 1864 in North Virginia – but often followed the same pattern of the infantry firing volleys, and charges and counter-charges. As a result, many of the battles were little more than 'hammering matches' which resulted in heavy casualties, with some 97,000 at the **Battle of Gettysburg** in 1863. The Confederates sustained 50 per cent casualties on the third day during Pickett's Charge, which, according to some analysts, was a turning point in the war as the South never recovered either militarily or psychologically.

KEY TERMS

Massed volley A line of soldiers firing their weapons at the same time.

Mexican War The war followed the US annexation of Texas in 1845 and was won by the USA, whose forces advanced a long way into Mexico. It led to a loss of much northern Mexican territory.

Battle of Gettysburg One of the most important battles of the American Civil War. The defeat of the South, some have argued, made its overall defeat inevitable, but the North was unable to follow up its victory and the South was able to hold North Virginia.

The accuracy of the rifle meant that the cavalry played a less important role. Cavalry could not charge infantry ranks without sustaining high losses and this therefore led to a change in its role. The cavalry became the scouts or carried out raids against supply trains, but when it came to an actual battle the troops often dismounted and fought as infantry.

The developments to the rifle also meant that artillery was less important as the range and accuracy of the rifle-musket made artillery vulnerable to rifle fire. Much of the artillery was therefore withdrawn to safer areas, but this limited its effectiveness. The artillery was also less effective against soldiers who were well dug in. As a result, it was the development of the rifle-musket that was the crucial weapon of the war. However, it was not just the development of the rifle-musket that determined the outcome but the numerical advantage and communications of the North, in terms of rail and eventually steamboats, which ultimately gave it victory.

The Wars of Unification

The Franco-Austrian War

Although, for the most part, developments in artillery did lag behind other weapon developments, the French were able to make use of their superior artillery. Their rifled cannon, known as the 'Napoleon', was so superior to anything that the Austrians possessed that it determined the outcome of virtually every battle. Its range of 3500 yards was some 1500 yards further than the guns of the Austrians, which meant that the French could position their guns outside the range of the Austrian guns while being able to attack and destroy their artillery.

It could be argued that this artillery superiority should have been balanced against the better rifles possessed by the Austrians, which should have been able to stop the mass attacks of the French. However, this was not the case, as the Austrians relied heavily on **Slav** conscripts who did not understand the orders of their commanders, showing that the advantage of better weapons did not always mean that the side would be victorious.

The Austro-Prussian War

One of the most significant developments in the nineteenth century was the Dreyse needle gun. This rifle had two advantages:

- It could be loaded and fired four or five times more quickly than a muzzle-loaded rifle.
- It could be loaded and fired from a lying or prone position, which allowed the firer to take cover.

At first, there were some technical difficulties with this gun, but its effectiveness in the war against Austria in 1866 encouraged its wider adoption.

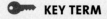 **KEY TERM**

Slavs People from eastern and central Europe, often the Balkans, but also Russia. The Austro-Hungarian Empire contained many Slavs.

This development had a considerable impact on tactics as the defenders now had an enhanced range and firepower, which alongside trenches gave them a great advantage. In the main battle at Sadowa it was the firepower of the rifle that was a major element in the Prussians' victory as they attacked the Austrian flanks with their Dreyse rifles, using the advantage of firing from a prone position, while the Austrians were fully exposed. Other factors such as the incompetence of the Austrian leadership were also important, but the technical advantage was reflected in the casualties in the battle, with 44,000 Austrians compared to the 9000 Prussians. It was therefore hardly surprising that the war was over in a mere seven weeks.

The Franco-Prussian War

As with the Austro-Prussian War, the Prussian victory was just as dramatic. However, as with the Franco-Austrian War of 1859, the Franco-Prussian War is another example where superior weapons, or at least superior rifles, did not bring about victory. The French, like the Prussians, also possessed a breech-loading rifle, the Chassepot, which had twice the range of the Dreyse, and they also had an early version of the machine gun, the *mitrailleuse*, which could fire 200 rounds a minute. However, the machine gun had been kept secret and therefore hardly any of the French soldiers knew how to use it! Despite this, the French possessed greater defensive firepower and should have had an advantage, but because of poor leadership and organisation were defeated.

The Prussians were helped by their superior artillery power, and it was this that determined the outcome of the two major battles. As in the war against Austria, the breech-loading rifled steel cannons, made by **Krupp**, were superior to the French cannons and had a far greater range and accuracy, which allowed them to destroy the French artillery. This meant that they were able to bombard and inflict considerable damage on the French while staying out of range themselves. They were also lighter and therefore more mobile, which along with the greater range of the Prussian cannons, gave them a considerable advantage. Both major battles, those at Metz and Sedan, were, according to some historians, ultimately determined by the superior artillery range of the Prussian forces, with the historian Neil Stewart (2002) describing the victory at Sedan as a 'stunning victory for the modernised artillery; the Prussian infantry were barely needed'.

It could, therefore, be argued that the Wars of Unification were a turning point in weapons. Despite the Wars of Unification witnessing the emergence of new, more powerful and accurate rifles, their dominance ended and it was the artillery that was the most decisive weapon.

Developments in weapons in the period 1871–1914

This belief in the superiority of artillery on the battlefield was encouraged by other developments that took place between the ending of the Wars of Unification and the outbreak of the First World War. These included:

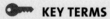

KEY TERMS

Mitrailleuse A French gun with a large number of barrels so it could fire either multiple rounds at once or several rounds in rapid succession.

Krupp Major German industrial firm and armaments manufacturer.

- High explosives, such as TNT, were developed, with no smoke to give away the position of the gunners.
- Artillery range was developed to reach up to five miles, but by 1914 this had become some twenty miles, although some could even reach 50 miles.
- Recoilless cannons meant that the rate of fire was more rapid. Prior to this development they could fire only three or four rounds a minute, but by 1914 were similar in rate to a rifleman.

However, it was not just in artillery that developments took place that would have a profound effect on the nature of warfare.

The rifle underwent significant changes, which made battles more deadly and increased casualty rates. The most significant development was the magazine rifle:

- Instead of loading one bullet at a time, rifles could take up to nine in the loading chamber.
- Loading time decreased and therefore the rate of fire increased, with firing rates of up to a bullet every four seconds.
- Cartridges also became smaller, which meant that soldiers could carry more, increasing from 60 rounds during the Austro-Prussian war to 200 by 1914, further adding to the firepower of an army.
- Metal cartridges and the use of cordite, which was smokeless, meant that rifles could be fired without smoke obscuring the firer or showing his location.

However, perhaps the most significant development in this period was the machine gun as this played an important role in ensuring that battles and wars were attritional and further added to the strength of the defender.

The machine gun was developed from the French *mitrailleuse* and the American Gatling gun, but they depended on hand-cranked revolver cannons, whereas the machine gun developed by Hiram Maxim was fully automatic and:

- fired 600 rounds per minute
- was water-cooled and belt-fed, improving reliability and effectiveness
- was much lighter, weighing only 40 pounds, and could therefore be manually wheeled or carried.

Despite these advantages, there was initial resistance to the machine gun as many officers thought that it took away from bravery and courage. However, its success in the colonial wars of the 1880s and 1890s convinced many of its value. In these wars, where European powers often had only small armies, the machine gun enabled them to overcome troop shortages. It played a vital role in the British victory over the Sudanese at Omdurman in 1898, with some 11,000 Sudanese killed compared with just 28 British. This development meant that numerical superiority was no longer a major factor.

The Russo-Japanese War

The war between the newly emerging modern power, Japan, and Russia was influenced by developments in weapons and communications technology. Japan had built up its forces so that they were locally superior to those of Russia. However, it was to be sea power that determined the outcome, as Japan was able to launch a surprise attack on the Russian fleet at Port Arthur and then transport a large force to land, unopposed, on the Liaodong peninsula. Both sides also resorted to underwater attacks, using torpedoes, as Japan attacked the harbour at Port Arthur, destroying a cruiser and two battleships. Minefields were also used by both sides, with the laying of defensive and offensive minefields in an attempt to keep the opposing navy in port or to sink ships in shallow waters. On the other hand, guns on ships achieved very little, with only direct hits inflicting damage, and they were unlikely, as they required close-range firing. Yet, it was domination of the seas by the Japanese, in part through their excellent use of wireless telegraphy (radio) to send orders and report enemy movements to their ships, which gave them superiority and allowed them to land their forces on the mainland.

The First World War

Initially, developments in weaponry had little impact on the nature of the war. The First World War began with both sides expecting it to be a war of movement that would be over by Christmas 1914. However, the halting of the German advance at the first Battle of the Marne in September 1914 resulted in both sides' determination to hold their positions. In order to remove themselves from enemy fire they dug a series of continuous trenches and this would become the dominant form of warfare for most of the remainder of the war. The nature of the war had been determined by the weaponry and technology available. Technological developments had meant that large numbers of troops could be moved to the battlefield relatively quickly, while developments in weapons, particularly the machine gun and artillery, meant that troops could not afford to be exposed to the firepower of the enemy. The weapons now had greater firepower, accuracy and range, all of which endangered the combatants and ensured that they had to take cover. As a result, the war gave advantage to the defenders, with the construction of a network of trenches that ran for some 700 miles down the Western Front. This can be seen most clearly in the numbers lost in the German attack on the French fortress of Verdun. It was only in the final months of the war that attacking forces were able to regain the initiative.

Even the trenches themselves were affected by the firepower of the weapons. The front-line trenches were zigzagged to prevent a shell blast or rifle fire running the length of the trench and inflicting even more casualties. The firepower also ensured that a series of trenches running back from the front line were constructed so that more men could be brought up to the front, while, at the same time, providing better shelter from enemy fire. Thus, a series of support and reinforcement trenches were constructed behind the front line, making it even harder for an enemy attack to break through and helping to explain why twice as many casualties were inflicted on the attacker as the defender during the war. The defensive nature of warfare was further reinforced by the use of barbed wire. Rows of wire, often up to 30 metres deep, only added to the problem that attacking armies would face as artillery attempts to destroy it usually ended in failure and simply turned no-man's land into a quagmire which it was even harder for the attackers to cross. This type of warfare resulted in the development of specific trench weapons, with the use of flamethrowers and gas; it could be argued that tanks were developed to cross the ground between trenches.

Weapons development had created stalemate on the Western Front, but also led to the belief that further developments in weaponry would bring the stalemate to an end. Therefore, from 1915 onwards both sides attempted to develop new weapons in order to achieve a breakthrough.

Developments took place in the following areas:

- chemical warfare
- tanks
- artillery
- infantry weaponry
- air warfare.

Chemical warfare

The development of chemical or gas warfare appeared to offer the promise of a breakthrough. It was first used by the Germans at the second Battle of Ypres in 1915 and disabled four miles of British lines. This was particularly important for Germany's war effort as it was fighting a war on two fronts and was suffering from a shortage of manpower compared with the Allies. It also had the potential to develop this form of warfare as its chemical industry was far more developed than that of either France or Britain. At first, chemical warfare caused much fear among soldiers and appeared to offer both a physical and psychological threat, spreading panic among those soldiers who were affected. Chemical warfare was developed further, so that by 1917 **mustard gas** and **phosgene** were used, delivered into enemy trenches by shells. However, despite these developments in chemical weaponry it had little overall impact on the conduct of the war. There were many shortcomings associated with the use of gas, the most obvious being that it was dependent on the direction of the wind, as it could be blown back to the very trenches from which it was fired, as happened to the British at Loos in 1915. Moreover, the development of ever more effective gas masks lessened the impact and meant that it was little more than an irritant.

KEY TERMS

Mustard gas A gas which causes large blisters on exposed skin and in the lungs.

Phosgene A colourless gas, which caused about 85 per cent of the 100,000 deaths due to chemical weapons.

Tanks

The development of tanks appeared to offer the possibility of advance while protecting soldiers from the fire of machine guns. However, there were many problems associated with the tank, which rendered its use limited, and it would not be until the Second World War that it would have a decisive influence. Its reliability was still very limited and many tanks broke down after only a few days of use. They were very slow, with a speed of only two miles per hour on the battlefield; that, and the weakness of the armour plating, meant that they were an easy target for enemy artillery, particularly once the Germans had developed an armour-piercing bullet. There was also the problem that there were initially, at least, not enough of them, which meant that they were too widely dispersed across the battlefield to have an impact. At the Battle of the Somme, where the British first used tanks, they had just 49. However, by the time of the Battle of Cambrai in 1917, the British were able to put over 350 into the field; but although they were able to achieve a breakthrough this could not be sustained as many were destroyed and even more broke down. Therefore, although the tank undoubtedly had potential, as was seen in the Second World War, its role was still limited; but it would be wrong to ignore the role they played in the breakthrough in 1918.

Artillery

The static nature of the war ensured that artillery played a significant role in the nature of the fighting, causing an estimated 70 per cent of the casualties. The lack of movement meant that once artillery guns were in position they did not have to be moved, which had been a problem in previous conflicts. However, the type of artillery, with shrapnel, available at the start of the war was designed for wars of movement and the flat-firing trajectory of the guns meant that they did little damage to trenches. Changes were made, and **howitzers** and mortars, with looping trajectories, could inflict greater damage, while heavier artillery could destroy barbed wire. Such developments ensured that the soldier was never safe as the range and accuracy were continually improved, meaning that soldiers back in **billets** away from the front line could be hit.

Despite these developments, initially at least, artillery had little impact on the nature or outcome of the war. An artillery barrage of the enemy front line soon became associated with an infantry attack and resulted in the withdrawal of troops from the front trenches to areas of greater safety, thus inflicting less loss of life. The artillery fire also usually failed to destroy the barbed wire, which only added to the problems faced by those soldiers who had survived crossing no-man's land. Not only that, but artillery shells had churned up no-man's land, creating crater holes and mud, which served to make the attack even more difficult. Once the barrage ended, it gave the defenders time to return to the front line and take up positions to repulse the attack.

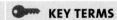 **KEY TERMS**

Howitzer An artillery weapon that fires projectiles at a high trajectory which then fall with a steep descent.

Billets Soldiers' accommodation.

It was only when the artillery was integrated into the infantry's attack that it played an important role in the outcome of battles. It was the use of the **creeping barrage**, which moved just ahead of the advancing infantry, that played the most important role. Although the aim was not to destroy the enemy troops, it forced them to take cover and therefore made the infantry's attack more likely to succeed, as it was not under continual fire from enemy machine guns. Therefore, it was more a change in the use of artillery rather than developments in the actual weaponry that had an impact on the nature and outcome of battles. However, artillery did increase its range with guns during the war, and as with previous conflicts this often allowed them to be located out of the range of enemy fire. The 'Big Bertha' gun, for example, designed by the German armaments firm Krupp, was seen in Germany as a wonder weapon, particularly after initial success against the Belgian fortress of Liège, but it was less successful against the stronger French fortress of Verdun. However, this development also had another impact as when firing, the crew had to move 300 yards away and fire it electronically and even then they were still so close that they required cotton wadding in their eyes, nose and ears. Despite these precautions they had to fire it with their mouth open to prevent the gun from blowing out their eardrums, even from that distance.

Infantry weaponry

By the final year of the war, improvements and developments in weaponry allowed greater mobility to return to the battlefield, and combined with new tactics, allowed a breakthrough to be achieved in 1918. The development of lighter machine guns, such as the Lewis gun, and mortars made the infantry more mobile and resulted in the organisation of heavily armed, mobile platoons of just 40 men who seized key positions, which were then secured by a second wave of attackers. Instead of being used for purely defensive purposes, the lighter machine gun could be carried and used as an offensive weapon, but the success of this was due also to developments such as the creeping barrage (see above), flamethrowers and rifle bombers. The success of July and August 1918 was due not just to the development of and improvements in the weapons, but to a combination of factors, which also included the use of tanks, aircraft, armoured cars, machine guns mounted on motorcycles and lorries carrying troops. Transport, weapons and greater co-ordination all played their roles and would provide a model for the Second World War.

Air warfare

The role of aircraft changed significantly in the First World War. At the outset they had been used primarily for reconnaissance purposes, replacing the cavalry, but by the end they were used as part of the attack on trenches, to stop infantry advances and disable gun and supply lines. Initially, pilots had been armed with just pistols and hand grenades, but a breakthrough was made in 1915 with the development of a fixed, forward-firing machine gun, which was synchronised to fire through propeller blades. On their own, aircraft achieved little, but in

> 🔑 **KEY TERM**
>
> **Creeping barrage** Instead of just bombarding enemy lines with artillery before the infantry advances, the creeping barrage involved the artillery fire moving forward in stages; it was first used at the Battle of the Somme. It required precise timing so that the infantry was not hit by its own artillery.

conjunction with other developments in weaponry they played a useful role in the breaking of stalemate and breakthrough in 1918. Both sides also developed bombers, but again their influence was limited. However, military planners were starting to believe that the bombing of civilians could be important in damaging morale on the home front, a view which would be developed much further in the Second World War. As with the ground war, the air war was decided by resources and mass production, an area in which the Allies were able to produce more planes than the Germans.

The Second World War

The weapons used to fight the Second World War were usually the same as those used in the First World War, but were improved versions and better utilised or more reliable.

The initial success of German armies in *Blitzkrieg* used weapons – the tank, motor vehicle and aeroplane, particularly the *Stuka* dive-bomber – that had been available in the First World War but were more reliable and better co-ordinated. This brought speed back to the battlefield and transferred the advantage from the defender to the attacker (see page 67). In particular, tanks were much more reliable and could move at far greater speeds than had been the case in the First World War. Their effectiveness was seen in the German advances in western Europe, but also in the great tank battles on the Eastern Front, at places such as **Kursk**, in 1943, which involved over 10,000 tanks.

The increased reliability of the combustion engine also meant that mobile artillery played an increased and more effective role in battles, as was seen in north Africa at the third Battle of **El Alamein** in 1942.

However, perhaps the greatest contrast with the First World War was improvements in aircraft. *Stuka* dive-bombers played a crucial role in determining the outcome of *Blitzkrieg* in the early years of the war as they provided air cover for tank and infantry assaults, as well as attacking retreating enemy forces. Such power ensured that trench warfare would not be the dominant method of warfare, as had happened in 1914–18. Flexible and hardy aircraft like the Spitfire and Hurricane were not only important in the successful defence of Britain during the Battle of Britain but could also be used in support of troops. The Mustang jet fighter was especially effective from 1943, when it was used to escort bombers in raids over Germany. Aircraft had also allowed Britain, and later the USA, to continue to attack Germany before the **Second Front** was launched in 1944. However, the impact of these raids on the outcome of the war was limited and their greatest effect was in sustaining morale at home, showing to the public that the enemy was still being hit and providing propaganda victories. Moreover, many of the attacks achieved little in the first part of the war because the raids were not accurate, with only one aircraft in three getting within five miles of its target and its bombs being even less accurate.

KEY TERMS

Kursk A major battle on the Eastern Front in July and August 1943, it was one of the largest armoured clashes. It was the first time a German strategic offensive was halted before it could break enemy defences and reach strategic depths. The Russian counteroffensive was their first successful summer offensive of the war.

El Alamein Named after an oasis and railway junction in the north African desert. The third Battle of El Alamein in 1942 is sometimes seen as a turning point as it was the first decisive victory since the start of the war.

Second Front The attack on mainland Europe through France, which was finally launched with D-Day in June 1944. The other front was the Eastern Front, where Russian troops were fighting Germany.

Figure 2.1 Bomb damage in London following a German air raid in 1940.

Figure 2.2 Damage inflicted on Dresden by British and US air forces in 1945.

Later in the war, air power did have an impact. The Allies were able to build many more planes than the Germans and air superiority allowed the Allies to destroy not just Germany's air force, the *Luftwaffe*, but also much of its war economy. Air power was able to do this as industry and lines of communication were destroyed and oil production was so reduced that by the end of the war German planes were being pushed on to the runway to save fuel. Some have argued that the attacks also had a knock-on effect on the German war effort, as men were withdrawn from fighting to operate air defences, while others have argued that the effects have been exaggerated. By the final year of the war, bombing had denied Germany half of its weapons and equipment.

Air power had an even more devastating impact in the Far East. By 1945, the Americans had seized islands that were well within the range of the Japanese mainland for US bombers. This allowed them to attack not only Japanese cities, which being mainly built of wood created firestorms that led to some 8 million refugees, but as a consequence to disrupt the Japanese economy. Air power had ensured that the Second World War was 'total war' and that civilians were often as involved as those fighting on the front. Although the First World War had seen some air attacks on civilians with **Zeppelin raids** and, later, heavy bombers, they had not been on the scale of the Second World War. It was therefore air power that had the greatest impact on the nature of warfare in this period, with the images of the destruction of cities such as London, Coventry, Hamburg and Dresden showing the extent to which civilians were affected.

The bombing of cities and industrial areas was important in destroying the enemy's economy and represents a change, if a controversial one, in the nature of warfare. However, it was not as controversial as the use of the atomic bomb in August 1945. The dropping of the two bombs on the Japanese cities of Hiroshima and Nagasaki was a clear demonstration of how the nature of warfare had changed. The development of weapons with powers of mass destruction of both buildings and civilians brought an end to the war and spared the USA the loss of large numbers that would have perished in an assault on mainland Japan, but it also made clear that warfare was no longer limited as it had been at the start of the period.

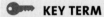

KEY TERM

Zeppelin raids German airships that travelled at about 85 miles per hour and could deliver about two tons of bombs. They were used in raids against British cities.

3 Developments in communication and transport

▶ *Did developments in communications and transport change the nature of warfare?*

The previous section considered the impact of weapons technology, but just as important were developments in non-military technology, such as communications and transport. The development of the steam engine had a significant impact on nineteenth-century warfare as the steamboat allowed troops to be transported across oceans and facilitated the development of overseas empires and the subsequent wars. On land, it was the development of railways that had the greatest impact as they allowed large armies and supplies to be transported to the battlefield in a much shorter period of time than was possible by horse or on foot. Railways could move troops fifteen times faster than their marching speed. This allowed both troops and animals to conserve their energy. However, once troops got beyond the railhead they still had to march and animals were still needed to haul supply wagons. Therefore, the condition of the roads in the areas of conflict still played an important role in moving both troops and supplies in the final few miles. Although there had been considerable improvements in both road design and construction, roads outside cities were usually in a poor condition and tarmacadam was still not being used on a large scale, meaning that roads became very dusty in dry spells but very muddy in wet weather, making transport very difficult.

In terms of developments in communications, the telegraph, radio and telephone had the most dramatic impact as they allowed far greater co-ordination of action on the field of battle. The development of the electric telegraph allowed the instantaneous transmission of messages from headquarters. However, as with transport developments, soldiers still relied on flags, **bugles and runners** on the battlefield until later in the period when the field telephone changed that, first being used in the Second Boer War and then more widely in the Russo-Japanese War before becoming commonplace in the First World War, allowing greater co-ordination between units, and in the Second World War between artillery and infantry advances.

The Revolutionary and Napoleonic Wars

Although both the Revolutionary and Napoleonic Wars were fought on a massive scale, with French forces often much larger than their opponents, and over vast areas, stretching from the Iberian peninsula in the west to Moscow in the east and Egypt in the south, this did not mean that the methods of transporting troops were any different to those of early eighteenth-century wars. The problem of supplying armies had been a limiting factor in their size in the eighteenth century. This was partly overcome by the French adopting a system of foraging rather than a convoy system of supplies, which would have relied on horses and carts carrying goods. This process was made easier by breaking the army up into a series of self-sufficient corps, which were spread out over a large area, allowing for more rapid movement by living off the land. Ironically, therefore, the large French armies had returned to a more primitive form of obtaining supplies. Although this did initially overcome the problem of supplying much larger armies than had been possible in the wars of the eighteenth century, it did not work when less fertile lands, such as Spain, were invaded, nor did it work when they invaded Russia as the defenders destroyed all means of both sustenance and shelter.

 **KEY TERM**

Bugles and runners
Messages on the battlefield were conveyed by a bugler conveying signals by playing a brass instrument or by soldiers literally running between lines with messages for commanders.

The armies themselves relied largely on marching to get to the battlefield, with only the cavalry mounted, and this limited the speed with which reinforcements could be brought to the front. The speed at which armies could move had been improved by economic developments before the war, which had resulted in the construction in parts of western Europe of more reliable, all-weather roads.

However, it was a different picture the further east one moved, reflected in the amount of material and cannons the French had to abandon during the retreat from Moscow because of the conditions of the roads in winter. The French certainly took advantage of developments in road construction and by carrying less baggage (for example by abandoning the use of tents and sleeping in the open instead) they were able to achieve far greater mobility. Such was the success of these methods that the allied forces abandoned their baggage trains and adopted a similar method to the French.

Therefore, although the wars saw the emergence of mass armies, the primitive methods of transport available meant that there was a return to old-fashioned methods of living off the land to feed the armies so that what speed there was did not get sacrificed by waiting for the arrival of slow-moving baggage trains.

The Crimean War

The Crimean War witnessed some significant changes in transport and communications technology with the development of the steam engine and the electric telegraph.

The impact of railways

It was the development of the steam engine, which could be used to power both rail transport and steamboats, that was to have the most dramatic impact on the nature of warfare and would have the greatest impact on strategy until the development of the internal combustion engine and air transport. In the Napoleonic period, an army could move only as fast as a soldier could march and, similarly, if soldiers had to rely on horses and carts to bring in supplies that also limited the distance over which an army could range. However, the development of railways removed that limitation and meant that soldiers could be carried, provided there was a rail line, much closer to the field of battle, and its importance would be seen throughout the remainder of nineteenth- and early twentieth-century wars. The development of railways meant that:

- soldiers could move much more quickly
- more troops could be moved to the battlefield
- supplies could be taken to the battlefield more easily
- soldiers were fresher when it came to fighting as they had not had to march vast distances.

All of this meant that armies became much bigger and the limiting factor would be the size of the population of the nations fighting, providing the potential for armies to become much larger than had been seen in the past.

These developments were evident in the Crimean War, where the development of the steamship allowed the British and French to transport both men and supplies to the region in less than three weeks. The war also witnessed the construction of the first purpose-built railway to move men to the battlefield. British engineers constructed a 25-mile-long line linking the port of Balaclava to the front line. Such a development meant that some 240 tons of supplies reached the front line daily, a figure previously unheard of. If it had not been for the incompetence of the command, this development would have brought the conflict to a much swifter conclusion.

The impact of the electric telegraph

In terms of communications, the most important development was the electric telegraph. This allowed messages to be sent over long distances and allowed leaders at home to stay in touch with commanders in the field, giving politicians a far greater role in the conduct of the war than had previously been the case. However, the development had little impact on the battlefield during the Crimean War and, as with the Napoleonic Wars, messages on the battlefield were still carried by runners or sent using flags or drums.

However, if the electric telegraph had little impact on the battlefield, it had a massive impact on public opinion and the conduct of war. Newspapers were able to take advantage of the development to provide up-to-date coverage of battles to the public. This led to far greater awareness among the public about what was happening, with reporters in the Crimea using the specially laid undersea telegraph, which was linked to the European network. It was this that made the British public aware of the awful conditions and inadequate medical facilities. These stories encouraged greater newspaper readership and led to the growing importance of public opinion in strategic considerations.

The American Civil War

The American Civil War of 1861–5 saw the most effective use made of railways to date. They played a vital role, largely because of the geographical area over which the conflict was fought. Their importance is made clear by the fact that armies often stayed close to railways, both to protect them from sabotage and attack and because they brought in supplies. This becomes even clearer when one considers that many battles were fought around key rail centres, such as Chattanooga, Atlanta and Nashville, or close to rail lines. Perhaps surprisingly, they were also used for reconnaissance purposes, with locomotives sent ahead to scout an area as they could withdraw much more quickly than the pursuing cavalry! They were also used for transporting heavy guns and artillery to areas of conflict.

The rail network also had a considerable impact on the outcome of the war. The North or Union possessed a far better rail network, with a study of the Baltimore and Ohio rail company revealing that of its 30,000 miles of track, only 9000 miles were in Confederate territory. The North also had a more advanced and reliable network and locomotives, while in the South many lines did not cross state boundaries and served just local areas. The Northern states were quick to realise the importance of the rail network, particularly after the Confederacy had used rail to bring in reinforcements to help secure victory at the **first Battle of Bull Run**. The Union responded by appointing **Daniel McCullum** as military director and superintendent of railways with total power over them. He ensured that the rail network was run by those with experience in the rail industry and not by military men, and he insisted that wagons were emptied quickly and reused so that marshalling yards did not become clogged, but perhaps his greatest feat was the rebuilding of the bridge over the Potomac River in just nine days. The 400-foot bridge had been destroyed by Confederate troops and prevented the North from moving both men and supplies south.

However, in terms of the impact of railways on the military outcome, this was best seen in the use made by the Northern general Sherman in his sweep south that brought about the end of the war. His army was supplied by a single rail route of three lines covering 500 miles from Louisville to Atlanta, and as he wrote in his memoirs: 'That single stem of railroad supplied an army of 100,000 men and 32,000 horses for the period of 196 days between 1 May and 19 November 1864.' Without the railway it would have been a logistical impossibility as it would have required 36,800 wagons each with six mules!

The Wars of Unification

The development of the rail network had an even greater impact on the nature and outcome of the Wars of Unification than it did on the Crimean War. Railways and steamships were used effectively by the French in 1859 to deploy troops to the front against Austria and again by the Prussians in 1866 in their war against Austria. The greater use of railways was matched by the further development, use and integration of the electric telegraph.

The Franco-Austrian War

Railways were used to great effect by the French to transport some 120,000 men to the battlefield in northern Italy in less than two weeks, whereas the Austrian army marched, often at no more than three or four miles per day. The French army was further boosted by the arrival of some 70,000 men by steamship. This gave the French a considerable advantage as not only did the soldiers arrive first on the battlefield and could choose where to fight, but they arrived much fresher. However, this potential advantage depended on the arrival of supplies and weapons and the lack of co-ordination sometimes meant that they did not

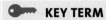

KEY TERM

First Battle of Bull Run
Also known as the Battle of First Manassas. Fought in 1861 in Virginia, it was the first major battle of the Civil War. It resulted in victory for the South.

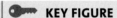

KEY FIGURE

Daniel McCullum (1815–78)
A Scottish-born American, he was a railroad engineer, general manager of the New York and Erie Railroad, and became major general in the North's army. He was a skilled manager and developed the first modern organisational chart.

arrive, reducing the advantage. However, lessons were learned, particularly
by Prussian planners, as was seen in their war with Austria in 1866 when it
was realised that greater planning and communication were needed to take
advantage of the opportunities provided by the technological advances.

The German Wars of Unification

Prussian generals learned lessons from the French use of railways in the
Franco-Austrian War and made sure that they did not make the same mistakes.
The Prussian general staff ensured that rail and telegraph were integrated
into its planning, often sending its most talented officers into war planning.
Even Moltke, the commander of Prussian forces, spent time in the 1840s in the
Prussian army's rail section and would later argue that money would be better
spent on developing the rail network than on building more forts. It was soon
apparent that Moltke realised the potential that rail construction offered the
army as he organised rail mobilisation exercises and in 1843 and argued that
'every new development of railways is a military advantage'.

The commanders were able to take advantage of the dramatic growth in the
Prussian economy in the period after the Napoleonic Wars, which saw the
amount of track more than treble and give Prussia a great advantage over its
continental rivals. Not only that, but it was agreed that the army would have
first call on the rail network when it was needed. This would continue to be
an advantage for Germany through to the First World War, when given the
nature of the development of its rail network the Germans were able to move
large numbers of troops relatively quickly to an area near Aachen on the
Belgian border in order to begin the implementation of the Schlieffen Plan (see
page 114).

The rail network was crucial in the Prussians' victory of 1866 over Austria as
they were able to deliver a force of some 250,000 men over 300 miles using five
separate lines. This allowed the Prussians to rapidly converge on the battlefield,
whereas the Austrians made little use of their own limited rail network.

The Russo-Japanese War

The absence of an adequate rail network had an impact on the outcome of the
land war. The incomplete Trans-Siberian railway around Irkutsk meant that
Russia was unable to transport troops rapidly to the area around Port Arthur,
which gave the Japanese time to consolidate their initial gains and secure the
area, while Russia attempted to fight a holding campaign until troops could be
brought in. It was Russia's inability to bring in sufficient troops that allowed the
Japanese to gain victory over a European power in a land battle at Yalu Bridge in
1904.

The First World War

Transport

In the period leading up to the First World War, a number of important transport developments had taken place. All the major continental powers had drawn up plans for mass attacks, made possible by the development of strategic rail lines. The Germans, as we have seen, had constructed a vast rail network which converged near the border with Belgium, around Aachen, which would allow them to transport large numbers to the west. Such developments allowed Moltke to deploy 1 million men in his initial assault into Belgium. Russia had also invested heavily in the development of its rail network and, although it was not as advanced as Germany's, it was increasing at a rapid rate.

However, although this might appear to offer the potential to move large numbers of men, it depended on reliability and planning. Railway timetables on which such large-scale movement depended were inflexible, while rail lines were liable to sabotage. There was also still the problem of getting supplies to the front line and the system was unable to keep pace with the initial rapid advances. If the rail network on the Western Front was unable to keep up with the military needs, it was even worse on the Eastern Front and by 1916 the Russian network had virtually collapsed. It was not just struggling in terms of moving and supplying troops, but also in supplying towns and cities with food. The chaotic nature of the system and the priority given to the movement of troops often meant that wagons taking grain to the cities sat in sidings and rotted, while people in the cities went unfed and prices rose at an alarming rate, contributing in no small measure to the **March 1917 Revolution**.

Figure 2.3 Germans troops being transported by train to the Western Front in 1914.

KEY TERM

March 1917 Revolution
Sometimes called the February Revolution, depending on which calendar is being used. It resulted in the overthrow of the last Russian tsar, Nicholas II, and his replacement by a Provisional Government. This was overthrown in the October Revolution when it was replaced by the Bolsheviks or Communists.

However, it must also be remembered that rail lines did not run all the way to the actual front line and, therefore, the last few miles would still depend on the traditional method of transport – feet. Perhaps this is seen most clearly during the adoption of the Schlieffen Plan, when Moltke's forces still had to march some 450 miles at a rate of over twenty miles a day and in the face of determined resistance. It would therefore not be until the next war, when reliability had been improved, that the rail system would play a crucial role in the outcome of the war.

Similarly, the other major development, namely the combustion engine, appeared to offer the potential of greater mobility for troops, but in practice often failed to meet the needs of armies. The combustion engine also had the potential to deliver large numbers of men to the front, but not only was the engine still in its infancy and unreliable but it could be used only where roads had been built. The road network, much like the rail network, was often overwhelmed, not just because of the number of military vehicles, but also because of civilians fleeing the battle area in whatever transport they could find, causing traffic jams. This did not prevent London buses being used to carry soldiers to the front in the early days of the war. French soldiers were taken to the Battle of the Marne in Parisian taxis, with the cost as on the meter! However, as the area around the battlefield became churned up and wet winters created further mud, it made many roads and tracks impassable for vehicles, and soldiers were forced once again to turn to the traditional method of walking to get to the front line, as was the case when they walked out of Ypres down the **Menin Road**. This also had an impact on the movement of supplies and weapons as, like the troops, they were delayed by the sheer volume of traffic and the physical conditions of the roads, many of which became little more than quagmires. As a result, armies were often forced back to using old-fashioned methods of moving and supplying troops.

KEY TERM

Menin Road The name, after the place to which it led, of the road leading out of Ypres to the front line, down which many British troops went.

However, despite these drawbacks, all sides were still able to supply large numbers of men to the front so that manpower was maintained and, until the latter stages of the war, neither side had an overwhelming numerical advantage. This resulted in the armies of both sides being larger than anything that had been seen before and, despite the heavy casualties, having the ability to replace the injured men.

The Second World War

Transport brought an element of mobility to the Second World War, which had been absent from the First World War. However, the transport that made mobility possible in the Second World War had been present during the First World War: the motor vehicle, the aeroplane and the tank. The difference between the two wars was in the range and reliability of such modes of transport. The developments in transport brought back mobility to the battlefield which had been seen during the Napoleonic Wars, but unlike those wars they did not depend solely on the pace of marching; instead, there was the co-ordinated use of technology.

The development was seen most clearly in the use of *Blitzkrieg* by German forces at the start of the war. The rapid movement of troops gave the attackers the advantage of surprise and allowed them to seize key points such as command and communication centres, which disrupted attempts by defenders to organise resistance. Aeroplanes were used to drop paratroops behind enemy lines and to seize key points, such as bridges. This rapid movement depended on co-ordination between different units and was made possible by improvements in communication, with radio available in aeroplanes, troop transporters and tanks. The rapid movement of these forces had a demoralising impact on defenders and often led to rapid surrender, with such tactics and use of transport allowing German forces to sweep through Poland in 1939 and much of north-west Europe in the early summer of 1940. This was perhaps most evident in the rapid 250-mile advance to the Channel coast, which led to British and French forces having to be evacuated from the beaches at **Dunkirk**.

The importance of this rapid movement of troops is seen in the fact that only a small proportion, possibly no more than ten per cent, of the German army was made up of such rapid-moving divisions, but it was these who were responsible for the victories as their speed made it virtually impossible for defenders to regroup and reorganise. The rest of the army that followed on behind to 'mop up' any remaining resistance still relied on being transported towards the front by train or by marching.

Although transport played a crucial role in the west, it must be remembered that such developments in transport failed to deliver the same rewards in the east, clearly revealing the limits to such tactics. However, the failings were not just down to transport. *Blitzkrieg* was much more effective in smaller areas, whereas the vast space in Russia allowed troops to fall back and regroup. This meant that, unlike in the west, German supply lines were extended and became vulnerable to attack and, as time wore on, to the harsh conditions of the Russian winter, something that German transport was unable to overcome. The fast-moving Panzer, or tank units, which had been so successful in the west, became isolated and unable to be supplied. Moreover, as in the Napoleonic Wars, the Allies learned from their earlier errors and *Blitzkrieg* also lost its element of surprise. As in the Napoleonic Wars, the Allies adopted similar tactics and with the development of more mobile artillery were able to not only repel the German advance, but as in north Africa, in 1942, make considerable gains themselves.

One development of the war was the use of airborne assaults. This became a feature of warfare as planes and gliders brought troops close to, or even behind, enemy lines. Such assaults were crucial in the German seizure of Crete in 1941, which began with an airborne assault, although this method was less successful in Operation Market Garden, when the Allies tried to encircle German industry in the Ruhr.

KEY TERM

Dunkirk With the rapid advance of German forces, the British and French were driven back to the beaches at Dunkirk. In a remarkable achievement the British navy and a flotilla of small boats rescued some 338,000 troops in the period from 27 May to 4 June 1940.

Transport would play a crucial role in the final outcome of the war. The Allies' ability to transport 156,000 men across the English Channel on D-Day in June 1944 allowed them to seize a bridgehead in Normandy from which they would eventually be able to spread out across France and north-west Europe to defeat Hitler's Germany. The seizure of crucial transport and communications points had been possible only by the use of gliders bringing in troops to secure key points, such as Pegasus Bridge near Caen, preventing the Germans from destroying the canal crossing.

Chapter summary

The rapid industrialisation and technological developments of the period had an impact on the nature of warfare. In the nineteenth century those with the economic advantages were usually victorious, whereas in the twentieth century it was usually those states with economic endurance that were victorious. In terms of the impact of industrialisation, the American Civil War was a turning point and, with the exception of the Wars of Unification, most conflicts lasted for years instead of for a few weeks. Industrial developments and the associated weapons were also crucial in changing the nature of warfare from the offensive to the defensive and it was only with the Second World War that there was a return to the offensive. Moreover, industrial developments, particularly the steam engine and the development of rail networks, allowed the scale of warfare to increase dramatically as ever-increasing numbers of troops could be moved quickly to the theatre of conflict.

Refresher questions

Use these questions to remind yourself of the key material covered in this chapter.

1 Why were industrial developments important in the outcome of wars?

2 What was the impact of the Industrial Revolution on the development of military tactics and strategy?

3 What changes did technological developments bring to the conduct of warfare?

4 In what ways was the American Civil War a turning point in the development of warfare?

5 Why were economic factors important in the outcome of wars?

6 Why were most wars not short?

7 In what ways did the development of the rifle change the nature of warfare?

8 Why did the importance of artillery change during the period?

9 Why did warfare change from offensive to defensive in the period from 1789 to 1918?

10 How and why did the role of the cavalry change in this period?

11 Why did sides with superior weapons not always win?

12 Why did the size of the war zone increase during the period?

13 What was the impact of the development of rail networks on warfare?

14 Why was there stalemate in the First World War but not in the Second World War?

In-depth studies and key debates

The examination requires you to study three topics in depth and for this unit they are:

- The French Revolutionary Wars 1792–1802
- The American Civil War 1861–5
- The Western Front and the First World War 1914–18.

This section will go into more detail about the three topics and introduce you to some of the key debates about them, so that you will have enough depth of knowledge to be able to evaluate passages that are set on any of these three topics.

Key debate 1: how important were developments in weaponry in the outcome of the French Revolutionary Wars?

There has been much debate as to the importance of developments in weaponry in the French Revolutionary Wars. Some have argued that it was not developments in weaponry, such as lighter artillery, that brought about French successes, but rather changes in tactics and organisation. In these interpretations, historians have sometimes argued that the changes in organisation had begun in the final years of the monarchy, while those who have focused on tactics have suggested that it was simply born out of necessity as the mass armies were quickly thrown in to the conflict with little training. Even those, such William H. McNeill in *The Pursuit of Power* (1982), who have argued that the success was due to developments in the use of weaponry, have agreed that many of the changes were inherited from the earlier period, particularly the reforms of the 1760s carried out under auspices of Jean de Gribeauval.

There is some evidence to suggest that success was due to developments in weaponry:

- Lighter artillery with standardised parts was an advantage and allowed the French to move the artillery which until then had often remained in a fixed position on the battlefield.
- Jean de Gribeauval's reforms had created an artillery that had standardised calibre and ammunition, making the artillery more accurate and mobile.
- The rate of fire was improved by the reforms and this meant that cannons could be grouped together in effective batteries.
- The artillery pieces used at Valmy in September 1792, at extreme range, so discomfited the Prussians that it persuaded them to withdraw from French soil.
- The recovery of Toulon in 1793 depended on the accuracy and rate of fire of the new French field artillery.

- The ability to carry and deploy field artillery was crucial in the Italian campaign.

It could be argued that the following factors were responsible for the success of the Revolutionary armies:

- The organisation of manoeuvrable divisions, which combined infantry, cavalry and artillery, provided greater flexibility and allowed armies to expand and draw their supplies from across a wider area.
- The use of divisions meant that the armies could converge on the battlefield from different directions.
- The use of 'shock tactics', or the storming of enemy positions, surprised the enemy, who were unable to sustain the high losses this often entailed.
- The new arrangements of attack columns turned the army into a form of 'human battering ram' and although they sustained heavy casualties, the enemy also suffered heavy losses which it could not sustain.
- The key element in French success was the weight of numbers and it was this that made possible their tactics and ability to sustain heavy losses.
- The French armies were much larger than those of their opponents.
- The concept of the 'nation in arms', combined with the ideological nature of the conflict, drove the French army to success.

The success of the Revolutionary armies, after initial defeats and the possibility that France would be overrun, shocked much of the rest of Europe. It started the move towards 'total war', where all civilians were involved, and marked a significant change from the more limited wars of the eighteenth century. Napoleon built on many of the changes and developments outlined above, but it should be remembered that by 1796, before he had made an impact, the French Revolutionary armies had extended French territory to an area not seen for many years and had brought in, according to the historian Neil Stewart (2002), 'a revolution in warfare every bit as significant as that ushered in by Napoleon'.

Key debate 2: how significant were developments in transport in the American Civil War?

There is a great deal of historical controversy about the factors that led to the victory of the North over the South. Although it was the North that emerged victorious, some have argued that at many points the war could have gone differently and resulted in a different outcome. Most historians accept that there were many reasons for the North's ultimate victory, whereas other interpretations focus on just one or two causes. Many have focused on the resources of the North, one of which was transport, and in particular railways, while others have looked to the economic and numerical advantages, and others have stressed the weakness of the South.

In arguing that developments in transport were significant, the following issues might be considered:

- Railways were crucial because of the large area over which the war was fought.
- Many of the battles were fought around key rail centres such as Chattanooga, Atlanta and Nashville, showing the importance of controlling rail hubs to be able to move troops rapidly.
- The North possessed a far better rail network than the South.
- The rail network of the North was more reliable, as were their locomotives, and this was used effectively for moving artillery and reconnaissance.
- The Confederacy had used the rail network effectively to bring in supplies to secure victory at the first Battle of Bull Run and the North learned from this.
- The North clearly recognised the importance of the rail network in its appointment of Daniel McCullum.
- Sherman's sweep south was sustained only because of the rail network.
- The Anaconda Plan recognised the importance of rivers and how their control could be used to strangle the South, and this depended on using steamboats.
- Steamboats were important as they could carry enough supplies to support an army of 40,000 and 18,000 horses for two days.
- In 1862, river gunboats were important in the capture of a number of the South's fortresses; similarly, they were used to capture Memphis.
- The North used ships to blockade the South and this helped to prevent it from selling cotton to Europe to finance the war.
- Union gunboats, in conjunction with forces, were able to control nearly all of the Mississippi by August 1862, and this was completed in 1863, with the result that the North could maintain control in the west.
- The large number of ships possessed by the North enabled it to move its troops and strike coastal targets, such as New Orleans, and this hit the morale of the South.

In arguing that it was factors other than transport that secured the victory of the North, the following issues might be considered:

- Some historians have suggested that the blockade of the South was not effective because of the 3500 miles of coastline which could not be policed.
- It has been argued that the result depended on the number of men and guns the North possessed, what historians have termed 'Big Battalions'.
- Some have suggested that there were divisions within the Confederacy over issues such as states' rights and resistance to a variety of war measures, and some groups were alienated from Southern war efforts, including some planters, non-slaveholding whites and slaves.
- Some have argued that morale was an issue and have suggested that the South lacked the will to make the required sacrifices, with some suggesting that there was a lack of nationalism, while others did not want to fight to

defend slavery and a lack of will was made worse by the economic and financial situation.

- Leadership has been seen as a factor, with some interpretations focusing on generalship, while others have looked at the management of issues such as the economy and finance.

It is certainly true that by the winter of 1864–5 the will of the South was drained, as seen in the desertion rate. However, it is vital to ask what caused these desertions and some have argued that it was defeat in battle, the occupation of the South's land and the re-election of Lincoln in 1864. Southern armies were defeated from mid-1863 onwards and that helped to drain morale and encourage the North. Transport played an important role in those victories, but it should be remembered that greater overall resources allowed the North to triumph and sustain heavy losses. By applying its advantages, such as in transport, victory, it could be argued, was inevitable.

Key debate 3: how important were developments in weaponry in the First World War?

The failure of the strategic plans at the start of the war in 1914 and the development of trench warfare over the next few months, which it can be argued was due in part to the machine gun, meant that leaders and strategists hoped that the development of new weapons would end the deadlock. In particular, the development of chemical weapons and the use of the tank were seen by some as crucial, while other have looked at developments to existing weapons, such as artillery, in being important. However, some historians have also argued that the new weapons achieved little and that it was a change in organisation and tactics that was vital, while others have argued that it was the entry of the USA and developments on the home front in Germany that were key.

In arguing that developments in weaponry were decisive, the following could be considered:

- Chemical weapons were useful in the advances of 1918.
- The Germans were able to disable four miles of British lines near Ypres in April 1915 because of the use of gas.
- Chemical weapons provided an element of shock and were a useful psychological weapon.
- Tanks appeared to provide protection against the machine gun and to permit greater mobility.
- Tanks were successful at the Battle of Cambrai, when 378 were used.
- Tanks, by the end of the war, removed the need for an artillery barrage as they were able to destroy barbed wire.
- Tanks offered an element of surprise.

However, it can be argued that the new weapons were limited in their effectiveness and therefore it was other factors that were more relevant:

- It has been argued that the success of chemical weapons depended on wind direction and could be blown back against the attackers, as happened at Loos in September 1915.
- This argument has been further developed as armies developed protection against chemical weapons, making them less effective.
- Technological advances were not always effective as the early tanks were very slow, vulnerable and unreliable. They had a top speed of only one or two miles an hour on the battlefield.
- The tank's effectiveness was limited as its armour plating was vulnerable to artillery.
- The tank's success was further limited as there often too few tanks either available or sent into action to be effective, as happened at the Somme, where only 49 were used.
- To be effective, tanks needed to be used in conjunction with infantry so that when the tanks broke through enemy lines the infantry could hold the ground seized, but this did not happen.
- Even when large numbers were used at Cambrai, the tank's effectiveness was limited as many broke down, with the British losing 300.
- This problem was compounded by the fact that even if tanks survived the early onslaught, they often lasted only a few days in battle before breaking down.

There is some justification to suggest that new weapons helped in 1918, but in terms of the tank it was probably the psychological impact that was the most important. Although they had potential, it was not really seen in the First World War. Instead, in terms of weaponry it was probably developments to existing weapons, such as artillery and the machine gun, that were crucial. The lighter and more mobile machine gun meant that it was no longer simply a weapon of defence. Artillery evolved so that its tactics were more varied, in particular, the creeping barrage. A more accurate approach to destroying enemy positions was seen from the British artillery and this increased the importance of the artillery on the battlefield.

Study skills: thematic essay question

How to develop analysis and write a paragraph that shows synthesis

If you have already studied units 1 and 2 of the OCR course, the essay writing skills that you have developed are similar to those needed for unit 3. However, there are two key differences. On page 54 we stressed that the title of the unit, thematic study, makes it clear that the essay section should be approached thematically rather than chronologically, particularly if you want to reach the higher mark range. In addition, in this unit there is a significant emphasis on synthesis.

In answering essay questions you are required to make connections, comparisons and links between different elements of the period and aspects of the topic; this is that crucial element of synthesis – the comparison between different parts of the period – to show similarities and differences between events or people. It is not simply enough to list examples from across the period in each paragraph; you must make direct comparisons between them. You do not need to make comparisons across the whole period in every paragraph, but the whole period needs to be covered in the essay.

As with essays in units 1 and 2, you should aim to write analytically. This is perhaps the most difficult but most important skill you need to develop. An analytical approach can be helped by ensuring that the opening sentence of each paragraph introduces an idea, which directly answers the question and is not just a piece of factual information. In a very strong answer it should be possible to simply read the opening sentences of all the paragraphs and know what argument is being put forward.

Consider the following question:

> How far did developments in transport and communications change the nature of warfare in the period from 1789 to 1945?

Possible opening sentences for an answer in response to this question could be as follows:

- The development of railways resulted in states being able to raise much larger armies than had been the case during the Revolutionary and Napoleonic Wars.
- The development of the electric telegraph expanded the range of military command and political interference, although there was initially less impact on the battlefield.
- The development of the combustion engine and air transport had a significant impact on the nature of warfare.
- More advanced means of communication increased the range and scale of military operations than had been the case at the start of the period.
- As the period progressed, the developments in air transport became particularly important as forces could be dropped behind enemy lines to seize key strategic points or airborne attacks could even seize large areas.

You would then go on to discuss both sides of the argument raised by the opening sentence, using relevant knowledge about the issue to support each side of the argument. The final sentence of the paragraph would reach a judgement on the role played by the factor you are discussing in changing the nature of warfare. This approach would ensure that the final sentence of each paragraph links back to the actual question you are answering. If you can do this for each paragraph you will have a series of mini-essays, each of which discusses a factor and reaches a conclusion or judgement about the importance of that factor or issue.

Developing synthesis

Some of the opening sentences have already hinted at comparisons between different wars across the period, but this comparison would need to be developed and more of the period covered if an answer was to reach the highest level. The two responses below illustrate a weak approach (Response A) that does not really illustrate synthesis, and a strong approach (Response B), which shows a high level of synthesis.

Response A

Developments in transport were a factor in changing the nature of warfare in the Wars of Unification. The Prussians, through the developments in their general staff, made extensive use of the rail network in both their wars against Austria and France and this had a significant impact on the nature of both wars as it allowed them to bring large numbers of soldiers to the battlefield quickly and in a better physical condition than if they had been forced to march, and this can be compared with both opposing forces. Railways gave forces the crucial advantage of arriving first on the battlefield, not only in superior numbers, but also in peak condition and fully supplied, as Moltke stated, 'every new development of railways is a military advantage'. The use of railways in the defeat of Austria allowed a force of some 250,000 to arrive across a 300-mile front and converge rapidly on the enemy and, most importantly, avoid a frontal assault. Similarly, against the French it enabled the Prussians, through sheer weight of numbers, to outweigh any weaponry advantages that the French had. As a result, transport developments, in this instance the railways, had made clear that rapid mobilisation was essential and would allow sweeping plans of attack to be put into place.

Response B

Transport developments, which in the mid-nineteenth and early twentieth centuries usually meant the railways, had a significant impact on the nature of warfare. **In both the American Civil War and the Wars of Unification** it was the rail network that played a crucial role in the victories of the North and the Prussian forces as they delivered large numbers of troops and supplies to the battlefield so that the size of the armies deployed increased dramatically and allowed the larger force to overcome any other disadvantages it might face. **However, in contrast, the development of the rail network had the opposite effect in the First World War. During both the American Civil War and particularly the Wars of Unification, the rapid deployment of troops was a considerable factor in victory as the rail network allowed troops to be deployed over a wide area and implement sweeping plans of attack. However, in the First World War the rail network allowed so many troops to converge on an area near Aachen that it blocked the theatre of operations and helped to ensure that instead of a war of movement and a quick, decisive victory that had happened in both 1866 and 1870–1, it led to a war of attrition in the form of trench warfare.**

Analysis of the responses

Response B is the stronger answer and displays high-level synthesis:

- Response A simply explains the role of the rail network in the nature and outcome of the Wars of Unification but there is no link or comparison between that war and other conflicts.
- There is sound detail in Response A, and there is some argument and analysis about the importance of the rail network, but there is no judgement about leadership or comparison with other factors.
- Response B compares the importance of the rail network and the use of railways in three different wars – as illustrated in bold type – and shows synthesis across much of the period, with examples from the middle and later periods.
  There is sound factual detail in Response B, which is sufficient to support the argument, and own knowledge is being 'used' and not simply imparted.

Activities

1 Write paragraphs similar to Response B for the other themes that were considered in the opening sentences above (page 96).
2 Try writing paragraphs for essays from the essay questions below.
3 In order to ensure that you have demonstrated synthesis across the period, highlight the examples of synthesis in your paragraphs and make a checklist to make sure that, over the course of the essay, your paragraphs cover all of the period from 1792 to 1945.

The focus of this section has been on planning and writing analytically and developing synthesis. Use the information in this chapter to plan answers and write a paragraph to each of the questions below which shows a high level of analysis and synthesis.

Essay questions

1 Assess the impact of industrialisation on the nature of warfare in the period from 1792 to 1945.
2 'Technological developments changed the nature of the battlefield, but did not decide the outcome of battle.' How far do you agree with this view of warfare in the period from 1792 to 1945?
3 'Developments in weaponry determined tactics on the battlefield.' How far do you agree with this view of warfare in the period from 1792 to 1945?

Study skills: depth study interpretations question

How to evaluate the interpretations

On pages 57–60 we considered how to structure and plan an answer to the depth study interpretations question. This section looks at how to evaluate, or apply own knowledge to one of the interpretations to judge its strengths and weaknesses. After you have started your essay explaining the two interpretations and placing them in the context of the wider historical debate about the issue, you need to go on to look at each interpretation in turn, to judge their strengths and weaknesses.

A good paragraph will:

- remain focused on the question
- directly link own knowledge to the view offered in the passage about the issue in the question in order to explain whether the view in the passage is valid or not
- use relevant and accurate knowledge to evaluate the view
- evaluate a range of issues mentioned in the passage.

Read the question and the two interpretations below about the impact of tanks in the First World War. Then look at the response, which gives a strong evaluation of the strengths and weaknesses of Interpretation A.

> Evaluate the interpretations in both of the passages and explain which you think is more convincing as an explanation of the impact of tanks on the outcome of battles in the First World War.

PASSAGE A

Adapted from John Terraine, *The Smoke and the Fire*, Sidgwick & Jackson, 1980, pp. 152–4.

The idea that tanks were war-winning weapons not recognised or used properly by ignorant generals is a myth. All tanks of that vintage were clumsy, slow and vulnerable. They had weak armour, lack of springs and poor ventilation. It is so much easier to ignore mechanical weakness and blame the 'high commands' for failing to perceive the potential of these 'wonder weapons', and wastefully using them in 'penny packets'. The truth is that the French ordered 400 of the heavy Schneider tanks straight off the drawing board in 1916. Haig, without ever seeing a tank, anticipated 'the surprise and demoralising effect they seem likely to produce'. Not until the Battle of Cambrai in 1917 was anything better than a 'penny packet' actually available to commanders. Then 324 fighting tanks and 54 more in reserve were used. During the last victorious hundred days in 1918 no less than 2000 tanks were engaged. However by 4 November only 37 were available. German anti-tank methods were improving all the time and a third of tank crews became casualties.

PASSAGE B

Adapted from C.R.M.F. Crutwell, *A History of the Great War*, Oxford University Press, 1934, pp. 267ff.

It is not easy to explain the violent hostility of the military leadership to the strenuous and helpful efforts of the politicians to improve the weapons at their disposal. The indispensible weapons of victory so eagerly offered by civilians were angrily rejected. Lloyd George [British Minister of Munitions] was regarded as a squandering megalomaniac when he insisted upon the great programme of machine guns, tanks and shells which, when completed, was thankfully accepted by his bitterest opponents. The history of tanks is a classic example of the dogged determination with which the British generals fought against the most fruitful of all modern improvements in the art of war. By using the early tanks in small groups, 'penny packets', it was hoped to protect the infantry. It is easy to deplore this premature disclosure and the correct tactical use of a new weapon is difficult to determine without experience. Not until the Battle of Cambrai, when the triumphant power of a massed force of tanks profoundly changed the character of trench warfare, do we see the correct tactical employment of the new weapon, which had hitherto been wasted.

Response

There is certainly some credibility in the view that generals have been unfairly criticised for their failure to see the importance of tanks and then using them in the wrong way. Terraine argues that it was not always justified to see them as war-winning weapons because they had severe technical problems. Thus, it took some vision on the part of the Allies to deploy them. The criticism made is that Haig wasted them during the Somme campaign and thus deprived the British of an element of surprise[1]. However, given the very heavy losses faced by the infantry, it does not seem irresponsible to deploy whatever aid was available as the use of the tanks which were stationed at nearby Flers. The idea of mass tanks being used in conjunction with aircraft and 'bite and hold' artillery tactics and infantry which avoided strong points had emerged by the end of the war and Terraine is right to stress the scale of these deployments, but also right to point out that the tanks were vulnerable and that casualties among crews were high[2]. By 1918, the morale and shortages of material among German troops in the west, together with the exhaustion of German forces after the failure of Operation Michael, were the context. Haig made effective use of tanks but they were, indeed, not the ultimate reason for the victories of 1918, so Terraine's analysis is convincing[3].

Analysis of the response

1 The view of the passage is explained.
2 Evidence is used to support the claim that it is a valid view.
3 Detailed own knowledge is then applied to reinforce and support the evidence in the interpretation and reach a judgement.

The paragraph could continue by considering the weaknesses of Interpretation A before a judgement is reached about the overall validity of the view of Passage A. Advice about reaching a judgement is given on pages 182–4.

Activity

- Use information from this chapter to evaluate Interpretation B.

It might be helpful to consider the following questions to help you structure your answer:

- What is the view of Interpretation B about the impact of the tank in the First World War?
- What evidence is there in the interpretation to support this view?
- What knowledge do you have that supports this view?
- What knowledge do you have that challenges this view?
- Check your work and highlight the evaluative words that you have used.

CHAPTER 3

Planning and preparation for war

All countries plan for the wars they expect to fight. Throughout the period, states made alliances with one another in the belief that this would give them a greater chance of victory. At the start of the period these alliances were often short lived and did not bring about success, but by the time of the First and Second World Wars it was the stronger alliances, and economic powers, which emerged triumphant, suggesting that the manpower and resources which the alliances provided were important factors in determining the outcome.

Control of armies was also a factor in determining the outcome of wars. In the eighteenth century, armies were under the command of the monarch, who often devolved power to a relative or an aristocratic general. During the nineteenth century, command structures became more sophisticated owing to the creation of general staffs, and this devolution of power continued for most of the period. This chapter analyses the significance of planning and preparation under the following headings:

★ Alliances, plans and their effectiveness

★ War plans and their success

★ The organisation, command and control of armies

It also considers the debates surrounding three in-depth topics:

★ How far was French success due to the weakness of the coalitions?

★ How significant in the defeat of the South was its failure to secure alliances?

★ How far did alliances determine the outcome of the First World War?

Key dates

1793	First coalition formed against France	1813		Sixth coalition
1798–1802	Second coalition against France	1905		Schlieffen Plan devised
1805	Third coalition			
1806	Fourth coalition	1914	**Aug.**	Plans of attack put into practice
1809	Fifth coalition		**Sept.**	Failure of plans of attack

Alliances, plans and their effectiveness

▶ *How effective were alliances and military plans in the period from 1792 to 1945?*

The alliances in the Revolutionary and Napoleonic Wars

Until the French Revolutionary Wars, wars were fought between royal families or dynasties in the interests of those families and dynasties. The armies were controlled by royal families and they fought to preserve or enhance their power, rather than that of the nation or the people. The alliances that were made were therefore between the various rulers and were often personal in nature, and often cemented by marriage agreements. However, the situation began to change towards the end of the eighteenth century with the American Revolution (see page 5) and French Revolutionary Wars. Both of the conflicts, although they were fought against monarchs, were fought for ideals, such as independence or liberty. The Revolutionary Wars would have an impact not just on the size and tactics of armies, but also on the nature of alliances as nations came together to stop the export of the French revolutionary ideals to the rest of Europe as they were a direct challenge to monarchical rule.

The nature of the coalitions in the Revolutionary and Napoleonic Wars

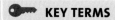 **KEY TERMS**

Decree of Fraternity The French Republic offered support to any state wishing to overthrow its rulers and establish a democratic system.

First Coalition This comprised Britain, the Netherlands, Spain, Piedmont, Naples, Prussia, Russia, Austria and Portugal.

The French Republic posed a threat to European monarchs with its **Decree of Fraternity**. The powers were also concerned that France had annexed Nice and Savoy, while Britain was particularly worried about the threat Revolutionary France posed to the Austrian Netherlands, as it could be used as a base from which to invade Britain. It was this concern that meant Britain was the driving force behind the **First Coalition**, which emerged between March and September 1793. However, there was no formal treaty binding the powers together, and despite diplomatic efforts which brought other countries to join it, it was only ever a loose group of nations, as shown by Russia refusing to commit soldiers to it when Britain failed to send money to support its armies.

The coalition enjoyed some success during the summer of 1793 and Austria and Spain both invaded France, but the failure of allied commanders to join forces and attack Paris allowed the French to survive. The coalition was simply not strong enough, and the allies were unwilling to co-ordinate their efforts, with the result that from June 1794 the French enjoyed a series of military successes which continued until all members of the coalition, except Britain, had been defeated. France was also able to weaken the coalition by making separate peace agreements with members of the coalition, with Prussia agreeing at the

Treaty of Basel in April 1795 to give up land on the left bank of the Rhine in return for land on the right bank, which also freed French troops to attack other opponents. Piedmont-Savoy also withdrew from the coalition and the war against Napoleon in the Italian campaign.

A **Second Coalition** was formed in 1799 following the British victory against Napoleon in Egypt. However, quarrels between members of the coalition allowed France to survive after a series of defeats. Austria failed to support Russia in Switzerland and sent its troops north, which allowed the French to attack in Switzerland, leading to a Russian withdrawal.

The Third Coalition, consisting of Britain, Austria, Russia and some smaller powers, was formed in 1805. However, military victories by Napoleon at Ulm in October 1805 forced the Austrians to surrender and then victory at Austerlitz in December 1805 against an Austro-Russian army caused a rapid Russian retreat and Austria to agree to peace with the Treaty of Pressburg. The lack of co-ordination between the powers of Austria and Russia is seen most clearly in the fact that the two sides were using different calendars, with the result that Russian forces turned up too late to save the Austrian forces.

At various stages during this period and during the War of the Fourth Coalition, 1806–7, Napoleon was able, either by military or diplomatic pressure, to bring Austria, Prussia and Russia under his direct influence and each, in turn, became his ally. This weakened the potential of any coalition, even if the states had been unwilling to ally with Napoleon.

It was concern over French domination in the German-speaking territories formerly under Austrian control and the creation of the Confederation of the Rhine that led to the creation of the Fourth Coalition in 1806. The coalition consisted of Britain, Prussia and Russia, but once again Napoleon's military skill rendered the coalition short lived as Prussia was defeated at the battles of Jena and Auerstädt in October 1806. Napoleon's subsequent attack on Russia and his victory at Friedland in June 1807 convinced Russia of the need to make peace, leaving only Britain of the original members of the coalition undefeated.

The result of these battles had left Napoleon as master of much of Europe, but he was aided by the weakness of his enemies as, although they formed a series of anti-French agreements, they were unable to overcome their mutual suspicions and jealousy, often being tempted away from coalitions by the offer of territory or forced out by military defeat.

Napoleon's disastrous Russian campaign of 1812 encouraged the creation of another anti-French coalition. Once again, this was not an alliance, but it did include all the great powers of Britain, Russia, Prussia and Austria. Numerical superiority enabled Austria, Prussia and Russia to win the Battle of the Nations and this victory encouraged the victorious powers to turn the coalition into a formal alliance with the Treaty of Chaumont in March 1814. For the first time, the powers agreed not to make a separate peace with Napoleon and to continue

KEY TERM

Second Coalition This comprised Britain, Russia, Austria, Turkey, Portugal and Naples.

Viscount Castlereagh (1769–1822)

Robert Stewart, Viscount Castlereagh, was British foreign secretary from 1812 and was central to the management of the coalition that defeated Napoleon. He killed himself in 1822.

Klemens von Metternich (1773–1859)

The Austrian foreign minister from 1809 and chancellor from 1821 until he was forced out by the revolutions of 1848. He led the Austrian delegation at the Congress of Vienna, which resolved many of the problems following the defeat of Napoleon.

Napoleon III (1808–73)

Also known as Louis Napoleon. He was the only president of the Second French Republic in 1848–52 and then became emperor from 1852, having been forbidden to be president for a second term, until 1870. He wanted to restore French influence in Europe and this was one reason for his involvement in the Crimean War.

Jefferson Davis (1808–89)

A US senator and representative from Mississippi before he became president of the Confederate (Southern) States of America during the Civil War.

the fight until he was defeated. Even so, these coalitions were still only loose associations and any joint military planning was, at best, minimal.

By the later stages of the Napoleonic wars, therefore, alliances were more effective as **Viscount Castlereagh** and **Klemens von Metternich** maintained the coalition. Napoleon's **Hundred Days** campaign failed because of Prussian–British alliance and military cooperation at Waterloo, which led to his final defeat and exile.

Alliances and the Crimean War

Although the Crimean War was fought by France, Britain, Turkey, Austria and Piedmont against Russia, it was not so much the alliance as Russia's inability to take advantage of its numbers and geography that determined the outcome of the war. There was little co-ordination between the allies, who were fighting for very different causes, with Britain fighting to preserve the balance of power in Europe, while **Napoleon III** wanted to restore *gloire* to France and win the support of Catholics by attacking **Eastern Orthodoxy**.

If the alliances had little impact on the actual outcome of the Crimean War, they did have a particular impact on Austria in the long term. Austria had become more fearful of Russian expansion and therefore abandoned its alliance with Russia, joining Britain and France. Austria contributed little to the actual fighting, but at the end of the war was diplomatically isolated and this contributed to its defeats against France in 1859 and most importantly against Prussia in 1866, when its former ally, Russia, did not come to its aid.

The South's failure to gain allies in the American Civil War

As the South lacked the resources of the North it realised that its best hope of success was if Britain and/or France joined the war on its side. As a result, **Jefferson Davis** tried to secure European support and recognition. However, in the end no foreign power either recognised or intervened on behalf of the South. Whether this was the result of good fortune, the North's diplomatic skill or the South's incompetence has been a matter of debate among historians, but the failure to gain support certainly had an impact on the war.

The South needed to at least be able to purchase military supplies so that it could fight the war, with many Southerners believing that British and French demand for cotton would bring them to an agreement. In order to attempt to force the British and French to support them, the South introduced an **embargo** on cotton. This ploy failed; it limited the amount of money coming into the South and actually angered many Europeans. However, the South was able to secure European loans and bonds, with which it was able to purchase British armaments which would allow it to continue the war.

There were occasions, as after **Second Manassas** in 1862, when Britain and France considered mediation, but as it would have necessitated recognition of the South they pulled back. Although it has been estimated that British war material for the South extended the war by as much as two years, it is also probably correct to argue that the policy of neutrality benefited the Union. The South needed to establish that it was a recognised, independent nation, which Britain refused to acknowledge. Without Britain recognising the South and going to war on its side it was always unlikely that they would win and therefore the failure to bring about an alliance and British neutrality had an impact on the course of the war.

Bismarck's policy of preventing Austria and France gaining allies in the Wars of Unification

Prussian victories over both Austria in 1866 and France in 1870–1 were dramatic and quick. Although much of this was due to better strategic planning (see page 117), organisation (see page 119) and weaponry (see page 71), the task was made much easier by the isolation of each nation so that Prussia fought them alone.

The isolation of Austria

Following the joint Austro-Prussian seizure of the provinces of Schleswig-Holstein in 1864–5, some have argued that Bismarck used it to force Austria into a confrontation. However, the historian A.J.P. Taylor (1958) argued that Bismarck's diplomacy towards Austria was more 'calculated to frighten Austria than to prepare for war'. Whatever Bismarck's plan, he was able to exploit the situation and isolate Austria:

- Russia would not support Austria following the Crimean War (see page 104).
- Britain, with the death of **Viscount Palmerston**, followed a policy of what later came to be known as '**splendid isolation**'.
- Bismarck was able to secure French neutrality, if not support, because France believed the war would be drawn out and they would gain from it.

Although it can be argued that the lack of allies was important because Austria was on the verge of bankruptcy and economically behind Prussia, there were some factors that favoured Austria:

- the Austrian army was larger than the Prussian army
- many German states supported Austria; however, any attempts at co-ordination between them were ineffective
- if the war was short, industrial power would have little impact.

It would therefore appear that it was not the lack of allies that resulted in the defeat of Austria at Sadowa but factors such as strategic planning, organisation and weaponry.

 **KEY TERMS**

Hundred Days The period from when Napoleon returned from exile on Elba, following his defeat in 1814, to his defeat at the Battle of Waterloo in 1815. During this time he rallied his forces and was able to raise an army and renew the war against the allies.

Eastern Orthodoxy Refers to the Eastern Orthodox Church, which broke from the Western Church in 1054. It is called 'Eastern' because of the geographical location of most of its members.

Embargo A trade ban.

Second Manassas Also known as the second Battle of Bull Run and was the culmination of a major campaign by the Confederate Army under Robert E. Lee. The battle saw heavy casualties, but in the end the Union left flank was crushed and driven back to Bull Run.

Splendid isolation This term, coined in 1896, refers to a desire not to be allied to other countries, therefore allowing freedom of action. It was called 'splendid' because Britain had made the decision from a position of strength and it allowed it to focus on its empire rather than be dragged into European affairs.

 KEY FIGURE

Viscount Palmerston (1784–1865)

Known as 'Pam' and twice prime minister, Palmerston was in government almost continuously from 1807 until 1865. He was known for being a strong defender of British interests.

Franco-Prussian War

The diplomatic situation in 1870 certainly favoured Prussia, but as with the war against Austria it was less the lack of allies that brought about French defeat. In 1870, the diplomatic situation was as follows:

- The dual monarchy of Austria-Hungary was divided. Although Austria would have liked revenge against Prussia, the Hungarian government was opposed to war, making resistance to the Prussians more difficult.
- Russia promised to support Prussia if Austria supported France, and this also helped to keep Austria out of the war.
- Italy offered to support France, but made very high demands.
- Britain distrusted France.

Despite this situation, many expected a French victory as France had a larger population and had been successful in both the Crimean War and the war against Austria in 1859. It would, therefore, seem that the French defeat was due to Prussian superiority, particularly in terms of mobilisation and the strategic use of railways (see page 85), and the use of the Krupp breech-loading artillery, particularly at Spicheren and Wörth, but must notably at Sedan.

The wars of the mid-nineteenth century

Alliances were much less important in the wars of the mid-nineteenth century: the French withdrew from their alliance with Piedmont in 1859; the German states added little to Austria's war efforts in 1866; in the Crimea, Austria did not give any support militarily and the British, French, Ottoman and Piedmontese did not effectively work together. However, it could be argued that in the mid-century it was not the effectiveness of actual alliances but the absence of alliances that was decisive: Austria was deprived of any major European power as an ally; France was isolated; the Confederate States could not secure recognition and alliance.

The wars of the early twentieth century

Alliances meant that powers could not concentrate their forces and had to take into account different possible enemies. But it did not mean that powers had to face any co-ordinated unified military strategy and the pooling of resources until the twentieth century. The alliance of the group of Balkan nations against Turkey in 1912–13, during the **first Balkan War**, showed the limitations of even a regional alliance of powers with a common enemy.

Given the military limitations of alliances it may therefore seem surprising that European powers were so anxious to obtain them after 1879, but as the next section shows, it was the desire of Germany and France in particular to build up a series of alliances.

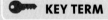

KEY TERM

First Balkan War The war was fought in 1912–13 between the Balkan League, made up of Serbia, Bulgaria, Greece and Montenegro, and Turkey. Turkey suffered defeats but the League squabbled over the division of former Turkish land and this led to a second war between members of the League.

Alliances and the outcome of the First World War

An alliance system had developed in Europe during the final part of the nineteenth century and the early twentieth century. France and Russia, having been isolated by Germany, had come together in the **Dual Alliance** of 1893 and signed a military convention, which provided for mutual aid if either was attacked by Germany. Russia also supported Serbia as a fellow Slavic nation.

Britain had signed the ***Entente Cordiale*** with France in 1904 and although this improved relations between the two powers, it was not a military alliance and was intended to improve colonial relations and prevent the two being drawn in to the Russo-Japanese war on opposing sides, as Britain had signed an alliance with Japan in 1902. The *entente* was further extended in 1907 when Britain reached an agreement with Russia, but once again this was largely designed to settle colonial disputes in Central Asia.

These agreements did not really have much military significance and there is no evidence of France and Russia undertaking any joint planning sessions. However, they did create fear and distrust in Germany and encouraged the **arms race**, which served to further increase tension in Europe. Despite the *ententes*, Britain continued to hold talks with Germany about a possible agreement, but Britain refused to guarantee that it would remain neutral if war broke out. This failure ultimately led to increased talks with France and resulted in the French moving their Atlantic fleet in 1912 from Brest to Toulon to give it greater security against the growing Austrian and Italian threat.

Despite the First Lord of the Admiralty, Churchill (see page 110), claiming in the House of Commons that Britain still had freedom of action, it is unlikely that the French would or could have taken such action without being confident about British actions in the event of a German attack. There were also naval conversations between the two, which led to an agreement in 1913 on technical arrangements, such as signals, should the two nations be fighting a war on the same side. In 1914, under pressure from the French, the British also entered into naval talks with the Russians. It could therefore be argued that although Britain had not signed alliances with either France or Russia there was some moral obligation to support them in the event of war, and this impression was given further weight by staff talks between Britain and France after 1906.

Although Germany and Austria-Hungary were allied through the Dual Alliance of 1879, which did have military clauses, it did not mean that the Austrian chief of the general staff, **Franz Conrad von Hötzendorf**, shared his military plans with Germany, even if each year he presented plans to the Austrian emperor for war against either Italy or Serbia. The industrial developments of the preceding years meant that the two sides were evenly matched, even when Italy joined Britain and France through the Treaty of London in 1915.

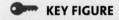 **KEY TERMS**

Dual Alliance Also known as the Franco-Russian alliance. Germany had allowed its alliance with Russia to lapse and with France wanting support against Germany and Russia against Austria-Hungary the two nations overcame ideological differences to sign the treaty.

Entente Cordiale A series of agreements between Britain and France signed in 1904, which resulted in an improvement in relations between the two countries. It resolved issues of colonial dispute, particularly in Africa, and helped to end years of hostility.

Arms race Used to describe the rapid build-up of arms and competition between European countries in the period before the First World War. It involved the increase in size of both armies and navies.

KEY FIGURE

Franz Conrad von Hötzendorf (1852–1925)
An Austrian field marshal and chief of the general staff of the Austro-Hungarian forces 1906–17. He was their leading military adviser during the crisis of 1914.

Central Powers The term used to describe Germany, Austria-Hungary and Turkey, who were allies against the Entente Powers of France, Britain and Russia in the First World War.

Verdun The battle lasted from February to December 1916. The German aim was to inflict heavy casualties on the French so that the French army would collapse. One reason why Britain launched the Somme offensive was to take some pressure off the French. The French line held, but the battle of Verdun resulted in some 700,000 casualties.

Lusitania A British ocean liner, torpedoed and sunk on 7 May 1915. It caused the death of 1198 passengers and crew, 128 of whom were American. Germany had breached international laws by firing on a non-military ship. However, the ship was carrying munitions. Its sinking helped to shift public opinion in the USA in favour of joining the war.

The relative industrial weakness of Russia was matched on the side of the **Central Powers** by Austria-Hungary and Turkey, while the economic powerhouses of Britain and Germany cancelled each other out. Both sides were, for the most part, able to supply their forces with sufficient armaments throughout the war, although Russian forces suffered from a shortage of weapons and clothing, while a shell shortage in Britain in 1915 created a political crisis and led eventually to the downfall of the prime minister, Herbert Asquith. Although the Germans had to fight a war on two fronts, they were able to supply their forces and this was made easier in 1917 when the Russian revolution led to the withdrawal of Russia from the war.

It might even be argued that the alliances, rather than being a strength, were a weakness; the Entente was close to defeat when Russia withdrew in 1917 and Germany was able to move all its troops to the Western Front, suggesting that the alliance with Russia had brought the Entente Powers little benefit. The entry of the USA did ultimately more than cancel out the Russian withdrawal. It could also be argued that the weakness of the alliances had an even greater impact on Germany as the sudden collapse of its allies, Bulgaria, Turkey and Austria-Hungary, in 1918 helped to bring about the German surrender in the autumn of 1918.

However, despite the alliances, co-ordinated action between allies did not occur, at least in the early years of the war. The first inter-allied military conference of the war took place at Chantilly in July 1915 but resulted in little being agreed, despite Joffre commenting that only with co-ordination would they succeed. A second conference at the same venue some five months later did result in agreement about co-ordinated attacks, but no overall command of the forces of the Entente Powers. However, the military pressure that France was under, with the German attack on **Verdun** in 1916, was a factor in encouraging Haig to launch the Somme offensive in order to try and relieve some pressure on the French. Similarly in 1917, with the withdrawal of Russia from the war and mutinies in the French army, the British accepted the full burden of the war.

The withdrawal of Russia from the war allowed Germany to concentrate all of its forces in the west and encouraged them to change from pursuing a defensive war to a more aggressive approach. However, this advantage was short lived as the USA joined the war in April 1917 following the sinking of the **Lusitania** in 1915 and the unrestricted submarine campaign to starve Britain, which resulted in the sinking of US ships. This shifted the balance towards the Entente Powers. Although it took some time for US forces to be transported to Europe, their involvement and arrival gave the Entente Powers access to a vast array of resources, both economic and manpower. Not only was this a massive morale boost for the Entente, but Germany, already weakened by the British naval blockade, was unable to meet the demands of war. While the Central Powers, largely Germany, produced just 19 per cent of the world's manufacturing output, the Entente Powers, including the USA, produced some 65 per cent. Similarly, the Central Powers were now heavily outnumbered and it soon proved impossible for Germany to continue to support its less economically developed allies.

It was the alliance with the USA that ultimately tipped the balance in favour of the Entente Powers, forcing the Germans into the desperate gamble of the **Ludendorff or Spring Offensive** of 1918, which ended any possibility of a German victory, with the commander stating in September 1918, 'We cannot fight against the whole world'. This offensive, however, did come close to success and forced the Entente Powers to appoint a supreme Allied commander, General Foch, following a meeting at Doullens on 26 March 1918. Such an appointment was unusual, and was seen again only with Eisenhower's appointment in the Second World War, as few nations were willing to accept their armies being placed under the command of a foreign power. This perhaps shows the extent of the crisis that the Entente Powers faced in those final months.

Yet, it was adversity that resulted in the dramatic breakthroughs of the summer of 1918. The Entente Allies worked more closely together, and therefore the development of more sophisticated artillery cover, and large numbers of tanks and planes allowed these co-ordinated assaults to take them deep into enemy positions. As a result, they were able to break through the **Hindenburg Line** at the very time that Germany was struggling; its alliances were falling apart as members of the Central Powers sought terms with the Allies.

Alliances and the outcome of the Second World War

Even before the outbreak of the Second World, the then Conservative MP and later prime minister, Winston Churchill, had been the major proponent of a Grand Alliance to defeat Nazi Germany and its allies. However, initially at least, Churchill's plans did not come to fruition. France collapsed in 1940, and the USSR sided with Germany through the **Nazi–Soviet pact** (1939) and then, when invaded in 1941, suffered a series of defeats. With the USA neutral until Japan's attack on **Pearl Harbor** in December 1941, Britain had stood alone against Germany and its allies, Italy and Japan.

It was therefore only at the end of 1941 that a Grand Alliance between Britain, USA and the USSR came into being. Despite different priorities between the three powers, they were united in their goal of defeating Nazi Germany, Italy and Japan. That Churchill viewed the alliance as essential in achieving victory is clearly demonstrated by his series of hazardous journeys and difficult summit meetings throughout the war. He was willing to appease Stalin over his demands in eastern Europe, in a way that he had not been prepared to accept Hitler's demands, in order to keep the alliance together.

The Nazi–Soviet pact had been crucial in allowing Germany to avoid the disaster of a war on two fronts, which had impeded their progress in the First World War, and allowed Hitler to take control of nearly all western Europe before turning his attention eastwards. His alliance with the Soviet Union in the early years of the war also ensured sufficient supplies of war materials, particularly of oil, and the Soviet Union continued to supply these even when they were being warned of an imminent German attack.

KEY TERMS

Ludendorff or Spring Offensive Launched in the spring of 1918 by General Ludendorff, this was a series of German attacks along the Western Front and saw the greatest advance by either side since 1914. It was the final assault by the Germans and an attempt to achieve victory before US troops arrived in numbers. When it failed to bring victory the German command realised it could not win.

Hindenburg Line A German defensive position built in 1916–17 to counter expected Anglo-French attacks in 1917.

Nazi–Soviet pact An agreement signed between Nazi Germany and Communist Russia in August 1939. It allowed Germany to avoid fighting a war on two fronts and gave Russia short-term security from attack.

Pearl Harbor The US naval base in Hawaii and home to the US Pacific fleet. It was attacked by the Japanese on 7 December 1941 and resulted in the USA joining the Second World War.

Winston Churchill

1874	Born
1905–8	Parliamentary undersecretary Colonial Office, Liberal government
1908–10	President of the Board of Trade
1910–11	Home secretary
1911–15	First Lord of the Admiralty
1917–18	Minister of munitions
1919–21	Secretary of state for war and air
1924–9	Chancellor, Conservative MP
1939–40	First Lord of the Admiralty
1940–5	Prime minister
1951–5	Prime minister
1965	Died

Early life
Churchill was born at Blenheim Palace near Oxford and was the son of the well-known politician Randolph Churchill. His privileged background saw him attend Harrow before going on to Sandhurst to train as an army officer. He went to India in 1896, where his involvement in a military expedition almost saw him killed. He went to the Sudan in 1898 and took part in a cavalry charge at Omdurman. Then, during the Boer War he was a war correspondent.

First World War
In 1911 he had been appointed First Lord of the Admiralty, where he was renowned for offering advice to senior commanders. A supporter of war in 1914, he believed his military experience made him a strategist and he supported the attempt to hold Antwerp against the German advance, which failed. He then backed the Gallipoli campaign, another disaster, which would be used against him by opponents throughout his career. The failure led to his demotion but he was appointed minister of munitions when Lloyd George became prime minister.

The inter-war years
Churchill had changed to the Conservatives during the war and was appointed chancellor in 1924. Here he was remembered for taking Britain back on to the Gold Standard at a rate which damaged British exports. With the fall of the Conservatives in 1929 and the establishment of a National Government in 1931, Churchill was out of office until 1939. During this period he is most remembered as a critic of the policy of appeasement and the failure to rearm.

The Second World War
As the likelihood of war returned, Churchill was brought back into government as First Lord of the Admiralty and was heavily involved in the disastrous Norway campaign of 1940. However, this did not stop him replacing Chamberlain as prime minister in May 1940. He did much to raise morale with his wartime speeches, particularly when Britain was fighting Germany alone. However, still believing in his own military abilities, he often interfered in military planning, annoying many of the generals. Perhaps his greatest contribution was in developing and securing the wartime alliance with the USA and Russia, although he angered Stalin by delaying the launching of the Second Front.

Post-war
Despite being seen as a hero, he lost the 1945 general election, but was returned to power in 1951, although he was largely a figurehead. He remained in office until his retirement in 1955 and died in 1965.

As with the First World War, it might be argued that it was the weakness of Germany's alliances, particularly with Italy, that had the most significant impact. The economic and military weakness of its major ally, Italy, added to Nazi Germany's difficulties. Troops often had to be sent to areas, such as north Africa, Greece and Yugoslavia, where Italian troops had lost control, and this further stretched German resources and delayed the attack on Russia. Moreover, the weakness of Romanian and Italian troops fighting on the Eastern Front allowed Russia to take advantage. Italian weaknesses in north Africa ultimately required the creation of the Afrika Corps and drew more resources away from Europe.

However, the situation was made worse in 1943 when Italy defected and left Germany with another front to defend.

In contrast, the Allies had, after the entry of the USA into the war, superior resources available. Britain supplied Russia with significant numbers of tanks and armoured vehicles via the **Arctic route**, which kept Russia's forces going during the early period of the German invasion until it was producing sufficient weapons of its own. Frequent meetings between Churchill and **Franklin Delano Roosevelt** ensured that the Anglo-American alliance remained secure and there were also meetings with Stalin.

Despite animosities, particularly between Churchill and Stalin, over the launching of a second front, with Stalin keen for it to be launched to relieve pressure on Russian forces in the east and Churchill's focus on an attack through the Mediterranean, the alliance remained intact and allowed sufficient forces under the unified command of Eisenhower to be built up in southern Britain during 1944 in order to launch **D-Day** and the reoccupation of western Europe. The alliance also ensured that the main focus of attack was in Europe against Hitler, before attention was turned to defeating Japan in the Far East. The economic resources that were at the disposal of the Allies, it can be argued, made victory inevitable, but the degree of cooperation ensured large-scale operations such as D-Day could be successfully launched. Germany simply lacked the resources to be able to resist attacks from both the east and west, as had also been their concern in 1914.

2 War plans and their success

▶ *Why, and with what consequences, did war plans emerge in the second half of the nineteenth century?*

The development of war plans and their role in the Wars of Unification

The modernisation of warfare with industrial and technological developments (see page 62) impacted on strategic planning. It was particularly the development of rail networks, first seen in use during the American Civil War, and their ability to move large numbers of troops to the battlefield at a far greater speed than had been possible at the start of the period, which resulted in developments and changes in strategic planning. The growth in the size of armies, as seen in the Prussian and French forces during the Franco-Prussian War, and their greater range also meant that careful planning was important. The availability of rail networks alone did not mean troops would arrive at the battlefield; it required planning. When this failed it could have serious results, as was seen with the Austrian reserve force in 1866, which got lost and missed the

Battle of Sadowa, or the French armies which found that many of their guns and much of their ammunition had been left behind before Sedan.

However, co-ordination of rail and telegraph did have benefits, seen most clearly in the Prussian forces during the Wars of Unification. While it would be wrong to argue that planning alone was responsible for their quick and decisive victories in 1866 and 1870–1, it was certainly important, and the careful integration of the new technology and the refinement of mobilisation plans allowed Moltke to achieve a decisive victory at Sadowa in 1866, allowing some 250,000 men to be brought to a front of some 300 miles by five separate rail lines. This was not repeated but improved on in 1870 when through careful planning Prussian mobilisation was even faster, and has been contrasted with that of the French, which was described as 'a disturbed ants' nest' by the historian Brian Bond (2014). As a result, one of the lessons drawn from the Wars of Unification was the importance of rapid mobilisation using a co-ordinated rail network, which allowed for sweeping attacks over a large front; something repeated in 1914 but with far less success.

The Anaconda Plan

Lincoln, leader of the North, thought that the outbreak of unrest in America in 1861 was little more than a minor insurrection, but this was soon proved hopelessly wrong. However, it was also apparent that it would take time to train and equip a force to put down the unrest and it was in that context that Winfield Scott, general-in-chief of the Union (North) army, supported the Anaconda Plan. The aim was to put pressure on the South through a naval blockade and win control of the Mississippi River. Scott believed that this would prevent the South from obtaining resources and squeeze the life from the South, hence the name Anaconda, forcing the South to surrender. The plan was to cut the South in two and it built on plans that had been drawn up before the war.

Scott wanted all ports in the states that had broken away from the Union and formed the Confederacy to be blockaded and a column of some 80,000 men to use the Mississippi to thrust through the Confederacy. This force would then be followed by a more traditional army that would secure the victories, ending with a battle below New Orleans, with the result that once they captured the forts there the Confederacy would be cut in two.

However, the plan faced opposition, with a faction in the north arguing that it was passive and what they wanted was a swift victory. They argued for a quick attack on the Confederate capital at Richmond, which was only 100 miles from Washington. As a result, Lincoln ordered General McDowell to march on Richmond. This, it has been argued, changed the nature of the war, with some even questioning whether the Anaconda Plan existed. The historian Rowena Reed (1978) suggested that it was imposed on events afterwards to give some sense of order to them. Instead, she has argued that the war was a series of

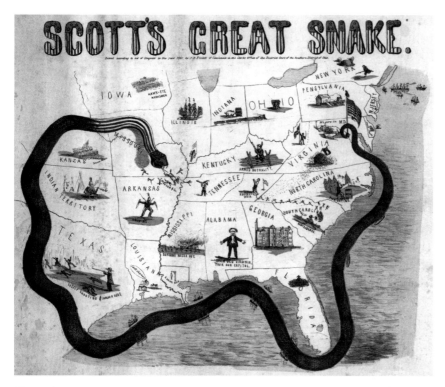

Figure 3.1 A contemporary cartoon map illustrating Scott's plan to crush the Confederacy's economy. It is sometimes called the Anaconda Plan (see page 112).

independent campaigns because the government in Washington was unable to control its generals.

However, there are two questions that need to be considered. First, did the Anaconda Plan actually exist or was it, as Reed suggested, imposed on events afterwards to try and explain them? Second, if the plan did exist, what was its value in bringing about victory? Some have argued that the value of the blockade was limited as three-quarters of all attempts to avoid the blockade succeeded, while the South was also not prevented from gaining supplies. However, those who support the concept of the plan have suggested that it was decisive and that by the end of the war Southern forces had been strangled, arguing that the collapse of the Army of Northern Virginia in 1865 followed soon after the loss of Wilmington. Moreover, they have also argued that it did help to bring about a collapse in the South's economy which encouraged a loss of both confidence and morale.

The failure of war plans in 1914

The short nature of the Wars of Unification had led military strategists to conclude that any future wars would be over quickly, and all the major powers drew up plans based on this assumption. The plans therefore focused on the need for the rapid mobilisation of troops and a decisive initial attack. This was particularly important for Germany which, as a result of the development of the alliance system, faced a war on two fronts: in the east against Russia and in the west against France and Britain. It was this that led to General **Alfred von Schlieffen** drawing up his plan in 1905. However, it was not just Germany that had drawn up plans. France, with Plan 17, planned to attack Germany through Alsace-Lorraine, while Russia's Plan 19 envisaged an attack into eastern Prussia, and Austro-Hungary, on the insistence of Germany, planned an attack against Russia.

The Schlieffen Plan

Despite, or perhaps because of, the detailed plans, they all soon failed, showing the weakness of strategic planning, which would continue for much of the war. The Schlieffen Plan was very detailed and based on a very strict timetable drawn up before the war and then modified, but simply serving to show the difficulty of translating distant plans into action on the ground. The plan was based on two assumptions drawn from the 1870 war with France:

- The French war effort would be disorganised, as it had been in 1870.
- Russia would be disorganised and take eight weeks to mobilise.

Not only were both of these assumptions wrong, but changes were also made to the plan which further lessened the likelihood of success. Schlieffen had been correct that an attack on France through the heavily fortified area around Alsace-Lorraine would fail and therefore it was necessary to avoid this area. In order to achieve this, he planned to swing the huge force of some 1.5 million men through Luxembourg and Belgium in a 'right hook' and encircle Paris, believing that this would lead to the surrender of France. Despite having been practised and carefully calculated, it failed for a number of reasons and clearly revealed the limits to strategic planning. It failed because:

- The attack through neutral Belgium drew Britain into the war because of Britain's 1839 treaty which promised to uphold Belgian neutrality.
- Moltke, who was commander-in-chief, weakened the right flank that attacked through Belgium to protect Germany's western borders from a French attack.
- Belgian resistance and the actions of the British Expeditionary Force slowed down the Germans' advance so that they were behind their timetable.
- The force used to attack through Belgium was made up of new recruits, who lacked the experience to destroy the resistance and cover 450 miles at over 20 miles a day.
- Although the troops were moved to the Belgian border by railway, the lines were liable to attack and supplies could not keep up with the advance.

The problems were clear evidence that despite developments in both transport and communications, as outlined in Chapter 2, they were still not sufficiently reliable to allow the strategy of rapid deployment of large numbers of men and horses to work. The attempt to encircle Paris, and hence the Schlieffen Plan, ended at the first Battle of the Marne on 9 September. This brought an end to the mobile war and resulted in the development of trench warfare, which would last on the Western Front until the end of the war.

Other war plans

Although the other plans were less elaborate, they also failed, even before the Schlieffen Plan had been stopped. The French Plan 17, which consisted of a mass frontal attack through Alsace-Lorraine, by French troops wearing red caps and trousers, was easily shot to pieces by a smaller German force, with over 300,000 French casualties. This showed that the old-fashioned concept of bravery was not sufficient to win battles and that the advantage had shifted to the defender. The Russian Plan 19 was defeated by a German counterattack at the Battles of Tannenberg and the Masurian Lakes, which also resulted in 78,000 Russian casualties at Tannenberg, 92,000 taken prisoner and only 10,000 escaping. Similarly, the Austrian offensive against Russia was also defeated.

Although the plans had yielded some victories, they were not decisive, ending the original view that the war would be over by Christmas. By the end of September 1914, the war had become one of attrition, particularly in the west, and would see little movement until 1918.

3 The organisation, command and control of armies

▶ *How far did the organisation, command and control of armies change in the period from 1792 to 1945?*

The organisation of armies during the Revolutionary and Napoleonic Wars

In the period before Napoleon, the command of armies had been the prerogative of the monarch. However, in practice they often gave command to a relative or a member of the aristocracy, although there were still occasions when the monarch commanded the army in the field. But it must also be remembered that once a battle had started, there was very little that could be done to change the course of a battle as officers tended to follow a prearranged plan. Perhaps the most important decision that a commander could make was whether to fight, and if so, where and when. Therefore, in most instances the armies of the eighteenth century were unitary forces under sole command. However, the growth in the size and nature of armies meant that changes in organisation and command were required. There was already evidence of some change in the organisation of the French army before the fall of the monarchy.

The Revolutionary Wars

The 'old-style' regimental army had begun to be reorganised during the Revolutionary Wars into divisions of 12,000 men, which combined infantry, cavalry and artillery into single fighting units. There were a number of benefits of this development, most notably that the division was able to move with greater speed and flexibility than a large army. It also meant that each division could gather its supplies from different areas and that divisions could advance individually on the battlefield, with the result that they could converge from a range of directions, throwing the enemy into confusion.

The larger forces that were seen in the Revolutionary Wars could not be deployed effectively in line and could not be controlled or disciplined in the way that the professional soldiers of the earlier eighteenth century had been. It was these developments that meant changes were needed in the organisation of the army. Not only this, but **Lazare Carnot** and French commanders in the Revolutionary Wars, such as Hoche, also began to reorganise their forces to present less of a target to opposing infantry and artillery. Troops were therefore arranged into attack columns of 50–80 men across the front and columns of nine to twelve men deep. This arrangement allowed the forces to advance as a type of 'human battering ram' against the thinner lines of the enemy as they rushed across the battlefield in the face of the heavy fire of the defenders. Although the Revolutionary armies suffered heavy casualties in such attacks, the defenders also lost large numbers, which they were unable to sustain. However, although there was some progress in these areas during the revolutionary period, it was not until Napoleon's control over resources that the co-ordinated divisions had a great impact on warfare.

The Napoleonic Wars

Napoleon also successfully introduced the corps system. This system consisted of an army corps made up of three infantry divisions, a brigade of cavalry and guns. In many ways it built on the divisional system explained in the previous paragraph. However, it consisted of some 30,000 men and was therefore much stronger. Although it had the ability to fight on its own, in practice it was designed to combine with other corps and launch attacks against the enemy from a variety of directions. This system also had the advantage that large numbers of soldiers could be dispersed over a huge area to forage, allowing a large force to be maintained, but could be brought together quickly to attack the enemy. The relatively small size of each division gave the corps system the advantage of speed and mobility that had been lacking in the unitary forces.

The greatest triumph of this system was at Ulm in 1805, when the French army, which was dispersed over some 200 miles, came together to encircle the Austrians and then separated only to reassemble to defeat the Russian forces at Austerlitz. This was a tremendous achievement given the primitive nature of communications at the time and can be seen as a revolution in the concept of strategic movement that was then adopted by all armies.

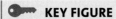

KEY FIGURE

Lazare Carnot (1753–1823)

A French politician and engineer, usually credited with organising the victories of the French in the Revolutionary Wars. He was one of the ministers of war for Napoleon from 1800 to 1805 and played a key role in organising the Revolutionary army, particularly conscription. He was exiled for supporting Napoleon in 1815 and died in Prussia.

Changes made in the command structure in the mid-nineteenth century

Napoleon's changes had allowed rapid movement and enabled him to sustain large forces in the field. In order to counter this challenge, other nations had to transform their military organisation. This was seen most notably in the changes made by the Prussians, who followed the French model. The Prussians removed the elderly generals and replaced them with younger men, such as Gerhard von Scharnhorst (see page 18) and Carl von Clausewitz (see page 118), who were willing reformers. They brought in a co-ordinated general staff and introduced the French system of divisions and corps. Austria also adopted French methods of organisation, with corps and divisions as well as skirmishers, attack columns and heavy cavalry. Although Russia was reluctant to reform its army, it did introduce the corps system.

The main reasons for the willingness of these nations to adopt the reforms were the defeats they had suffered at the hand of Napoleon and a realisation that without reform they would continue to suffer defeats on such a large scale. This view is further reinforced by the lack of reform carried out by Britain at this time, as the British, unlike all the other nations, had not suffered the defeats the other nations had endured.

The impact of the changes in the command structure made by Prussia in the mid-nineteenth century

The Prussians had brought in the most far-reaching reforms of all the allied powers during the Napoleonic Wars with the creation of the Prussian general staff, which developed both war plans and army doctrine. However, the general staff did not have control over the officers in the field, which came about only under von Moltke (see page 29), who was chief of the general staff from 1857 to 1888. His reforms brought a new professionalism to the Prussian army and would play a key role in the victories in the Wars of Unification. Von Moltke, like other members of the Prussian general staff, had been promoted through merit, and this system had a number of advantages:

- The members of the general staff were the best products of the War College, which was an institution not copied by other powers until after 1871.
- The general staff officers rotated duties at general headquarters and headquarters of field armies, corps and divisions, ensuring that they were in touch with the army.
- They were separate from the Ministry of War and thus avoided routine military administration, allowing them to focus on strategy and planning.

As the historian Larry Addington (1994) has argued, other powers were deficient in at least one of these three elements, which served to weaken them. The rotation between different elements ensured that members of the general staff had wide experience before they were viewed as fully qualified. However,

Carl von Clausewitz

1780   Born

1806–15   Fought in the Napoleonic Wars

1806   Captured at the Battle of Jena

1807–8   Prisoner in France

1812–13   Joined the Russian army

1815   Rejoined the Prussian service as a colonel

1815–30   Director of the Kriegsakademie

1830   Appointed chief of Prussian staff and sent to deal with Polish crisis

1831   Died of cholera

1832   His widow posthumously published *On War* about the philosophy of war

Early life

Born into a middle-class family in the Prussian Duchy of Magdeburg, Clausewitz entered the Prussian military service at the age of twelve as a lance corporal. He served in the campaigns against the Revolutionary French armies in the Rhine campaigns and then fought in the Napoleonic Wars. He entered the Kriegsakademie, or Prussian War School, in 1801, where he probably studied the works of Kant, and made a great impression on Scharnhorst, who would be the first chief of staff of the reformed Prussian army.

Napoleonic Wars

He fought in the Napoleonic Wars from 1806 to 1815, first for Prussia, but was captured at the Battle of Jena and was a prisoner in France from 1807 to 1808. On his return, he helped in the reform of the Prussian army. However, he opposed Prussia's alliance with Napoleon and left Prussia and joined the Russian army, fighting against Napoleon in his 1812 campaign. While fighting for the Russians he helped to negotiate the Convention of Tauroggen, which led to the coalition that finally defeated Napoleon. In 1815, with integration of the Russian–German legion into the Prussian army, he rejoined it as a colonel and was soon appointed chief of staff of Thielmann's III corps, serving at Ligny and Wavre during the Waterloo campaign.

After the Napoleonic Wars

He became director of the Kriegsakadamie, where he served until 1830, then he returned to active service. In 1830 it appeared as if war would break out again and he was sent to the Polish border, where he was chief of staff of the Prussian army. Following the death of the commander he took over and attempted to construct a barrier to contain the cholera epidemic which had broken out, but he succumbed to the disease and died.

Theory of war

His book, *On War*, is a major work on the philosophy of war and is based on the campaigns of Frederick the Great of Prussia and Napoleon. The work is a philosophical examination of war. He saw war as an instrument of state policy. He emphasised defence, but also argued that states need to involve the whole population. Clausewitz rejected intelligence, seeing it as false – described as the 'fog of war' – but only at a tactical and operational level. He argued that the fog prevented commanders from knowing what was happening and therefore they needed to be alert to developments. As a result, he developed the concept of military genius which combined intellect, experience, personality and temperament.

once they were qualified the chiefs of staff of the field commanders were highly valued for their advice and had the authority of the chief of the general staff. They ensured that war plans were adhered to and changes of doctrine were implemented.

The Prussian general staff was also far ahead of its rivals in other areas. Its strategic planning was of the highest level. It practised war games, studied previous campaigns and also mapped much of the country for military purposes. It was able to use these changes to respond to the technological developments in railways and telegraphs that had taken place. Members of the general staff worked in the railway section so that the rail system was integrated into war planning (see page 119) and as part of the war games there were rail mobilisation exercises. The increase in the speed of movement brought about by the railways and the increased communications resulting from the telegraph led to the control of armies passing from battlefield commanders to the general staff headquarters.

In much the same way that Napoleon's victories at the start of the nineteenth century brought about changes in structure and planning, even during the wars as the allies copied his methods and organisation, the same was true with the Prussian victories. Their decisive and quick victories made other nations realise that they had to copy the Prussian model, particularly the importance of a general staff in strategic planning. One of the other major organisational developments that resulted from these wars was the acceptance of the German concept of the 'nation in arms'.

The First World War and changes in the command structure

The First World War saw a return to traditional command structures and unitary armies because of the sheer size of the armies. The Allied forces, particularly the British, were accustomed to the small-scale colonial wars of the nineteenth century and it therefore took time for them to adapt to the demands of modern warfare. However, as the war progressed, changes were made. One of the most notable changes was the appointment of Foch as Allied commander as, until his appointment, combined arrangements between the British and French had been on a voluntary basis. However, after the Doullens Conference of 1918 he had authority for centralised planning and the carrying out of operations on the Western Front. Even when the Americans joined the war they agreed to this structure. However, his tactic was to persuade other Allied commanders to follow his plans, rather than to order them.

German leadership, at the start of the war, benefited from the changes in organisation of the nineteenth century. In the first half of the war this gave them an advantage in both leadership and trained manpower. The large, professional German army, in contrast to the volunteer army of the British, was able to fight the war according to Germany's plan. The structure meant that it was able to delegate command downwards, making use of individual fighting skills, and was therefore more flexible in its approach in comparison to the Allied forces. However, this advantage lasted only as long as the original professional army remained intact, and this came to an end in 1916 following the heavy losses at the battles of Verdun and the Somme.

Both sides also began to delegate command and developed much smaller units. The Germans trained their non-commissioned officers to take over in the event of the death of officers, so that by 1916 the concept of devolved initiative had become more common and was particularly important in the advances of 1918. This was seen most clearly in the organisation of stormtroopers to lead counterattacks. These were well-armed strike forces; in 1917 a German force consisted of eleven men armed with light machine guns, grenades, mortars and flamethrowers. Their task was to advance rapidly through enemy lines, thus bringing back mobility to the battlefield, while subsequent less well-trained units would deal with more heavily defended positions, such as machine-gun posts. This new form of organisation saw probably its greatest success in the Ludendorff Offensive in the spring of 1918. The British and French soon followed this example, particularly after their experiences on the Somme; with the British creating heavily armed units or platoons of some 40 men. They advanced in rushes moving from one shell and crater hole to the next, with men trained to use specific weapons, but unlike the Germans, the British schooled all their men in this technique so that the units following up the first advance were just as well trained.

Changes to the command structure during the Second World War

Fought over an even larger area than the First World War and with far greater mobility, the Second World War saw much continuity in the command structure. The end of the First World War had witnessed the development of small groups of shock troops, stormtroopers, and in many ways the Germans continued this in its use of small units in *Blitzkrieg*. However, such attacks also required high levels of co-ordination between a range of forces, which was made possible by developments in technology.

This brought Germany early successes, but the plans and command structure had been based on a series of short, fast-moving wars and not on the drawn-out campaign in Russia. Moreover, as the war continued, German command was hampered by the leadership of Hitler, who held full military and political responsibility for all decisions about the war both in terms of strategy and timing. Nothing could be done without his agreement. His early successes had been the result of shock and surprise, but once that went and there was a need for careful planning to fight an attritional and co-ordinated war, his weaknesses were revealed. He overruled his generals who wanted to fight a flexible defence and insisted on no retreats. As the war progressed, he sacked those generals who disagreed with him and made promotions based on loyalty to him. As a result, commanders were reluctant to make decisions without his approval. This was seen most clearly on D-Day when the quick movement of a Panzer force near Caen could have created difficulties for the Allies, but was not made because Hitler was still asleep and no one dared wake him.

The scale of the battlefield meant that in the West and in most theatres of war, with perhaps the exception of the East, flexibility in command was important. In the Far East, commanders such as Slim and Wingate relied on smaller groups who were able to show resilience and take the initiative when not fighting with the main armies in Burma. Also in the Far East, the USA began its two-pronged plan of **island hopping** in 1943. Admiral **Chester Nimitz** was in charge of the

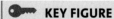

KEY TERM

Island hopping The policy pursued by the Americans in the Pacific of their troops seizing islands as they moved across the ocean towards Japan, rather than launching an attack directly on Japan.

KEY FIGURE

Chester Nimitz (1885–1966)

An admiral in the US navy and commander-in-chief, US Pacific Fleet.

force in the north, while **Douglas MacArthur** led the forces in the south, but the very nature of the fighting meant that platoon commanders had to take the initiative and make decisions on the ground. Similarly, with the Japanese, individual units did, and were expected to take considerable initiative and defend themselves independently of general orders.

In the war on the Russian Front the situation was somewhat different. The large Russian forces were under greater central command, with Stalin exercising close personal supervision. However, even he accepted the professional authority of his commanders, and as defence turned into advance even Russia followed the German model based on the mobile Panzer division with smaller armies and commanders making decisions.

As with the First World War, the Allies also appointed an overall commander, General **Dwight Eisenhower**, for D-Day. However, the command structure was very complex, with the 21st Army group under **Bernard Montgomery**, the US First Army under **Omar Bradley** and Canadian Second Army under Miles Dempsey, with more to be introduced once a bridgehead, or secure position within the enemy's territory, had been secured. As the advance through Normandy gathered momentum and more forces joined, the Allies reorganised their command so that by 1 August, Montgomery's 21st Army was composed of the First Canadian Army under Harry Crerar and the Second British Army under Dempsey, while a new US Twelfth Army Group under Bradley was created and composed of the US First Army under Courtney Hodges and Third Army under **George Patton**.

Despite these developments, once again, as with the end of the First World War, much also depended on smaller units taking the initiative to deal with German resistance, particularly in the advance through France, while high command dealt with bigger strategic issues such as the breakout from the Cotentin Peninsula and decisions over the crossing of the Rhine and opening up the Scheldt. British units took considerable initiative in campaigns such as Arnhem and the invasion of Germany. Although the British army was, much like the armies of the Revolutionary Wars, a citizen army, it did not have to be used in mass attacks. Instead, it had developed the initiative and expertise to fight in smaller platoons in order to achieve its objectives.

🔑 KEY FIGURES

Douglas MacArthur (1880–1964)

An American five-star general and field marshal of the Philippine army. He was given the medal of honor for services in the Philippines campaign.

Dwight Eisenhower (1890–1969)

A general in the US army, he was supreme commander of the Allied forces in Europe and responsible for the invasion of northern France on D-Day. He was US president 1953–61.

Bernard Montgomery (1887–1976)

Usually known as 'Monty', he was a senior officer in the British army and commanded the Eighth Army in north Africa, including at El Alamein. He commanded all Allied ground forces during the Normandy landings.

Omar Bradley (1893–1981)

Responsible for all US ground forces invading Germany from the west, with some 1.3 million men under his command. This was the largest body of US soldiers to serve under a single field commander.

George Patton (1885–1945)

A senior US officer, he led the US Third Army in France and Germany after the invasion of Normandy.

Chapter summary

States believed that alliances would help them to achieve victory in war and, although this was true to some extent, there were occasions when alliances were more of a hindrance. Germany discovered this in both world wars when the weakness of its allies meant that it had to deploy its own resources to try to aid them, thus deflecting Germany from its own aims. However, where alliances were combined with economic strength, they were usually successful, as seen ultimately against Napoleon, with the Treaty of Chaumont, and with the Allies in the First and Second World Wars. Nevertheless, where wars were short, alliances were less important, as was seen in the nineteenth century Wars of Unification, in which Prussia was successful without allies, although the weaker Piedmont did need help to drive Austria out of the peninsula.

War plans played an increasingly important role in the nineteenth and twentieth centuries. As the nature of warfare changed, so states developed increasingly detailed war plans, often based on the rapid deployment of forces to the front by railways. This may have brought early success, for example when only the Prussian forces deployed men quickly during the Wars of German Unification. However, when both sides had detailed plans and were able to move men rapidly to the front, the area of fighting became so congested that it resulted in failure, as was seen on the Western Front in the First World War. Plans were also usually so regimented that they lacked the flexibility that battle required, they took little account of resistance and therefore failed to bring about the quick victories expected, as was seen in both the American Civil War and First World War. However, where the command structure allowed the rapid movement of troops, as seen under Napoleon and again at the end of the First World War, and when smaller units took initiatives in the Second World War, be it through *Blitzkrieg*, island hopping, or in the advance through France, then breakthroughs were achieved, leaving the high command to deal with bigger strategic questions.

Refresher questions

Use these questions to remind yourself of the key material covered in this chapter.

1 Why were the coalitions against Napoleon short lived?

2 Why was the South so concerned to gain allies during the American Civil War?

3 Why was Bismarck so concerned to isolate his enemies?

4 Why were nations so concerned to reach alliances in the period before the outbreak of the First World War?

5 In what ways were the alliances of the Second World War a hindrance?

6 What was the Anaconda Plan?

7 Why did the war plans of 1914 fail?

8 In what ways did Napoleon change the command structure of French armies?

9 Why were there changes in the command structure in the mid-nineteenth century?

10 How similar were the command structures during the First and Second World Wars?

11 Why did command structures become more flexible by the end of the First World War?

In-depth studies and key debates

The examination requires you to study three topics in depth and for this unit they are:

- The French Revolutionary Wars 1792–1802
- The American Civil War 1861–5
- The Western Front and the First World War 1914–18.

This section will go into more detail about how planning and preparation impacted on the outcome of the three wars above and introduce you to some of the key debates so that you will have enough depth of knowledge to be able to evaluate passages that are set about them.

Key debate 1: how far was French success due to the weakness of the coalitions?

The period of the Revolutionary Wars saw France under attack, having thrown down a challenge to royalist Europe. Initially, the new Revolutionary army was a shambles and it ran away from its first battle near Valenciennes in April 1793. Yet, by 1794, it had been able to defeat its enemies and drive them from French soil. Some historians have argued that its victories were the result of a revolution in warfare, which was just as significant as the changes brought in by Napoleon, while others have argued that it was the weakness of the coalitions ranged against them that allowed it to initially survive and then go on the offensive and become a war of conquest and plunder.

In arguing that the success of the Revolutionary armies was due to the weakness of the coalitions, it could be claimed that:

- The coalitions were never formal alliances, and therefore it was easy for France to reach separate peace agreements with individual states and avoid fighting a united opposition.
- Allied commanders did not join their forces together to launch a co-ordinated attack against French forces, allowing French military success after 1794.
- France was able to defeat all members of the coalitions, with the exception of Britain, at some stage in the wars, showing that cooperation was essential.
- The Prussian agreement with France at the Treaty of Basel freed up French troops to attack other states.
- The Second Coalition fell apart after a series of quarrels, with Austria failing to support Russia.
- Defeats of individual states forced them to pull out of coalitions, which meant that France faced fewer enemies.
- The European powers were divided by jealousy and differing priorities.
- Once the powers agreed to a formal alliance, with the Treaty of Chaumont in 1814, they were able to defeat France.

However, it is also possible to contend that the success of the Revolutionary armies was due to other factors, such as organisation, the tactics used and the scale of the armies raised by France:

- The reforms that had started under the monarchy were implemented; the regimental army was reorganised into divisions of 12,000 men which combined the infantry, artillery and cavalry into a single unit.
- The organisation of the French army into columns provided less of a target for the enemy and allowed them to operate as a 'battering ram'.
- The divisional system gave the French speed and flexibility.
- The French used 'shock tactics', using columns to storm enemy lines.
- The French developed a 'mixed order' of attack columns, skirmishing and sniping.
- The Revolutionary armies, because of their composition and ideals, were able to sustain heavy losses, often in excess of twenty per cent.
- The *levée en masse*, which raised over a million men, allowed the French armies to be much larger than their opponents. This continued with the introduction of conscription.
- The ideals and ideology of the Revolution and the need to defend it provided forces with a *raison d'être*. This was unprecedented in Europe.
- France became a 'nation in arms' which united the country.
- The French, initially at least, were fighting to defend their homeland.
- The volunteer force was united with the regular army so that those who were less well trained were given some military order.
- Discipline was imposed on the French forces, which turned them from a shambolic army, which ran away at Valenciennes, into a strong fighting force.
- The French gained experience with so many battles and this created a battle-hardened army.
- The number of battles meant there was almost continuous warfare, which the opposition was unable to sustain.
- The French, through 'living off the land', were able to support large armies.
- The defending forces could not sustain the heavy casualties that the Revolutionary armies inflicted.

Although it cannot be argued that all of these changes were directly responsible for the victories of the French armies, they were certainly important as once many of the changes were in place it proved impossible for the Allied forces to defeat the French. Instead of the French having to defend their homeland, they were able to launch wars of conquest and spread the ideals of the Revolution. However, they were certainly aided by the weakness of the opposition they faced, and it is notable that the Allied armies introduced many of the changes that had been brought in by the French, suggesting that they considered such reforms essential if they were to succeed in stopping the French domination of Europe. Yet, it was ultimately a coalition of forces that remained united that defeated the French at Waterloo, although they were using some of the tactics and organisation that their enemies had brought in.

Key debate 2: how significant in the defeat of the South was its failure to secure alliances?

The economic superiority of the North has led many historians to argue that its success was inevitable. However, the South was able to maintain the war for some five years and, at least in the initial stages, come close to achieving victory or at least forcing the North to discuss terms. This was a remarkable achievement given the extent to which the South was outnumbered and lacked the war materials that the North was able to muster. It has led some historians to argue that if the South could have gained recognition from other powers, such as either Britain or France, and therefore secured aid, it would have been victorious. However, others have argued that unless Britain or France committed significant sums and manpower, which was always unlikely, the North would always win a war of attrition as it could afford to sustain the losses which the South could not.

There is certainly some evidence to suggest that the failure to secure alliances was a significant factor in the defeat of the South:

- The South was able to sustain the war from 1861 to 1865 without allies and against an economically superior enemy, therefore with recognition and help from Britain and/or France it could have been victorious.
- The South recognised the importance of alliances as Jefferson Davis spent much time and effort trying to secure agreements with Britain.
- Alliances would have helped in the procurement of weapons, although Southerners were able to secure loans and bonds, which allowed them to buy weapons, and therefore this was less important.
- It has been argued that the supplies the South gained from Britain extended the war by two years, therefore it could be argued that with further supplies it could have won, given how close it came in the early years.

Despite the failure to secure alliances with either Britain or France it does appear as if other factors played a crucial role. Historians have tended to focus on issues such as leadership and generalship, the economic resources of the North and the issue of big battalions, the financial resources of the two, internal divisions within the South and a lack of will or a lack of nationalism. In addressing other issues, the significance of the following might be considered:

- The South did all it could to secure alliances, but the problem was that Palmerston would not recognise the South.
- Lee argued that the South lost because the North had more men and more guns.
- The economic strength of the North was reflected in the population which was two and a half times greater, railway capacity which was three times greater and industrial production which was nine times greater, and naval supremacy was important. However, some have argued that states with smaller resources than their opponents have won wars in the past.

- States' rights meant that states put their own rights before those of the Confederacy and this divided the war effort. The governors of Georgia and North Carolina, it has been argued, followed obstructive policies, but others have argued that the scale of obstruction was limited.
- There was resistance in the South to various war measures, such as conscription, direct taxes and martial law, and some have argued that this sapped the 'will to fight', but this is not entirely convincing as during the war Davis was able to enforce the draft and suppress dissent.
- There were divisions within the South over slavery, but the North was also divided over some of Lincoln's policies.
- Some have argued that the South lost because it did not have the will to fight; this was because the Confederacy, given its short existence, lacked a strong sense of nationalism and therefore when it became difficult to sustain the war it gave up. However, given the differences of the South and the link to the slave economy, which was different from the North and gave the South its identity, this is difficult to sustain. This may even explain why the South fought for so long – to preserve a distinct way of life.
- The leadership of the South has been criticised for failing to produce men of strategic vision, such as Grant and Sherman. Lee has been blamed for defeat because his concern was the Virginia theatre and therefore he lost the West and, as a result, the war. However, this has been disputed as military conditions in the West favoured the North as there was much land to defend and control of the rivers was an advantage for the North.
- Comparisons have been made of Lincoln and Davis, with Lincoln seen as a better communicator, uniting various factions and keeping his commanders together.

It is apparent that there is much debate over why the South was ultimately defeated. Certainly, heavy losses and defeats in battle had eroded Southerners' will to resist. If morale collapsed it was because they were being defeated in battle. They had been successful in the first two years without alliances, suggesting that ultimately they were defeated because they had fewer resources. The Northerners always had advantages and they were finally realised with Grant's leadership and the 'big battalions' he spoke of. In order to best understand the outcome, the historian James McPherson (1988) has argued that each campaign and battle should be studied separately as there is no general explanation.

Key debate 3: how far did alliances determine the outcome of the First World War?

Alliances are usually seen to have been a key factor in causing the outbreak of the First World War and turning what might have been a local conflict into a global one. However, their impact on the outcome of the war is disputed. Some of the 'alliances' were little more than agreements or understandings, which developed only as the war progressed, while some alliances hindered states, particularly Germany. On the other hand, others have argued that alliances provided the Allies with the economic power they needed to secure victory.

In arguing that alliances determined the outcome of the First World War, it might be claimed that:

- The economic resources and manpower that the Americans brought to the war in 1918 were crucial.
- Germany was weakened by the sudden collapse of its allies, Bulgaria, Turkey and Austria-Hungary, in 1918 and this helped to bring about its surrender.
- The military defeat of Germany's allies hastened the end of the war: Bulgaria suffered heavy defeat at the Battle of Doiran, the Turkish army fled Damascus, while the Austro-Hungarian Empire collapsed and the Yugoslavs, Poles, Czechs and Hungarians declared independence.
- The surrender of Russia in 1917 put considerable strain on Britain and France and brought them close to defeat.
- The surrender of Russia allowed Germany to concentrate all its forces in the West and led to a change from defence to attack, which put pressure on Britain and France.
- The military alliance that developed between Britain and France allowed unified command to develop with the appointment of Foch in 1918.
- The Allies launched co-ordinated attacks towards the end of the war with artillery cover, tanks and planes, which did allow advances.
- The co-ordination of the Allies coincided with the collapse of German alliances and members of the Central Powers seeking peace terms, which aided the Entente Powers.
- Alliances were important in 1918 and that was the year the war came to a conclusion.

It can, however, be argued that it was other factors that determined the outcome:

- The German home front collapsed because of the British naval blockade.
- The German economy was unable to meet the demands of total war and support its economically underdeveloped allies.
- The economic output of the Allies was over three times greater than that of the Central Powers.
- Political unrest within Germany; there was a growing sense of revolution following the order from the German high command to launch the fleet to engage in battle with Britain and the refusal of the sailors to agree. It led to the establishment of workers' and soldiers' councils, which demanded an end to the war.
- Mobile tactics were reintroduced with the development of mobile infiltration and the use of stormtroopers.
- The use of surprise, along with the sheer scale of the assault, was important in the July and August 1918 Allied counterattacks.

- The use of armoured cars, light tanks, motorcycle machine guns and troop-carrying lorries to support the assault allowed the advance to keep going.
- The Allied attacks towards the end of the war were mobile and flexible, unlike the attacks in the earlier years of the war.
- The entry of American troops provided a morale boost.

General Ludendorff stated, 'We cannot fight against the whole world', which was in part due to the strength of the Allied powers and the blockade of Germany, but also acknowledges the weakness of Germany's own allies and their collapse in 1918. Germany had become increasingly isolated and therefore it was becoming impossible for it to continue the war, particularly after the failure of the 1918 Spring Offensive.

Study skills: thematic essay question

How to answer turning-point questions

The mark scheme used by examiners is exactly the same for turning-point questions as it is for other thematic essays. This suggests that the approach should be exactly the same as it is for other themes essays and that the structure should be thematic and not chronological. It is much easier to compare the significance or importance of different turning points if a thematic approach, rather than a chronological one, is adopted.

Look at the following question:

> 'The development of the Prussian general staff during the Wars of German Unification was the most important turning point in the conduct of war.' How far do you agree with this view on the conduct of warfare in the period from 1792 to 1945?

If we consider the question above, it is important to realise that the focus is on planning and the control of warfare. There are a range of events or wars which might be considered to be the most important turning point in the development of planning and control, including:

- the Revolutionary and Napoleonic Wars
- the Wars of Unification
- the First World War
- the American Civil War
- the Second World War.

In theory, an essay could analyse, evaluate and compare each of these events (in order to show synthesis), but it would make for a very cumbersome structure and would be difficult to undertake in 45 minutes.

It would be far easier to adopt a thematic approach, which would allow you to compare the events. The following themes could be considered:

- the development of war plans
- the control and training of officers
- the concept of 'nation at arms'
- command structures
- co-ordination of different elements of the military.

You would then select examples from the period and compare their relative importance and significance in terms of being a turning point for each theme. Ultimately, you would reach a judgement as to which event was the most important for each of the themes, before going on to reach an overall judgement as to which event was the most important turning point.

This means that the skills you have considered in the previous chapters are just as applicable to turning-point questions as to other essays.

Consider the following responses to the question above.

Response A

The development of the Prussian general staff during the Wars of Unification was an important turning point in the conduct of war for a number of reasons. The developments under von Moltke, who was chief of staff from 1857 to 1888, brought a new professionalism to the Prussian army, which would play an important role in their victories against both Austria and France. The rotation of duties for the officers at general headquarters was particularly important as it ensured that members of the general staff had wide experience, which meant that they were highly valued and respected, with the result that their war plans were adhered to. The training was of the highest level, practising war games and studying previous campaigns, but also in an age of increased technology they were given experience of working in the railway section so that they were able to integrate the rail system into war planning, which was reflected in their ability to deliver large numbers of troops to both Sadowa and Sedan in the Wars of Unification, while neither the Austrian or French forces were able to gather together such a concentration of forces. Such was the significance of these developments that other nations soon copied the model of the Prussian general staff, particularly in terms of strategic planning.

Analysis of Response A

Strengths:

- The paragraph shows good knowledge of the developments of the Prussian general staff.
- The knowledge is used to support an argument about the significance of the general staff in bringing about military success in the Wars of Unification.
- The paragraph offers a clear view about the significance of the general staff and its impact on various elements of the conduct of war.

Weakness:

- There is no synthesis or comparison of the development of the general staff with other developments to establish whether it was the most significant turning point. It simply explains why the development of the general staff was important and is more like a period study essay.

Response B

In terms of the development of strategy, particularly the strategic use of railways, the reforms and changes to the Prussian general staff were the most significant turning point[1]. This was more important than the strategic developments that took place under Napoleon, whose aim was to bring about a decisive battle in order to break the enemy army, which although successful at the start of his rule was less so in the 1812 campaign. The Prussian general staff recognised the military potential of railways and therefore sent some of their most talented officers to the rail section to integrate both rail and telegraph into Prussian war planning, which enabled them to move 250,000 men across 300 miles and converge on Austrian positions.

This was more decisive than the strategic developments under Napoleon as Austrian forces in 1866 were comprehensively defeated in just seven weeks and the outcome was decided by one major battle. Although there were occasions when Napoleon's strategy was successful, as in the twin battles of Jena–Auerstädt, it did not work in 1812 as Russia denied him a decisive battle by retreating, whereas in both 1866 and 1870 the use of railways enabled a large force, which proved decisive, to be delivered to the battlefield. However, in 1914 such strategic planning failed to deliver the knock-out blow that was seen in the Wars of Unification. Although it was expected that, as with the Wars of the Unification, the decisive element would be the speed of delivery of troops to the battlefield, this was not the case, and the unlike the sweeping offensives of the earlier period they did not succeed in 1914.

The strategic planning of the Prussians in both 1866 and 1870 was the most significant turning point because it transformed the nature of warfare, but by 1914 the planning and use of railways simply allowed nations to increase the size of their armies which, along with the inflexibility of rail transport, prevented the sweeping movements that the war plans required as the size of the armies simply restricted the movements of such numbers. Whereas in 1866 and 1870 the strategic plans and use of railways had enabled a quick victory, they were incapable of this in 1914[2].

The development of strategic planning during the Second World War was as important in the early years as it was during the Wars of Unification. Strategists had learned from the First World War and therefore the

adoption of more flexible tactics in the Second World War, particularly the use of Blitzkrieg by the Germans, was a significant turning point as it restored mobility[3]. However, this was successful only at the start of the war and did not deliver the decisive victory in the East against Russia, **whereas the strategic planning during the Wars of Unification did result in quick and comprehensive victories, supporting the view that in terms of strategic planning the 1860s was a greater turning point[4].**

Analysis of Response B

Strengths:

- The whole period is covered from 1792 to 1945.
- A clear view is offered: the Wars of Unification and the development of strategy by the Prussian general staff were the most important turning point in the outcome of war **[1]**.
- There is comparison between the Wars of Unification and both the Napoleonic Wars and the First World War, which is seen in emboldened text.
- The view is explained and justified **[2]**.
- There is also comparison with the Second World War, which also witnessed strategic changes **[3]**.
- The significance of the changes brought about by the Second World War is then compared with the success in the 1860s **[4]**.
- There is considerable comparison between periods and the significance of a range of events is evaluated.

Activity

Sample Response B compared the role of the Prussian general staff in strategic planning as a turning point for military success with other wars. Now write thematic paragraphs which compare the importance of the development of the Prussian general staff with other events in terms of co-ordination, command structures, the training of officers and the development of the concept of the 'nation at arms'.

Essay questions

1 To what extent was the First World War a turning point in the effectiveness of alliances in determining the outcome of wars?
2 'The most important turning point in the development of command structures was the reform of the Prussian general staff during the Wars of Unification.' How far do you agree with this view of planning and preparation in the period from 1792 to 1945?
3 'The co-ordination of forces remained a problem throughout the period.' How far do you agree?

Study skills: depth study interpretations question

How to evaluate

This chapter continues to look at how to evaluate, or apply own knowledge, to one of the interpretations to judge its strengths and weaknesses. In the first paragraph in answer to this type of question, you will have explained the two interpretations and placed them in the context of the wider historical debate about the issue (see pages 58–9), and in the second paragraph you will have evaluated the strengths and weaknesses of the first interpretation (see pages 98–9).

In the third paragraph you will evaluate the second passage and consider both its strengths and weaknesses by using your own knowledge. Read Passage A below about the military strategy of the North in the American Civil War, and Response A which follows.

PASSAGE A

From Paul Boyer et al., The Enduring Vision: A History of the American People, Houghton Mifflin, 2008.

To the extent that the North had a long-term strategy, it lay in the so-called Anaconda Plan. Devised by a hero of the Mexican–American War of 1848, General Winfield Scott, the plan called for the Union to blockade the Southern coastline and then like a snake to advance down the Mississippi River. Scott expected that the sealing off and dividing the South would make it recognize the futility of Secession and bring Southern unionists to power. But Scott, a Southern Unionist, overestimated the strength of Union support in the South. Furthermore, although Lincoln quickly ordered a blockade of the Southern coast, the North lacked naval power to seize the Mississippi. So while the Mississippi remained an objective, Northern strategy did not unfold to any blueprint like the Anaconda Plan.

Response A

The passage puts forward the view that the North's strategy, as seen in the Anaconda Plan, did not succeed. It argues that the aim of the plan to seal off and divide the South so that it would realise the futility of Secession was a failure, and this view is valid as the blockade of the South, which the plan envisaged, was not effective as over three-quarters of the attempts to avoid the blockade got through and the Southern armies were not prevented from obtaining supplies because of the blockade. The passage also argues that Northern strategy did not 'unfold to any blueprint like the Anaconda Plan'.

This also has some validity as the North was unable to impose its will on its commanders, with the result that the war became a series of independent campaigns, which depended on the general in charge, leading some to argue that the very concept of the Anaconda is a misconception and has been imposed on events for which there was no real overall strategy. However, this view can be challenged as, although the war was not a bloodless affair as was the aim of the strategy, the Union success in the West was vital to their overall victory, while the strangling of the South, which the name of the plan implies, did have some success by the end of the war, with the collapse of the Army of Northern Virginia, virtually all that remained of the Southern forces by 1865.

Activities

1 What are the strengths of Response A?
2 Identify places where the passage is evaluated.
3 What other information could you use to either support or challenge the view offered?

Now read Passage B on the North's strategy in the American Civil War and consider the following question:

> Evaluate the interpretation in Passage B and explain how convincing you think it is as an explanation of the reasons for the North's victory in the American Civil War.

Remember: in the examination you will have to evaluate two passages and reach a judgement as to which you think is more convincing, but this exercise will help to develop the required skills.

PASSAGE B

Adapted from Mark C. Vlahos, *Winfield Scott's Vision for the Army*, Lulu Publishing, 2015, pp. 4–5.

From a military point of view, the Anaconda Plan had deficiencies and did not take into account Southern initiatives. Its 85,000 men were not enough to hold ground as the army moved forward. The main weakness however was political, as the pressure to march on Richmond immediately was overwhelming and the proposal to 'squeeze the South to military death' was ridiculed, though in the end it was the only way to win the war. Lincoln set aside the plan and directed MacDowell to attack in Virginia. Scott's plan was not adopted, but reappeared in 1864 in an aggressive form. Ulysses S. Grant's two-front fight in Virginia and Tennessee pressed the Confederacy, while Sherman's march through Georgia helped to 'squeeze the South'. Scott's wisdom came from a lifetime of soldiering. While his strategic calculation of the numbers needed for the plan was way off, in actual execution over the next four years, it's easy to see that his plan was a prophesy.

Activities

Apply what you have learned in the study sections so far to respond to Passage B above. Before you start you should reread pages 98, 99 and 100.

It might be helpful to consider the following questions before you write an evaluative paragraph:

1 What is the view of Passage B about the reasons for the victory of the North?
2 What evidence is there in the passage that supports this view?
3 What own knowledge do you have that agrees with the view?
4 What own knowledge do you have that challenges this view?
5 How convinced are you by the view offered in the passage? Explain your answer.

Having answered these questions you are now in a position to evaluate the passage.

CHAPTER 4

The relationship between relevant domestic factors and warfare 1792–1945

The years between 1792 and 1945 witnessed considerable economic changes and also the growth of populations, cities and communications. However, perhaps the greatest change was in the role and power of the state. All these external factors affected the nature and conduct of warfare, leading to total warfare and world war on a new scale. This chapter will consider how war was changed by these developments, which produced warfare on a huge scale, and blurred the distinction between military and civilian combatants in profound and often tragic ways.

The chapter explores these developments under the following headings:

★ The organisation of the state for war

★ The importance of conscription as a factor in the development of warfare

★ The impact of public opinion on the changing nature of warfare

★ The influence of economic factors on the conduct of war

It also considers the debates surrounding the three depth studies:

★ Did the organisation of the state in the French Revolutionary Wars bring about a turning point in the history of warfare?

★ Did organisation and economic factors determine victory in the American Civil War?

★ Did Germany lose the First World War because of the home front?

Key dates

1792	Start of Revolutionary Wars	1916		Battles of Verdun and the Somme
1795–7	Napoleon Bonaparte's campaign in Italy	1917		USA joined the war
		1918		Armistice
1799	Bonaparte took power in France	1939		Germany invaded Poland. France and Britain declared war on Germany
1805–7	War of the Third Coalition			
1812	Napoleon's Russian Campaign	1940		Fall of France
1815	Napoleon's final defeat at Waterloo	1941	June	Germany invaded USSR
1854–6	Crimean War		Dec.	Japan attacked Pearl Harbor
1859	War of Italian Unification	1942		Japanese attacked US and European colonies in South Asia
1861–5	American Civil War			
1866–71	Wars of German Unification	1944		Invasion of France by Britain and the USA
1904–5	Russo-Japanese War			
1914	Start of First World War	1945		Surrender of Germany and Japan

Cabinet warfare The wars between monarchs in the eighteenth century that had limited aims and were often settled by diplomatic negotiations and relatively small territorial changes. These wars were fought by small professional armies.

Total war War which involves the whole resources, both economic and human, of the countries involved, often with regime change as an aim rather than merely gaining limited lands.

Nation in arms A concept found in the work of some military theorists in the eighteenth century, who argued that if the whole nation rallied to a cause then the larger and more committed armies would be greatly superior in moral force to the mercenary, professional armies that were the norm.

Revolutionary France In 1789, the French Revolution reduced the power of the monarch Louis XVI, who was eventually executed in 1793. After a period in which the monarch was forced to share power with the elected representatives of the people, a republic, a state without a king, was set up in 1792. In 1799, the Republic was overthrown by a successful general, Napoleon Bonaparte, who became emperor in 1804.

Home front The activities of civilians to support fighting troops. The term was not used until 1919 and then to describe the activities of civilians during the First World War, but it is applicable to earlier wars.

1 The organisation of the state for war

▶ *How did the state organise itself for war in the period from 1792 to 1945, and how this change and impact the nature and conduct of warfare?*

War was a major factor in the expansion of state power after the French Revolution. As warfare changed from the limited **cabinet warfare** of the eighteenth century into the **total war** of the twentieth century, so the state changed with it. To raise and support mass armies required a number of developments:

- Taxes had to be raised to pay for equipping and supplying larger forces.
- The state needed to control key areas of production for the needs of the military.
- The state needed to persuade or compel larger numbers of men into the armed forces.
- The state needed to suppress opposition to war or military service and to promote the support for war.
- There had to be improved transport for use in time of war.
- Medical care had to be developed to ensure that the wastage of manpower through wounds did not weaken actual or potential war effort.

In 1792, the concept of the **nation in arms** was relatively new and was put into practice by **Revolutionary France**. By 1945, the scale and destructiveness of war had increased to such an extent that the distinction between soldier and civilian had been blurred. The **home front** was as important as the purely military fronts. Civilians were legitimate targets as the maintenance of modern warfare depended on wholehearted support from the civilian population.

The Revolutionary and Napoleonic Wars

The starting point for modern war was the total war introduced by the French revolutionary regime after 1792. The decision to go to war against the monarchies of Europe was a dangerous one. The French regular army of the eighteenth century had been weakened by the widespread exodus of highly trained officers. The well-drilled forces of Austria and Prussia, the large armies of Russia and the highly effective navy of Britain presented formidable opposition. Reverses in war could and did provoke internal opposition among the many French people who were still loyal to the king and had little understanding of or sympathy for the revolutionary regime, which moved steadily towards extremism after war was declared.

The break with the past enabled the revolutionaries to embark on a new course which required a more powerful state. The idea of a nation in arms was not new, but the revolution gave dedicated leaders the chance to put it into practice. France's huge asset was its large and relatively young population. It had over 30 million people compared to Britain's 5 million, Prussia's 6 million or Austria's 20 million. Russia had more, but could not really organise them effectively. The total war of the Revolution involved:

- mass recruitment through the *levée en masse*
- political indoctrination
- brutal coercion to enforce authority
- the taking over by the state of industry and workshops
- the rise of officers with talent rather than from the traditional elite class
- the exploitation of civilian resources.

The result was an unprecedentedly large army. By 1794, the Republicans had succeeded in raising 800,000 men. As this army was ten times the size of eighteenth-century armies, the state had to ensure that it was armed, fed, clothed and motivated. Frantic improvisation ensured that 3000 workers manufactured 700 muskets a day by 1794. Uniforms were made by ordering tailors and dressmakers to work for the state. Cobblers were required to produce ten pairs of shoes for the army a week. An astonishing 7.5 million revolutionary journals were supplied to maintain devotion to the cause, along with 100,000 republican song sheets containing morale-boosting songs like the *Ça Ira* ('It'll be Fine') and the **Marseillaise**.

KEY TERM

Marseillaise Now France's national anthem, it was the marching song of revolutionary troops from the south who marched to the support of the Republic in 1792. It urges the spread of revolution and the destruction of tyranny and calls all French citizens to take up arms. It was less widespread at the time than the *Ça Ira* song.

Figure 4.1 The Revolutionary Army of the North.

Inflation This is when prices rise. It was a feature of most of the longer wars of this period, as they created shortages and also increased the amount of money in circulation, as governments spent more and printed more money. More money and fewer goods led to higher prices.

Living off the land Armies took what food they could find from farms and villages rather than relying on their own supplies provided by the state.

KEY FIGURE

Charles, Duke of Brunswick (1735–1806)

A leading Prussian military leader, a veteran of the wars against France in the eighteenth century and commander of Prussian forces which suppressed a revolt in the Netherlands in 1787. His threats against the French people provoked resistance and his forces were defeated at Valmy in 1792. He was killed in battle against Napoleon.

To ensure that the money was available, a new paper currency was introduced based on the value of confiscated property – the *Assignats*. When **inflation** threatened, prices were controlled by direct order and profiteers ruthlessly arrested and executed. Internal opposition was met by the harshest possible means of mass execution. The armies took what they needed from the lands in which they operated. Reports of the war in Germany in 1793 referred to confiscation and plunder of villages, the murder of anyone who resisted or hid food and the abuse of women. The minister for war, Lazare Carnot, was the key figure in the development of modern warfare. He increased not only army size but the production of artillery, and played a key role in organising the Revolutionary army, particularly conscription.

The mass armies, in turn, affected tactics. The larger forces lent themselves to mass columns of shock troops. The need to **live off the land** led to the creation of mini-armies. The greater political motivation allowed for forces to be split far more than in the traditional armies of the *ancien régime*, whose commanders feared desertion if men did not stay firmly together on marches and on the battlefield.

Behind the armies was the revolutionary state, sending out political representatives to stiffen the resistance of troops and meting out revolutionary discipline. The Revolutionary Wars were a fight for survival, not for limited territorial gains, so involved the total commitment of the civilian population. Hoarding, trying to escape conscription, criticism of the regime and breaking the restrictions on price control were seen as undermining the war effort and were treated as treason.

In the wars in the countryside, there was little time for mercy. The civilian population feared the reprisals if foreign armies entered France. The Prussian **Duke of Brunswick** had threatened to burn Paris down so the whole nature of war had changed from formal manoeuvres to a life-or-death struggle.

To wage this war the state assumed greater powers than any absolutist king in French history. The Revolution had started as a movement for liberty, but revolutionary liberty involved restriction of legal rights, plunder, control, conscription and a heavy reliance on political indoctrination. This in turn transformed the nature of the wars being fought.

The classic example was Napoleon Bonaparte's campaign in Italy. His armies were divided into mobile divisions. They were led by a young, ambitious officer who had taken advantage of the opportunities of the Revolution. The troops lived off the land and did not rely on supply depots. They were highly motivated and their general was famous for leading from the front.

Napoleon made use of the artillery supplied by the revolutionary war machine and his victories led not to a modest truce but to the establishment of new states in Italy in 1797. The traditional warfare of his opponents, moving in much larger units and deploying more slowly and formally, led by older generals and with troops relying on regular supplies, was less effective; nor did they have the same political motivation or inspiring revolutionary leadership to urge them on.

There are limits, however, to the nation in arms. The mass levy was difficult to organise. France was not altogether a nation in the 1790s but more a collection of provinces with different languages and traditions. The peasantry in many regions was unwilling to leave their farms and often fled to avoid conscription. Many deserted – perhaps 20,000 a year – either to avoid the rigours of military life or to join the growing counter-revolutionary forces. After all, the existence of mass propaganda does not mean that it was effective.

The industrial capacity was limited when most production was done in small workshops. Also, the 'new' tactics did not emerge solely from the revolutionary concepts, but had been advocated by theorists of the old regime. Revolutionary hordes did not always triumph because of superior morale, and a lot of the revolutionary victories owed much to effective leadership or weaknesses of opponents.

However, all that being said, the achievements of the revolutionaries in creating a state dedicated to victory were considerable. In terms of the development of warfare, the concept and the example of total war were to prove hugely influential in the future. The key elements of state control of taxation, money supply, production, supply of resources, manpower, propaganda and discipline and control of the civilian population became essentials of the longer conflicts of the remainder of the period. The relative weakness of the eighteenth-century state meant that, in practice, total war was not entirely achievable. By the twentieth century, however, the growth of communications and the techniques of government meant that total war was much more a reality, with increasingly destructive consequences.

The Napoleonic period 1799–1815

Napoleon had risen to power in 1799 because of the Revolutionary Wars. What he brought was a total unity of the military command and the civilian state in one person. The generals of the Revolutionary Wars had had to work with the state authorities. Napoleon commanded both and so anticipated the twentieth-century dictator commanders like Stalin and Hitler. The militarised state was a model for the development of Prussia after 1806. In the whole of Napoleon's rule from 1799 to 1814, war predominated and there were only a few months of peace. As soon as he returned to power in 1815 for the 'Hundred Days', then war started again. The total war extended to the empire which he created in Europe. His armies, even larger than those of Carnot, became international forces.

With the total resources of the state behind him, Napoleon was able to add considerably to the artillery deployed. He added hundreds of guns to the French forces. These were specifically intended to destroy enemy forces with solid **shot, grape shot and canister shot** and, after 1803, **shrapnel**.

 **KEY TERMS**

Shot, grape shot and canister shot Shot is what was fired from cannons. Round lumps of metal were solid or round shot; pieces of metal were known as grapeshot; and canister shot, consisting of small metal balls packaged in a brass container, was an anti-personnel device similar to grapeshot, but made up of larger pieces of metal.

Shrapnel A British invention. A spherical case shell contained bullets and a timed fuse. When fired, the explosion broke the case and sent the bullets flying among the enemy. The British commander Wellington used it quite extensively.

Artillery

Eighteenth-century warfare had relatively limited casualties from artillery. By 1814, it was inflicting twenty per cent of casualties, but by 1914–18 it would account for 75 per cent. The productive capacity of the military state was changing the nature of warfare as well as increasing the numbers involved. The Battle of Wagram in 1809 involved the use of mass cannons – 500 guns on both sides and very heavy casualties – 33,000 French and 37,000 Austrians. By 1812, Napoleon was able to take a staggering 600,000 men into an invasion of Russia. This was equivalent to about an eighth of the population of Britain in the 1790s. Although Napoleon suffered over 500,000 casualties, he was able to raise very large armies again in 1813 and to endure 73,000 casualties at Leipzig in 1813. Even after his defeat and return to France in 1815, he raised another 72,000 men to invade Belgium. There were 400,000 artillery rounds fired by both sides at the Battle of Leipzig.

Mass mobilisation

The mobilisation of French manpower and resources was copied by the states that Napoleon fought. Austrian, Russian and Prussian armies expanded and had to be fed, clothed, sheltered and armed. The scale of warfare thus grew, the battlefields became larger and the scope greater. There was also much greater involvement of the civilian population. In Spain, which France had invaded in 1808, there was brutal warfare between France's regular armies and local resistance groups of guerrillas. The Russian population and irregular groups harried Napoleon's retreat from Moscow in 1812. Invading troops did not respect the rights of civilians. Prussian and Russian forces that entered France in 1814 left a trail of devastation in the villages they passed through. Britain had little respect for the ships of neutral countries which it seized as part of its naval blockade, and destroyed the Danish fleet in Copenhagen rather than letting it ally with France. The brutality of a Napoleonic sea battle more than matched the increasing destructiveness of land warfare when the resources of an ever-increasing state power were put behind the armed forces.

State power

The features of state support for this increasingly large-scale and brutal warfare were the raising of taxes and loans, the censorship and control over criticism and resistance to war, the resort to economic warfare, the raising of larger forces and the attempts to engage the population in support for the wars. This varied from country to country. France and Britain produced more propaganda than Russia or Austria. Britain depended less on coercion into the armed forces. British and French financial organisation and taxation were more developed. Britain's **income tax** of 1797 was the most developed wartime financial measure, but Britain did not have conscription legislation. Levels of repression were greater on continental Europe than in Britain. The type of warfare introduced by Revolutionary France was not replicated totally in any other European country, but it influenced them all.

KEY TERM

Income tax A key element of wartime finance. Before this, taxation had been mainly on property or on sales. Income tax was on all forms of income above a certain amount, so ensured that richer people paid more than the poor. It was unpopular and was removed in 1816 but restored in the 1840s and has remained the main British tax.

The American Civil War

This was the most protracted major war of the period between 1815 and 1914 and it affected a country which was deeply suspicious of the power of government. The US constitution had very carefully restricted the authority of the federal government, and there was a strong belief in the rights of the individual states and the need to maintain the freedom of the individual from central and local government. This meant that there was a great reluctance to wage anything like total war in the initial stages.

By the end of the war, there had been in both the North and South a significant increase in the power of the state and the scale and nature of the war. Some of the changes remained after the war and amounted to a second American Revolution. As the war developed into a lengthy struggle, so the power of the state had to grow to meet its demands. This, in turn, changed the nature of the war. As the state was able to raise larger armies, equip them with more powerful weapons and involve the civilian population more, so the fighting became more costly and extensive, and involved civilians more and more. It was a pattern that was to be repeated in the twentieth century.

As with tactics and strategy, the lessons of the American Civil War regarding the organisation of the state for war were lost on political and military leaders, who preferred to take as their models the much shorter European wars of 1856–71 (see page 9), which did not develop into long conflicts and so did not require such an expansion of the power of the state.

The Confederacy of states formed in the South had been one of the least taxed and controlled areas of the world before 1861. The white majority was left free to manage the African American enslaved workforce with minimal interference from either state or federal governments. There was little to pay in the way of tax, and the state made few demands. Those migrating to the territories to the west were freer still. After the initial enthusiasm for war had waned, the Confederate leadership were forced to resort to conscription to meet the dangers of an invasion by Union forces with greater numbers. This was heavily resisted, although a larger army was raised. In addition, there was more taxation, more resort to loans and finally the widespread printing of money by the government, which resulted in considerable inflation.

The imposition of a trade blockade by the North had hit the Southern economy, and the South faced a much more direct form of economic warfare when Union forces marched in a destructive campaign through the Southern heartlands, hitherto unaffected by war. Resistance at local level made it harder for the South to implement a policy of total war, but, by pre-war standards, the power of the state – in arresting dissidents and enforcing **martial law**, in taxing, borrowing and finally in undermining the currency and in forcing men into the military – exceeded any infringement of the rights of the states by federal governments before 1861.

KEY TERM

Martial law When the normal civilian legal system is replaced by the legal authority of the army, which places civilians under its authority and treats them as though they were military personnel.

The North went further in state control, which partly explains its victory. The suspension of civil rights and the arrest of dissenters and opponents were harsher, especially in the early days of the war. There was less chance to evade conscription, although substitution was allowed and there was a range of reserved occupations. The control of the federal government over finance went further, with a new banking system and the issue of the famous 'greenback' paper currency. The levels of inflation were far less than in the South, but there the population still faced rising prices.

However, in important respects, the war led to social and economic change on a new scale. The abolition of slavery in areas under Union control in 1863 was probably the greatest social change brought about by war in the period. This was extended by constitutional amendment to the whole of the USA. The expansion of Northern industry, the ending of the slave-dominated agricultural system, the new plans for the **settlement of the West** passed by the Union Congress and the expansion of railways saw a new growth of government power which would have been impossible outside the context of war. The mass armies raised led to a new destructiveness, especially in the later campaigns of 1864–5, when coupled with the heavier weaponry of the industrial age and a strategy of attrition. Without the growth of the state, neither side would have been able to develop the resources which led to this, nor would the armies have been so large. When Europe launched its own wars in 1914, and again in 1939, the armies were even larger, the weapons more powerful, the strategies even more geared to attrition and the willingness to wage war on civilians even greater.

KEY TERM

Settlement of the West The rapid expansion westwards in the USA in the nineteenth century owed a lot to the power of the US government, for example in the Homestead Act of 1862 regulating the allocation of lands to settlers. The Native Americans felt the full power of modern military might.

Figure 4.2 Economic warfare: Union troops destroy Southern railway lines, 1864.

The First World War

Despite assumptions that the war would not last long, the main protagonists assumed that a high level of state intervention was necessary. Unlike the American Civil War, there was not the assumption that the war could be fought without state control at the start. As in that war, the power of the government was a key element, but developments before 1914 made the state even more powerful:

- The growth of modern communications had encouraged a greater sense of nationalism and commitment to victory than in either the Revolutionary and Napoleonic Wars or the American Civil War. Until 1917, there was little sustained opposition or disagreement, and there was limited attempt to evade state compulsion.
- States had become more powerful by 1914 so it was harder to escape the controls of the state. The mass desertion or evasion of conscription that had been seen in many areas of France in 1792–1814 or in the Southern states from 1861 to 1865 was more difficult by 1914–18. The opening up of rural areas by roads and railways brought the power of the state closer. Telegraph and telephone helped to control the population. The fact of a patriotic majority supporting the war effort made it difficult for deserters or draft dodgers.
- The more efficient tax-collecting and administrative systems in a united Germany and Italy and an expansion of bureaucracies in Europe made raising money for war easier.
- The development of railways had made military movements easier and the state had little problem in commandeering railways. The French even took over Paris's taxis in the rush to get troops to the River Marne by 1914 to stop the German invasion.
- Many states had developed their police powers; for example, Russia's secret police had waged war against revolutionaries and terrorists. Modern police techniques like fingerprinting and photography had made it easier to control the population.
- In some states, like Russia, Germany and Austria, the state was already powerful and parliamentary institutions were weak. Thus, it was easy to make the transition to greater state control of resources. In other countries, like Britain and France, where parliaments were stronger, the growth of nationalism before 1914 led to a surge of support for government controls which had been regarded with suspicion in peacetime. The development of state intervention in welfare schemes and higher pre-war taxation paved the way. The British, notoriously reluctant to accept a powerful state for much of the period, consented to a large amount of government power in the Defence of the Realm Act in 1914. They had accepted government interference to help the old, the sick and the unemployed, and also higher levels of taxation and government regulation in the years 1906–14, so it was a natural extension to

see the powers of the state increase. The nationalisation of railways, the first conscription acts (1916) and rationing (1918) were new departures, but they built on a growth of state power. In Germany, the state tradition in military affairs was greater, and the levels of military control increased. From 1916 there was virtual military rule under Hindenburg and Ludendorff.

- There had to be greater links between government and industry to wage the type of warfare demanded by massive weapons deployed in a limited space on the Western Front. In Russia, businessmen and parliamentarians worked with the government to supply weapons. In Britain, business leaders were invited into government after December 1916. It was hard for workers to strike in most countries.

- In many countries there was an attempt to involve the whole population in the war effort. More women worked in heavy industry, and the very large armies together with high casualty rates meant there was a need for nurses. Propaganda developed in order to maintain morale, promote war loans and to ensure that the fighting forces received the gratitude of the nation.

- In all countries there was pressure on normal civil rights and liberties, where they existed for the people of the warring nations. In occupied areas, there was repression and brutality that anticipated the much more savage treatment of civilians in the Second World War. This did not develop as a result of the terrible losses of the war but was evident from the very start. Russian forces were brutal to occupied Germans in East Prussia. Germans treated French and Belgian civilians badly from the start. Austrian troops in Serbia behaved cruelly. All nations treated people badly who were seen as 'enemy aliens'. Naval bombardments of the British east coast in 1914 and 1915 showed little respect for civilians and air raids deliberately attacked civilian targets.

The huge demands for arms and war materials were largely met by an alliance between private industry and the state. Some areas were regulated and there were some state enterprises and nationalisation, but, in the main, big businesses were happy to work with the governments.

The war fell heavily on the masses of the people. Housing and services were neglected. In most countries there were high levels of taxation, both direct and indirect, and considerable shortages, particularly in Germany, Austria and Russia. In Britain, the pre-war dependence on imported food led to serious shortages as a result of the German submarine campaign. Economic warfare was waged energetically, by the British blockade and German **U-boats**, as in previous wars. Coupled with shortages, the tendency of governments to inflate their currencies meant higher prices. This was worse in some countries than others, and was a particular feature of the mass discontentment found in Russia in 1917 and Germany by the autumn of 1918. The high level of government involvement dictated that this was a war which was fought on the home fronts, as well as the fighting fronts, and whose effects took in the entire nation.

KEY TERM

U-boat An abbreviation for *Unterseeboot* or submarine. U-boats were a major threat in both world wars to Britain as they hit merchant ships bringing essential raw materials, food and war supplies from North America. The British relied on their surface ships to enforce the blockade of Germany.

Figure 4.3 Wartime industry during the First World War in Britain.

The Second World War

By 1939, Europe was dominated by dictatorships, so the exercise of state power had gone way beyond even the most stringent wartime conditions. In Russia, the Stalin dictatorship had led to a considerable amount of economic control and social engineering with a high level of repression of the civilian population. The state already owned industries and controlled agriculture through collective farms. It could control the employment and residence of the subjects and so, when war came, could exert the utmost discipline and control production to ensure a steady flow of war supplies. It could, and did, demand a high level of sacrifice, for example during the siege of Leningrad, which cost a million Soviet lives. Whole populations could be moved if the state felt they were a danger to security, and military operations could be conducted with no care at all for lives lost. There is continuity with earlier war efforts, but none in this period equates with the state-dominated war fought by the USSR.

The Fascist dictatorships did not put their countries on a war footing so quickly or with the same intensity. Neither Mussolini nor Hitler had enough faith in their subjects to require them to make extended sacrifices at the start of the war. Hitler hoped for rapid success by using *Blitzkrieg* tactics. This was to avoid the sort of drawn-out controls and sacrifice of 1914–18. It nearly worked. The war against France was over quickly. German forces were highly successful in Poland, the Low Countries, Norway, Greece and Yugoslavia from 1939 to 1941 without the Nazi state officially declaring total war. Conscription, censorship, a one-party state, coercion of the civilian population and cooperation with big business had already been well established by 1939. The Nazi victories made the regime popular and gave Germany access to a whole range of goods and raw materials, so there were fewer shortages. Casualties were relatively light, and the early successes in Russia in 1941 indicated that the war might be a short one. Germany had not yet faced heavy bombing raids, so restrictions on civilians did not increase dramatically. The exception was the war waged on the Jews and other racial enemies of the Third Reich. Here, war was conducted mercilessly and totally, resulting in millions of deaths in pursuit of an ideological aim.

However, the reverses in Russia in the winter of 1941, which extended to a long, drawn-out war of attrition in 1942, culminating in a disastrous defeat at Stalingrad in February 1943, saw Germany having to engage in total war. The restrictions increased as Allied bombing raids hit German cities; production had to be moved; intense control of the civilian population and increased propaganda efforts brought Nazi Germany closer to the type of war effort waged by the USSR. Industry remained in private hands, but Himmler's SS developed its own state within a state with special economic enterprises and considerable use of slave labour. By the time of the final campaigns in 1945, the full force of the violent Nazi state was brought to bear on the civilian population, 3 million of whom had already been killed by bombing raids and Russian invasion. The slightest hint of defeatism resulted in execution. Again, state power had increased beyond anything seen before. The use of that power to murder 6 million Jews once war had begun shows an extension of the state's control over civilians that is virtually unprecedented.

Britain, unlike Germany, adopted total war early on. Rationing, conscription, heavy taxation, control of transport, financial controls, extra police powers and internment of aliens were not new. However, the evacuation of children from cities for fear of bombing was probably the greatest intervention by the state in British history. It was accompanied by an extension of the welfare state, which was, too, unprecedented as hospitals had to be made available and childcare facilities were vital if women workers were to fill the jobs of conscripted men.

Once the USA had entered the war in 1941, it quickly caught up with the other participants in rolling out propaganda, state links with industry, conscription, and repression, for example the internment of Japanese Americans. There was also censorship, greater police powers, and controls over criticisms of the war or support for enemy countries.

The key elements in the greatest extension of total war that the world had seen were:

- The deliberate attempt to destroy morale and war production by the targeting of civilians. This had been a feature of wars since 1792, but the scale in this war was different. Examples of this include:
  - the bombing raids by Britain and the USA on Germany

- the heavy bombing of Japan by the USA followed by the use of the atomic bombs in 1945 on Hiroshima and Nagasaki
- the bombing by Germany and the use of V-1 and V-2 rockets and pilotless aircraft against Britain
- the reprisals against civilians in occupied areas
- the deliberate genocide of racial enemies by Germany with the connivance of its allies in France, Italy, Romania and Hungary.

Similarly, the repression and transportation by the USSR of whole populations are examples of the blurred line between civilians and troops. Any peoples seen as a possible danger to the Soviet war effort were ruthlessly removed.

- Considerable efforts were made by the state to use persuasion and propaganda to ensure that the war was fought to the bitter end. As there were very few attempts to bring about a negotiated peace, the persuasion could be seen as very effective. Only Italy decided to seek a separate peace and to overthrow its dictator in 1943. In other countries there was remarkable commitment to what was essentially a pointless struggle which neither Japan nor Germany could win, and to not countenancing anything but unconditional surrender on the Allied side, even though millions of lives might have been saved by a negotiated peace.
- State power had been considerable in the context of the time in Revolutionary France, in the American Civil War and in the First World War. However, it reached new heights between 1939 and 1945. In eastern Europe it continued for 40 years afterwards. In the USA it continued in the form of 'red scares' involving the persecution of suspected communists and the development of what Eisenhower called the **military–industrial complex**. In Britain, it persisted in terms of nationalisation of industries and an extension of the wartime welfare state in post-war Britain.
- The greater role of the state in providing ever-larger armies with more advanced weapons continued the growth in the scale of wars and the sheer size of the battlefields. The Battle of Kursk in the USSR in 1943 was the greatest tank battle in history; it took place over an area of 166 miles by 99 miles and resulted in half a million German casualties.
- The amphibious operation on D-Day was the greatest undertaken in the history of warfare. The US campaign in the Pacific took place in an area of thousands of miles. Without huge backing from the state to provide weapons, ships and men and without the total commitment of the population neither the USA nor Japan could have conducted warfare on this scale.

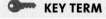

KEY TERM

Military–industrial complex The links between the top military leaders in the USA and the engineering, chemical and military industries. Eisenhower coined the phrase but it was widely used by critics of the Cold War who saw big industrial concerns benefiting from exaggerated defence requirements put forward by the military.

The growth in the state and its impact on warfare

The eighteenth-century state relied on a small administration and it had limited responsibilities. War was the most challenging of these, but warfare did not involve regime change and as it was not reliant on the support or enthusiasm of the people, it could be ended by the commanders and political leaders at will.

The Revolutionary War changed that. The Revolution had given the state more power. As France raised larger forces, its enemies had to respond, and even though the other European powers had not had a revolution, war drove them to make changes in order to meet the challenge of France.

The growth in state power in turn changed the nature of warfare. Although the wars of the mid-nineteenth century relied on some of the state-driven changes in military weaponry, transport and organisation, they did not require total war. However, the longer American Civil War did. After 1865, states had greater populations, more developed technology and industry and a good deal more popular nationalism. They were also increasingly powerful in their control and manipulation of their populations. All this culminated in the total wars of the twentieth century. Just as the First World War reflected the experience of previous wars, so did the Second. However, in terms of the growth of state power there was an unprecedented difference between the Second World War and any other previous war in history. The change was much greater than between the First World War and the American Civil War. It was also greater than the difference between the Revolutionary and Napoleonic Wars and the wars of the mid-nineteenth century. It culminated in an act which showed the huge gap between 1945 and the past. The atomic bomb was made possible only by the state harnessing the very highest level of scientific knowledge and pouring resources into the development of atomic power. It also reflected the willingness of the modern state to use any method to achieve its ends and to regard civilians as a legitimate target of war. This was only possible because civilians and military had become so interlinked. If repeated, the use of the much more powerful nuclear weapons now available will achieve the ultimate in total war: total destruction of the world and an end to human history. The state cannot achieve anything more decisive.

 # The importance of conscription as a factor in the development of warfare

► *How did conscription impact on the conduct of warfare?*

Conscription was a major feature of the military developments of the period between 1792 and 1945 and deeply affected the conduct of war. The eighteenth-century armies did have elements of conscription, but after 1792 the obligatory taking of men for the armed forces became an organised system of universal obligation to serve. The turning point was the French Revolutionary decree of 24 August 1793, which stated that 'the French people are in permanent requisition for army service'.

In the seventeenth century, there had been little idea of the state creating 'citizen soldiers' who would be taken into service but would not become permanent troops. The wars of the eighteenth century had required growing numbers of troops. These had been obtained by various means. Increasing populations meant that for some military life was an alternative to worse hardships such as unemployment, starvation or prison, and so there were volunteers. Some, of course, were genuinely attracted to a military lifestyle and were prepared to serve in foreign armies.

In the eighteenth century, the Prussian monarch Frederick the Great amassed an army of 187,000, but only 90,000 were Prussian subjects. Added to this were troops who were forced by their feudal lords to serve. Much of eastern Europe still had serfdom. In addition, there were local militias who were called on by states when necessary. The Swedes had developed a system in the late seventeenth century whereby local communities were responsible for keeping trained men and horses available for military service. The Prussians adapted this system so that there were local forces in each district that could be called on when there was a war but demobilised in peace. This system was limited in Britain to a volunteer English militia and was not attempted in Austria or Russia.

The idea of a general conscription was not developed in the period after 1815 for a number of reasons:

- Most states did not want armed civilians, but preferred closely controlled professional armies led by an aristocratic elite.
- Armies were also used for maintaining internal order, so needed to be totally loyal to the monarch and his elite military leaders.
- The system of warfare depended on complex manoeuvres by very well-drilled troops with a high level of training in rapid musketry.
- Wars were not generally fought for great national causes but for monarchs to gain glory and land, so it did not matter if armies were international in make-up.

There were theorists (see page 40) who thought that a national citizen army would revolutionise warfare, but the eighteenth-century state could not enforce mass conscription, nor could it organise the barracks and garrisons necessary for large permanent armies.

What was new in the French Revolution was the concept of a citizen army with mutual obligations between the state and the people. The people were 'sovereign' but that involved duties as well as rights, and a major duty was to defend the Revolution which had taken place in the name of the people. This involved creating a mass, enthusiastic force which would overcome the less motivated professionals. The system of obligation to serve was formalised by the *Loi* [Law] *Jourdan*, introduced by **Jean-Baptiste Jourdan** in 1798. This was different from the territorial militia and the serf conscripts of France's enemies. It aimed to create armed patriots like the ones who had defeated the British in

KEY FIGURE

Jean-Baptiste Jourdan (1762–1833)

Introduced the conscription law in 1798. He rose through the ranks to become a marshal of France under Napoleon and was a leading revolutionary general, fighting in the Netherlands and Germany. He was nearly guillotined after a quarrel with Carnot but went on to wage successful campaigns with the army of the north and in the Napoleonic Wars.

the American Revolution and also the patriots of the Low Countries who had resisted Prussian rule from 1787.

The French law of 1798 divided all men between the ages of 20 and 25 into 'classes' and men were selected from each class to serve for five years. This was decisively different from any previous conscription and provided the basis for Napoleon's armies. It was not the all-powerful military machine that later states were to develop as there were exemptions and richer people were able to pay for substitutes. There were still volunteers and mercenaries. However, the system was extended to the empire that the French created in Europe.

Contemporary Europe was deeply impressed by the French *levée en masse* and saw it as the key to understanding Napoleon's military successes. There was less need for armies to march in one disciplined unit and the new citizen armies had greater flexibility. The defeat of Prussia in 1806 led to a military reorganisation and the creation of a new state apparatus which allowed for the introduction of a conscription system in 1814. By that time, the state had abolished serfdom and created a war ministry and military training schools. The *Krumpersystem* saw ever more men being inducted into military training as there was a rolling programme of service. Thus, Napoleon spread conscription through his conquered territories and his enemies developed it as well.

Conscription and the growth of the state

Conscription depended on a reform of the whole apparatus of the state. French rule brought a new more uniform and powerful administration. Prussia, Bavaria, Baden and Württemberg introduced social and governmental reform, which was the only way a modern conscription system could work. Russia and Austria could not do this, so relied on creating local militias. There was no universal conscription in Austria until 1867 and none in Russia until 1874. This went some way to explaining Austria's defeat by France in 1859 and Prussia in 1866, and Russia's failures in the Crimean War (1854–6). Modern war needed mass participation and effective administration. Britain relied heavily on naval warfare and, here, conscription was of limited use. The infamous 'press gangs' concentrated on taking trained seamen from ports and from captured or intercepted merchant vessels. Britain's small but effective army was not a citizen army; the local militias were largely defensive and dominated by local gentry.

The spread of conscription

Conscription was not fully introduced in Britain until 1916. The idea had spread to Denmark in 1806, Sweden in 1812, Norway in 1814, Spain in 1810 and the USA in 1862.

An interesting example of national forces being created alongside a general modernisation of the state structure is Japan, which introduced conscription in 1868 as part of a general westernisation process and a destruction of the power of feudal lords and their armed followers (*Samurai*). The national army was strikingly successful in 1898 against China, which relied on local warlords, and against Russia in 1904–5.

Conscription and the nature of warfare

In the Napoleonic period, two results of conscription were a state much more organised for war and considerably larger forces. This in turn changed the character of warfare. Initially, the more committed French forces trusted to operate in independent corps had an initial advantage. However, as armies grew, the room for manoeuvre lessened. The Battle of Borodino in Russia in 1812 was little more than a mass slogging match as the size of the forces involved precluded much in the way of surprise or brilliant tactics. Napoleon could not surprise his enemies in the large-scale battles of 1813, and his final defeat at Waterloo saw the failure of frontal assaults against a determined British defence.

The larger conscript forces determined to some extent the nature of warfare, which was different from the complex manoeuvres of professional armies seen in the last quarter of the eighteenth century in the wars between monarchs and the exciting and rapid campaigns of Napoleon's Italian campaign and the War of the Third Coalition.

Conscription after 1815

The clash of national armies was not desired by the monarchs of Europe after 1815. Faced with the dangers of revolution, the kings preferred smaller armies. Conscription was abolished in France by the restored Louis XVIII in favour of a return to a royal army. Prussia retained its system of having a regular army and a reserve, the *Landwehr*. Its standing army of 156,000 was actually smaller than that of Frederick the Great (1756–86). Until the wars of the mid-nineteenth century, most European military activity was against internal revolts or in colonial policing or acquisition.

The most significant extension of conscription came with the American Civil War. Hitherto, the USA had small regular forces. Standing armies were distrusted, as they were in Britain, as agents of royal power. However, once the Civil War started it became clear that a quick victory would be unlikely and both sides introduced compulsory military service. Again, there was a need to accompany the maintenance of a larger army with administrative and financial reforms.

Conscription and the development of nation-states

The restored US nation-state after 1865 did not maintain conscription. However, the new nation-states of Germany (created in 1871) and Italy (1861), and the new joint state of Austria and Hungary (1868) needed conscription as a means of unifying their new citizens and guarding against their major enemies.

The new French Republic, too, needed conscription as a unifying element and as a means of being able to avenge the loss of two key provinces, Alsace and Lorraine, taken by Germany in 1871. Russia needed to keep up with this military modernisation given that all the major powers had universal conscription and even Japan had introduced it in 1868.

Forms of conscription

Conscription, which was introduced in all major countries except Britain and the USA, took a variety of forms. These were analysed in a book by Eliot Cohen (*Citizens and Soldiers: The Dilemmas of Military Service*, Cornell University Press, 1985). One form was the cadre/conscript model. A cadre or core of professional non-commissioned and commissioned officers trained a conscripted rank and file. There was a large reserve as trained soldiers had an obligation to remain 'on call' by the state and to renew their skills regularly while working in civilian life. The reforms of the Prussian army after 1859 reinforced this militarisation, and were the model for other European forces and for Japan. It permitted a rapid mobilisation as the reserve could be 'called to the colours' quickly. The Prussian victories against Austria in 1866 and France in 1870–1 owed a lot to rapid mobilisation and the Germans were able to gather forces of over a million men in a remarkably short time in 1914. The militarisation of the whole of society had considerable consequences for the country and paved the way for the war effort of the Second World War.

The second model was the so-called militia model. Conscription was into locally based forces led by part-time officers. This was less disruptive than the cadre model as it did not take so many people out of productive economic activity. It was the basis of the Swiss armed forces, which could be mobilised quickly and were seen as being effective – so much so that the German generals of the Nazi period were reluctant to plan to invade Switzerland.

The third model was the expandable/selective model. There was a small professional force and this was supplemented by calling up mass forces not in a reserve when necessary. This had been the situation for both Union and Confederate forces in 1862. It had taken quite a long time to establish mass, trained forces. It was also the British model in 1916. The forces could not conduct the type of independent unit-based fighting that the German army specialised in and had to, initially, be used as in the Battle of the Somme, in mass assaults which required basic military skills. With increasing numbers of trained and experienced troops, the British were able to adapt their tactics, and rely more on local initiatives and more highly trained units. The US forces coming to France in 1918 and again during the first campaigns of the Second World War faced the disadvantages of this system, which takes a long time to produce effective armies.

Developments after 1870

There were key developments in the post-1870 period which allowed for conscription to take place on a new scale. The first was the concentration of populations in urban centres and greater communications between administrative centres and rural areas. It was easier to enforce conscription, and state apparatuses had expanded even in countries which had been difficult to govern, such as Russia. The second was the engagement of the population with the preoccupations of the governments.

Conscription and society

There was genuine enthusiasm for the armed forces among many in Germany and for the navy and the empire in Britain. The alliance system had created fear among the population and the growth of nationalism had meant an enthusiasm for extreme solutions. For example, many in France wanted the war of revenge against Germany; many in Germany wanted to end 'encirclement' and to meet the supposed threat from Russia; many in Austria shared concerns of the threat from Serbia and wanted an end to separatist agitation; while many in Britain wanted to end the threat from the German navy. This is not to say that all of Europe wanted war, but the growth of newspapers, the spread of nationalist ideas and the belief in national power were notable features of the period. There was a wave of volunteers when war broke out, and conscription was widely accepted as a national duty.

The enthusiasm for militarism and the growth of mass nationalism were products of social and political change in the second half of the nineteenth century. Urban growth and the concentration of the population in large towns and cities had led to greater political awareness. The increase in the right to vote in many countries in Europe led to the development of mass political parties who often used the appeal of national expansion and the need for defence spending as vote winners. Examples of colonial movements can be seen in Germany and Britain. There was huge enthusiasm for naval expansion in both countries after 1890. In Russia, Pan Slavism – the belief that Russia should aim to unite all the Slav peoples in eastern Europe – had strong mass appeal. Even in the USA there was enthusiasm for the extension of US control over overseas territories, especially in the popular press. Conscription meant that there was less of a distinction between citizens and the armed forces.

So greater state power, widespread fears and national feelings, a larger and more concentrated population and a general militarisation of Europe all led to conscription raising armies on a new scale which had some of the enthusiasm of the French forces of 1792. By 1913, Russia had a **standing army** of 1.3 million. Germany recruited an extra 287,000 men in 1911, adding 38,000 in 1912 and another 63,000 in 1913. By 1914, the total size of armies in Europe had reached an all-time high (see Table 4.1, page 154).

 **KEY TERM**

Standing army
The permanent army maintained by a state in peacetime.

Table 4.1 Sizes of armed forces in the First World War

Country	Standing armies and reserves in August 1914	Mobilised forces in 1914–18
Austria-Hungary	3,000,000	7,800,000
Britain	975,000	8,905,000
France	4,017,000	8,410,000
Germany	4,500,000	11,000,000
Italy	1,251,000	5,615,000
Russia	5,971,000	12,000,000
USA	200,000	4,355,000

Army size was not in itself new: the French forces had reached nearly a million in the 1790s, but there were significant differences:

- The other nations of Europe has significantly smaller forces.
- The French armies often drifted away and were not really established in permanent barracks.
- The French forces were not armed, equipped, trained and organised to anything like the degree of the mass armies of 1914.
- The French forces were not deployed in a limited area and they did not face the huge artillery attacks that the conscripts of 1914 were subjected to. Casualty rates were therefore not nearly as high.

Conscription after 1918

What was remarkable about the conscription of the First World War was that despite the well-known horrors that men faced, it was maintained successfully and faced so little opposition for much of the conflict.

The Treaty of Versailles, which was signed as a settlement after the First World War, banned Germany from using conscription and limited its army to 100,000 regulars. This represented a view that far from uniting the nation, it had created a dangerous military culture. Hitler restored conscription in 1935 and Britain reinstated it in 1939. The Second World War was fought once more between large conscript armies but the impact of conscription varied far more than during previous wars (see Table 4.2, page 155).

For example:

- The French 'nation in arms' gave way before German attacks in 1940 and did not show the same spirit of national resistance.
- The German conscript army, trained by the core of regular soldiers, showed remarkable unity and resilience in the face of almost inevitable defeat. There was no recurrence of the unrest that had led to the armistice of 1918 and fighting continued way beyond a point when it could have achieved anything. The conscripted forces showed that they could work effectively as spare units in *Blitzkrieg* attacks and in complex campaigns.

Table 4.2 Number of divisions available over the course of the Second World War (a division contained between 10,000 and 20,000 soldiers)

Country	1939	1940	1941	1942	1943	1944	1945	End of war
Britain	9	34	35	38	39	37	31	31
France	86	105	0	0	5	7	14	14
Germany	78	189	235	261	327	347	319	375
Italy	6	73	64	89	86	2	9	10
Poland	43	2	2	2	2	5	5	5
Romania	11	28	33	31	33	32	24	24
USA	8	24	39	76	95	94	94	94
USSR	194	200	220	250	350	400	488	491

- Russian conscripted forces were able to sustain a war after vast losses of manpower earlier in the year against Germany, although there was more control, threats and political pressure. For all this, the Russian soldiers – the so-called 'Ivans' – fought in a determined way regardless of loss.
- British conscripted soldiers, after the initial defeats of 1940, managed to work in self-contained units and mastered a range of military skills. Both they and the US conscripts were able to sustain complicated amphibious landings, for example in Sicily and Italy in 1943 and in France in 1944. US conscripted men fought tenaciously and independently in campaigns in the Pacific to clear the Japanese from strongholds on islands. The British campaign in Burma relied heavily on the initiative and self-reliance associated more in the past with professional forces.

The citizen army and the conduct of war in the Second World War

In one respect, the existence of a citizen army did dictate strategy. The British leaders were reluctant to embark on an invasion of France, which might re-create the trenches of the First World War and lead to heavy casualties. D-Day was postponed until June 1944 despite Stalin's request that the Western Allies should invade France. As it was, the casualties in the campaigns of 1944 and 1945 proved to be as costly as the campaigns of the First World War and were endured with the equivalent bravery by men who were not professional soldiers.

The Germans showed a similar resistance to subjecting their citizen soldiers to the hardships that they had faced from 1914 to 1918. The rapid and heavily motorised *Blitzkrieg* campaigns were intended to produce fast results and avoid a war of attrition. It was only when this proved impossible after the failure to knock Russia out of the war that conscripts were called upon to sustain a long and bitter struggle with little chance of a quick result.

Most of the Western armies held out the prospect of survival and return to civilian life for their conscripts. Japan, in contrast, held out only the prospect of serving the emperor and fatherland. Japanese soldiers and their families did not expect to return alive and there was no consideration for avoidance of casualties that might weaken the resolve of conscripted men.

Thus, the impact of great conscripted forces differed from army to army, but what was common was the considerable increase in the size of the forces relative to the population and the compulsion placed on civilians to support the war effort in the spirit of the revolutionary ideal of the nation in arms.

No war had put the stakes so high for all those involved. The threat was of a total destruction of the way of life of soldiers and civilians that had few parallels in the period. A German victory in Russia would have created a slave state with a much-reduced population. Russian victory did divide Germany for over 40 years and imposed a radically different social and political system on part of it. There was little hope in Britain of any accommodation with a Nazi-dominated Europe and the defeat of France brought unparalleled national division and humiliation. Japanese defeat brought an end to the most cherished traditions and beliefs. Japanese forces were no longer considered invincible. Surrender, previously seen as dishonourable and virtually impossible for any Japanese leader, had to be accepted. The emperor, hitherto seen as divine, had to be accepted as a human head of state. In this context, conscripted soldiers and regular troops shared a sense of mission and purpose, and the distinctions became even more blurred. The most extreme struggle became necessary for survival, and mass conscription made this possible.

3 The impact of public opinion on the changing nature of warfare

▶ *What impact did public opinion have on the way wars were fought and won?*

The eighteenth century

Eighteenth-century wars were characterised by very limited appeals to public opinion, although some conflicts were popular. The British government was pressured into war against Spain by an account of an attack by Spanish ships on an English vessel, which resulted in a Captain Jenkins losing his ear in 1739. Wars of rebellion and revolt such as the American War of Independence clearly were influenced by public opinion. However, there were many so-called cabinet wars which were driven by high matters of state or monarchs' ambitions. The way wars were fought had little to do with public opinion and was dictated by the military class which controlled the armies.

The Revolutionary and Napoleonic Wars

The French Revolutionary Wars were driven more by opinion and there was a strong feeling within radical elements in Paris for war in 1792. When defeats

Figure 4.4 The Spanish artist Francisco Goya produced a series of works showing the horrors of the war in Spain from 1810 to 1820.

followed, the pressure for all-out war was influenced by the people of Paris and supported by provincial radicals. In turn, the revolutionary authorities stirred up patriotic feelings with a steady flow of songs, pamphlets and speeches. This set a precedent. Napoleon's wars were not uniformly popular but he did his best to engage public opinion by a series of carefully manufactured bulletins and also by paintings and prints showing heroic images of himself and his forces. This was not common among his monarchical opponents, but where he met national or popular resistance then there was a strong element of public opinion driving opposition and dictating the nature of warfare. This was especially true in Spain, where irregular forces driven by religious fervour and local patriotism engaged in violent and implacable warfare against French forces, leading to atrocities on both sides. These ideas were captured for posterity by the Spanish artist Francisco Goya (see Figure 4.4). A similar fervent opposition had been encountered in provinces of France during a lengthy civil war in the 1790s. There was also a patriotic movement in Germany in opposition to Napoleon, although this was more dominated by traditional elites.

The nineteenth century

In the reaction against the revolution, statesmen after 1815 tried to avoid having to appeal to public opinion, but some wars were popular. The campaign fought to free Greece from Turkish control in 1827, for instance, saw favourable public support in Britain. Public opinion was mobilised to support the Franco-British campaign in the Crimea, and Napoleon III's support of Italian nationalism in the war against Austria in 1860 was in part a response to public sympathy for Italy. The mid-nineteenth-century wars in Europe, however, were not long enough to require the mobilisation of public opinion. Bismarck was not moved by popular nationalism in his war against Austria, which was not supported by majority opinion in Germany, and the outcome depended on purely military factors. There was a great deal of enthusiasm on both sides during the Franco-Prussian War, but again the relatively short war did not require a massive propaganda campaign to ensure victory.

The exception to the short and decisive mid-nineteenth-century wars was the American Civil War. Here, both sides needed to maintain the morale of their supporters. The anti-war feeling in the North was considerable and Lincoln had to rally support. The so-called Gettysburg Address (see the box below) in 1863 was the most famous example of interpreting the war as one to preserve the essential principle of government by, with and for the people. The emancipation of the slaves defined the war as a moral crusade. Both sides used propaganda and enlisted music for their cause to maintain the public support needed as the war dragged on into a campaign of attrition. Without ongoing public commitment, the heavy casualties could not have been endured.

The Gettysburg Address

The address given by President Abraham Lincoln on 19 November 1863 to inaugurate a burial ground for the victims of the costly battle at Gettysburg in Pennsylvania, which was a turning point in the war, is one of the greatest wartime orations ever, although it was poorly thought of at the time for being too short. The speech sums up the nature of the war as a great struggle for a cause and the importance of rallying the nation.

Four score and seven years ago our fathers brought forth on this continent a new nation, conceived in liberty, and dedicated to the proposition that all men are created equal.

Now we are engaged in a great civil war, testing whether that nation, or any nation so conceived and so dedicated, can long endure. We are met on a great battlefield of that war. We have come to dedicate a portion of that field, as a final resting place for those who here gave their lives that that nation might live. It is altogether fitting and proper that we should do this.

But, in a larger sense, we cannot dedicate, we cannot consecrate, we cannot hallow this ground. The brave men, living and dead, who struggled here, have consecrated it, far above our poor power to add or detract. The world will little note, nor long remember what we say here, but it can never forget what they did here. It is for us the living, rather, to be dedicated here to the unfinished work which they who fought here have thus far so nobly advanced. It is rather for us to be here dedicated to the great task remaining before us – that from these honored dead we take increased devotion to that cause for which they gave the last full measure of devotion – that we here highly resolve that these dead shall not have died in vain – that this nation, under God, shall have a new birth of freedom – and that government of the people, by the people, for the people, shall not perish from the earth.

The later nineteenth century saw considerable efforts by supporters of national strength (nationalist groups who were determined to build up their countries' military power) to gain public support. The growth of a popular press, of colonial and patriotic organisations, and of literature designed to scare and alarm the public, made the widespread growth of militarism in Europe possible. Without the steady growth of armies, the spending on weapons, arms races and a belief in military solutions to political problems, the nature of the First and Second World Wars would have been very different.

The twentieth century

The enthusiasm for war in 1914 was not as widespread as is sometimes stated, but the war faced very little sustained opposition until the Russian Revolutions of 1917 and the collapse of the German home front under the pressure of shortages in 1918.

War was more popular in 1914 in western than eastern Europe because of the greater urbanisation in the west. Rural areas lacked access to the propaganda and nationalist enthusiasm. Peasant communities were more inclined to see war as another aspect of an intrusive and alien state impinging on their traditional way of life. In this respect, there was more continuity with the earlier part of the period.

Support for war was bolstered by a whole series of efforts by the state to maintain enthusiasm. The press was censored. There were reports of atrocities by the enemy and the ramping up of fears of invasion. Idealistic war aims were produced and given wide circulation. The talents of artists, writers and composers were enlisted to boost morale. Hostile opinion was suppressed. War, as in 1792, was converted into a popular cause and religion was commandeered to support it. Chaplains in all armies preached the righteousness of the cause.

Increasing civilian involvement in the conduct of war

In both world wars, the appeal to public opinion and public reactions to war meant that the character of war was affected. It became hard to conceive of a negotiated settlement with a demonised enemy. Without this possibility, warfare became increasingly unrestrained, with attacks on civilians, the use of weapons like gas, the mistreatment of minorities and an increasingly careless regard for loss of life or wasting of resources.

This had become apparent between 1914 and 1918; earlier wars had shown elements of it, for example the deliberate destruction of property in Sherman's march to the sea in 1864 and the British imprisonment in special concentration camps of the families of their enemies in the Boer War to put pressure on them to surrender. Japanese campaigns against China (1898) and Russia (1904–5) had been fought with a total disregard for casualties. Almost as soon as the First World War started, there were attacks on civilians and those considered to be unreliable minorities, and occupying troops acted savagely against civilians. This could be seen in Belgium in 1914 in the case of Germany and East Prussia in the case of Russia at the same time. By 1939, the availability of much more destructive air power meant an extension of efforts to smash the morale of the enemy's population.

Propaganda

Incitement of support for war by government using a variety of printed material had been a feature of warfare since 1792. All sorts of pamphlets, pictures and patriotic songs, pageants and theatrical events had been used. This was much more marked in France, where the Revolution had politicised the nation far more than in any other country. In the monarchies that opposed Napoleon on the mainland of Europe, there was far less need felt to mobilise popular opinion. The British governments did subsidise anti-Revolutionary propaganda to a degree but generally propaganda was much more developed in twentieth century wars as the need to mobilise civilians behind the struggles for national survival was much greater and the means open to governments were so much greater.

The development in the twentieth century of government departments devoted to propaganda was significant. Goebbels' Ministry of Public Enlightenment had existed since 1933. The Soviet state had devoted considerable resources to propaganda since 1917. Britain had promoted state propaganda in the First World War but its Ministry of Information in the Second World War drew talents from the world of literature, advertising, radio and the cinema. Propaganda films featured in all countries in the Second World War. Although some footage was shown of battles in the First World War, it was limited and the famous British film of the Battle of the Somme drew huge audiences but was not very stirring. However, by the Second World War it was very different and all sorts of powerful films deeply affected audiences and had high production values.

Radio allowed the patriotic exhortations of political leaders to reach a very wide audience, a development of the pre-war period and the growth of broadcasting. Even music was recruited for the war effort. Marching songs and patriotic anthems had always been important but a major work of art, the Russian composer Shostakovich's Leningrad Symphony, was produced as a response to the German invasion and its fame spread throughout the Allied countries. It remains probably the only classical masterpiece produced as a direct result of the war, although songs like 'Lili Marlene' and 'The White Cliffs of Dover' had more widespread emotional impact.

The more sophisticated propaganda also meant that war was promoted much more effectively. Goebbels presented the war in terms of a clash of civilisations; the British and Americans, as a crusade for democracy. The USSR saw a struggle against Fascism and for the people. Japan saw it as a struggle to fulfil a God-given **imperial destiny**.

 **KEY TERM**

Imperial destiny There was a traditional Japanese belief that the emperors were descended from the Sun goddess Amaterasu Ōmikami, and emperor worship was revived in the 1920s as part of the Shinto religion. The emperors were declared to be mortal, rather than gods, after the defeat of the Second World War, something that led some traditionalists to suicide. Given this divinity, many nationalists thought that the empire had a destiny to rule Asia and even beyond.

Josef Goebbels

1897	Born to a Catholic family in Rhineland
1921	Gained a doctorate in literature
1924	Joined Nazi Party
1926	Became local party chief in Berlin
1930	Took control of all Nazi press
1932	Organised an extensive propaganda campaign
1933	Minister of public enlightenment and propaganda
1938	Took a leading role in attacks on Jews in 'Night of Broken Glass'
1939	Gave his support to war
1943	Announced the implementation of total war
1944	Plenipotentiary for total war
1945	Killed himself in Hitler's bunker

Propaganda and war

Goebbels' ministry controlled press, mass rallies, radio broadcasting, film censorship, art and music. The war extended this control to occupied countries and he kept a close control over the propaganda messages received by German troops. He made strong use of film with 1500 mobile film vans. The propaganda deployed celebrated German victories in the early part of the war. To boost morale, Goebbels was careful to avoid over-obvious 'messages' and to promote light entertainment. When Allied bombing hit Germany, he was in the forefront of visits to bombed areas and did his best to sustain morale. He did not shy away from facing up to disasters like the surrender of large numbers of German forces at Stalingrad in 1943.

Goebbels took a leading part in promoting the concept of total war, which he introduced in February 1943 in a famous broadcast from Berlin. Early victories had spared the German people from total commitment of resources but Goebbels now led a campaign for more rigorous controls and utter devotion to victory regardless of cost. He emphasised the positives, for example the new 'wonder weapons' the V-1 and V-2 rockets.

Faced with inevitable defeat, Goebbels continued to be defiant in his broadcasts and unrelenting in his support for the annihilation of the Jews. Devoted to Hitler, he could not live without him and killed himself after Hitler's death. His wife and all his children died with him in Hitler's bunker.

The ideological appeal to public opinion and the support given by states meant that a more destructive war was possible with less restraint than in previous conflicts. Germany's war against European Jews was fought with a great deal of popular support. Popular racial hatred could also be seen in the USA's struggle against Japan.

The flood of propaganda on all sides was unprecedented, with whole areas of government devoted to 'information' or 'public enlightenment'. It is difficult to see quite how any regime by 1943 could have stopped the war given the enthusiasm created, so the only alternative was to wage it with increasing resources and brutality. The tendency begun in 1792 reached its greatest intensity with the bombing raids and wholesale mistreatment of civilians that characterised the war, while in military terms the loss of life exceeded that in any previous or, indeed, subsequent conflict.

4 The influence of economic factors on the conduct of war

▶ *What impact did economic factors have on the way wars were fought?*

The long period of war from 1792 to 1815 coincided with the British-led Industrial Revolution and a period of growth in transport and in commercial agriculture. There is a strong possibility that the demands of war stimulated economic growth. The growth of British trade and industry and an efficient system of public finance, which could tax effectively and raise money for war, had a major impact on the conduct of war. First, it gave Britain the ability to increase the strength of its armed forces to pay them, and equip them from British factories and forges. It also allowed Britain to subsidise its continental allies while focusing on lucrative naval warfare and an effective campaign in Spain (the Peninsular War 1808–14), which weakened Napoleon.

Economic warfare

Given the economic strength that Britain had shown in both the Revolutionary and Napoleonic Wars, Napoleon extended the conduct of war by deliberately waging economic warfare. This was not new in naval terms, as Britain had often imposed naval blockades on its enemies, restricting their trade. The British had extended restrictions on trade to neutral ships by the infamous Orders in Council. This is the name given to the orders of the British government which gave British naval vessels the right to stop and search any ship and confiscate it if found to be trading with the enemy. It was enormously unpopular with neutral nations.

Napoleon's Continental System was a more ambitious strategy based on his domination of Europe, and his ability persuaded his allies to join in a boycott of British exports. Hitting the British economy would make it harder for Britain to continue the subsidies paid to its allies – some £65.8 million in all – a vast sum at the time. It would also bring unemployment and social unrest. The subsidies which Britain paid to its European allies were often used to buy British-produced war supplies, so by reversing this, even more damage would be caused to Britain. Economic warfare was to be a major feature of longer wars when countries had the capacity to wage it. In the American Civil War, the disruption caused by the Union blockade hit supplies of Southern cotton to Europe. However, this did not produce the support for the South that the Confederacy had hoped for. Napoleon's economic warfare did provoke hostility, though. To enforce it required spreading French authority even further and was a factor in leading to French over-extension, by fighting in Spain and Russia.

Both France and Britain were able to sustain their war efforts economically. Both had developed financial institutions, which avoided the very high inflation experienced by Revolutionary France when it relied on paper money. Britain managed to get its people to accept a paper-based currency in 1797 and Napoleon copied Britain by creating a **Bank of France** in 1800. Both nations managed to spread the tax burden and to raise loans. Thus, economic and financial factors allowed for a long war. France relied much more than Britain on exporting a command economy to conquered nations and exploiting them. Britain relied more on its new industries; its trade and naval strength; and a more efficient enclosed agriculture, which generated better profits for landowners, which in turn provided capital for new industries.

Industrial development and war

The industrial and commercial growth of Britain and the wealth gained from conquest by France did not have much direct bearing on the actual development of war. The military leaders were conservative. Napoleon did not promote the use of air balloons to observe his enemies' battlefield deployment (balloon observation), even though such balloons were available, and Wellington was not interested in new technology that was developed, such as the **Congreve rockets**. Industries in the Revolutionary and Napoleonic Wars did not produce much in the way of technological innovation of weapons. Technology did not impact much on military methods, except for the development of lighter artillery. All depended on the eighteenth-century musket with socket bayonets. Napoleon's reliance on horse transport compared to his enemies' greater use of water transport was a factor in his defeat. However, no great industrial might on the part of any country was decisive in the period from 1792 to 1840, although population growth and increased economic activity maintained the larger armies.

Industrial changes after 1840 and the ability of states to benefit from economic change became more crucial. In this respect, the period 1792–1815 was much less important than the years after 1840. Greater economic growth was seen in continental Europe, especially in France and Prussia. As the gulf grew between the industrial economies of Prussia and Austria and of France and Austria, so the military balance swung towards economies that could produce greater changes in weaponry and also in transport. These gave European powers a significant advantage over forces in Asia and Africa, and allowed colonial domination and greater access to markets for manufactured goods. It also swung the balance militarily in Europe to those powers with more developed industry, science, technology and finance. Thus, Prussia with its industrial resources granted in 1815, its ores, coal, railways and large workshops, triumphed over the less developed Austria. Austria's limited economic development left it vulnerable to French forces in 1860 in Italy. The greater industrial development of the Union gave it ultimate victory over the less economically developed Confederacy.

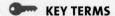

KEY TERMS

Bank of France Based on the example of the Bank of England, created in the 1690s. British financial stability was a major element in its military success after 1700 and the national banks controlled money supply and the activities of private banks, reducing inflation and encouraging lending to the state which modern wars required.

Congreve rockets Relatively small rockets were developed by the Indian Sultan of Mysore in the 1790s for use against the British and could travel 1000 yards before exploding. Sir William Congreve developed them from 1804 and they could then travel 3000 yards. Not very reliable on the battlefield, they were mainly used by the British navy.

Japan's economic and industrial growth gave it a victory over the much less economically advanced China in 1898.

The advantages of transporting troops by train were demonstrated first in their use to deal with internal disturbances, but the war of 1866 between Austria and Prussia revealed their military potential most fully. Prussian forces were mobilised quickly and were able to reach the battlefields of Bohemia in good order and ready for battle. Communication issues were crucial. Napoleon's failures in Spain and France are attributed by some military historians to problems of supply. The rapid deployment of troops by Prussia was a key element in its victories in 1866 and 1870–1, as well as its having the industrial capacity to equip its forces with the needle gun (see page 65).

An assessment of the importance of economic factors in the nineteenth century

It would be inaccurate to see all the outcomes and methods of war as being dictated to by economic factors. The rapid victories of Garibaldi in the south of Italy and Sicily in 1861 owed little to economic factors. Austria might not have had the volume of trade and wealth that Prussia had, but its industry was powerful enough to produce Škoda heavy artillery that could have been a formidable threat to Prussia had the quality of Austrian generalship been better in 1866.

For all the advantages the North had economically, its armies were often defeated by the Southern general Lee, and victory took four destructive years of fighting. Britain's economic might did not prevent military disasters, for example the futile Charge of the Light Brigade in the Crimean War or defeats at the hands of the Boers in 1899, who were reliant on agriculture and were fighting the world's greatest industrial power.

Later nineteenth-century developments

By 1870, economic growth had progressed to a level whereby the state could finance and supply very large standing forces and could develop technology which changed the face of warfare. The German levels of economic growth were striking and coincided with a rapid growth of the military and the development of newer weapons. However, US post-Civil War economic growth did not produce a vast army or any great interest in new military hardware. Economic growth in itself did not develop warfare, but it facilitated those forces which were influential in making Europe two great armed camps, raising army size and pursuing new weapons such as smokeless weapons, gas, iron-clad ships, prototype war planes, magazine rifles and machine guns, which *did* transform warfare. Economic progress also concentrated populations in cities, making them easier to control and enlist into forces and also more susceptible to nationalist and militarist ideas.

The period between the 1880s and 1914 saw what the historian William H. McNeill (1982) has called the 'intensification of military–industrial interaction'.

The early twentieth century

In Britain, concern about naval supremacy led to a 400 per cent increase in naval expenditure, from £10.8 million in 1884 to £48.8 million in 1914. The scale of this can be seen if it is remembered that £1 a week was a living wage at that time. The link between the state as a customer for shipbuilding and engineering and private firms was of the utmost importance and really saw a military–industrial complex. Great firms like Vickers and Armstrong in Britain were more than matched by the French company Creusot and the Krupp arms manufacturer in Germany and Škoda in Austria. By 1914, the state did not need (as the French Revolutionaries did in 1792) to take over industrial concerns to prepare for war, because the relationship was already in place. Russian arms manufacture expanded considerably after 1905.

By 1914, the great powers were confident in their industrial capacity to wage modern warfare; they had considerable reserves of manpower and had forged the economic links with industrial concerns to sustain a major war. They also had more developed transport infrastructures. Germany's railway building had permitted a highly complex plan to avoid war on two fronts.

Thus, the scale of warfare and its industrial-based nature had been determined before 1914 by economic developments and the state's ability to forge relationships with industrial producers.

The impact of economic factors on the First World War

The unexpected development of a long war of attrition forced states to develop their home fronts. In effect, the industrial countries turned themselves into 'what amounted to a single national firm for waging war' (McNeill). After a frantic few months, France realised the importance of allocating manpower and resources to the economy rather than merely waging war like an extended version of the mass enthusiasm of 1792. Big businessmen like **Louis Renault** were used to allocate resources and developed mass production. By 1918, he had 22,000 workers. Mass production was sustained by enlisting a new and more extensive workforce including women, children, veterans and even soldiers allocated to war production.

The French state co-ordinated the industrial effort through a minister of munitions, **Albert Thomas**, who recruited industrial managers and technical experts. This was similar to the situation in Britain, where **David Lloyd George** was a dynamic minister of munitions and the workforce was expanded by using more women and children. The British had more experience of mass production than France and, unlike France, no British industrial area had been conquered by Germany. War production expanded enormously, mainly using existing private industry. However, the demands of war led to increasing dependence on the USA and Canada for war products, food and credit. The ability to tap into the enormous industrial resources, even before the USA joined the war on the Allied side in 1917, gave Britain and France the ability to sustain warfare on a

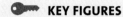

KEY FIGURES

Louis Renault (1877–1944)

An engineer and industrialist. He built his first car in 1898 and formed a company with his brother. He developed mass production of weapons and motor vehicles in the First World War and built the Renault FT tank. He was accused of collaborating with the Germans in the Second World War and died while awaiting trial.

Albert Thomas (1878–1932)

A French journalist who became a leading Socialist politician. He was put in charge of railways in 1914 and then rose to become a powerful minister of armaments, controlling resources and producing great quantities of arms. He lost office in 1917 but after the war was a key figure in the development of the International Labour Organization.

David Lloyd George (1863–1945)

A Welsh solicitor who rose in the Liberal Party to become chancellor of the exchequer in 1908. He was an energetic minister of munitions, working with businessmen and unions to raise war production. He was prime minister from December 1916 to 1922 in a coalition with the Conservatives.

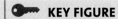

KEY TERM

War economy All economic resources are employed for the war and resources are controlled and allocated by the state for the war effort.

KEY FIGURE

Walther Rathenau (1867–1922)

A prominent German physicist and industrialist, he founded the famous electrical firm AEG. In the First World War he was in charge of the army's raw materials department and worked on developing chemical substitutes for imported raw materials unavailable because of the British blockade. He became minister of reconstruction in 1922 and then foreign minister. Hated by right-wing extremists for his policies and Jewish background, he was murdered in 1922.

new scale. The organisation of a **war economy** allowed the tank to be developed and to be used alongside air power to help to achieve victory in 1918. It allowed warfare on a new scale with millions of shells, heavier artillery than ever seen before and equipping of the greatest mass armies in the history of warfare to that date.

Germany too took over its industrial resources. It developed a programme to avoid dependence on imported military products like copper and nitrate. Businessmen such as **Walther Rathenau** of the General Electric Company (AEG) were used to allocate resources, and a special Raw Materials Department was created by the War Ministry. Key raw materials had to be rationed, especially food in Germany from 1916 and in Britain from 1918. Germany used conquered territories to maintain food supplies, but lacked access to large-scale purchases in North America. The shortages of food at home brought about by British economic warfare were a major cause of Germany trying to force a rapid end to the war in 1918, they also led to the loss of morale among many troops and on the home front which contributed to unrest and the decision to seek an armistice. From 1916, the military attempted to control war production with the Hindenburg Plan, but authoritarian demands for greater efforts yielded less than expected. In Britain, negotiations with trade unions, higher wages and rewards led to better results.

Russia, like the other countries, used businessmen and key committees of industrialists, and manufacturers managed to increase arms productions to new levels. Shell production went from 450,000 a month in 1915 to 4.5 million a month in 1916. The idea that Russian arms production was primitive and always inadequate is not accurate. However, industrial production did hit problems by 1917 and Russia's infrastructure was less efficient than other countries in bringing food to cities. This was a major factor in underperformance by troops and internal unrest, which effectively took Russia out of the war in 1917.

The later phase of the First World War from 1916 had brought industrial disciplines to civilian life, with resource allocation, the development of mass-production techniques, the application of new technology and managed economic and social life. It had also brought elements of welfare, with the state often having to introduce better health care to maintain production in the manner of enlightened factory owners in the nineteenth century. This varied from country to country.

The ability of Britain and France to manage their war economies and to have the advantage of US and Canadian economic support were major factors in the Allied victory in 1918. The British blockade was effective economic warfare, which Germany, even with its submarine campaign, could not entirely match. U-boat warfare, for all its threats to Britain's economy, was responsible for the USA entering the war and so in the wider sense was counterproductive in the same way that Napoleon's Continental System had been (see page 162).

The impact of economic factors on the Second World War

By 1939, no state was in any doubt that economic resources were going to be at the heart of conflict. Germany had already, by its Four Year Plan of 1936, been establishing the economic basis for war with at least some state control of industry and the development of *ersatz* replacement raw materials to avoid being defeated by any future blockade. The need for economic self-sufficiency dictated strategy for both Japan and Germany. Japan launched sudden attacks in 1941–2 to seize key raw materials in South Asia such as rubber, oil and metal, which had been threatened by a US embargo. Germany had seen the problems of fighting a long war and the decline of civilian morale in the face of shortages.

The war of 1939 was intended to be won quickly without imposing the total war economy that had failed in 1916. This depended on using tanks, mechanised vehicles and a strategy of rapid movement and avoiding strong points. Thus, economic factors dictated the way that the war was fought initially. Both France and Britain had faced economic problems in the 1920s and 1930s which had affected rearmament, and the build-up of forces was delayed and dominated by defensive strategies. However, the war was not primarily determined by economics from 1939 to 1941. France had greater manpower and resources but lost heavily before any long-term economic contest could be waged. Britain had resources and manpower which outstripped Japan, but still lost Singapore, its main base, to a rapid and skilful Japanese attack in 1942. For all its enormous industrial development in the 1930s, Russia faced a real danger of defeat in the German advance in 1941 at a time when the German economy had not been placed on a complete wartime footing.

Hitler was anxious not to subject the German people to the full economic control and rigour which had been seen in the First World War, although, like other countries, the army had a considerable economic planning staff. From 1943, however, it was clear that the war was likely to be even more drawn out than that of 1914–18 or the American Civil War, and that victory would depend on resources. With the entry of the USA into the war after the Japanese attacks on Pearl Harbor in December 1941, and Hitler's somewhat inexplicable decision to declare war on the USA, the economic balance swung heavily against the Axis powers. The sheer production ability of both the USA and the USSR, once the initial shock of German invasion had passed, allowed warfare to develop in a way that gave the Allies the initiative. The series of amphibious landings and invasions by Britain and the USA depended on the mass production of landing craft and naval superiority. The war in the air gave the initiative to the Allies because of their ability to produce large numbers of aircraft. The ability of the USSR to go on the counterattack in 1943 depended on the mass production of tanks and heavy artillery. The success of Britain in north Africa in 1942 depended on the mass build-up of supplies in Egypt and the shortages of fuel for the militarily superior German Afrika Corps, with its more skilful general Rommel.

Essentially, the situation in 1918 where superior resources supported Allied victory was reproduced in the Second World War after 1942. However, because the Nazi leadership were determined to fight to the bitter end, regardless of any real chance of winning, the war was protracted through 1944 and 1945, despite the economic advantages of the Allies. A similar situation emerged in Japan, where heavy bombing by the USA and the loss of key and irreplaceable shipping in naval battles in 1943 and 1944 left its rulers without the industrial resources to win. However, surrender was psychologically impossible until the total superiority of Western science, technology and industry was demonstrated by the prediction and use of atomic weapons in August 1945.

Thus, economic factors did a lot to determine the final outcome of the war, as well as how it was fought, but alone they cannot explain the nature and duration of the war, which was influenced by ideology and power politics.

Chapter summary

There was an interaction between the development of warfare and the power of the state throughout the period. Warfare became more ideological and dominated by revolutionary ideas. This required greater popular participation, and to oppose the Revolution required monarchies like Prussia to remodel their governments and armies more along the lines of the French. The development of conscription proved to be a major development. In order to feed, clothe and supply the larger armies, states needed to develop more powerful bureaucracy and more administrative personnel. In turn, the enlarged states could raise larger armies.

The wars of the mid-nineteenth century were not fought for a long period by massive forces because they were relatively short. The mid-century war which was most extended – the American Civil War – did involve larger forces, and saw the power of the state changed forever. The growth of national feeling, the development of an informed urbanised population and the growing fears of the late nineteenth century saw arms races, war scares, complex alliances and eventually war between the greatest forces ever assembled in history. This determined the whole nature of the First World War, as mass attacks to wear down human and economic resources dominated. The economic and scientific advances had led to weaponry which few attacks could overcome. The massive armies produced by the conscription of an enlarged population were used in costly frontal assaults.

The Second World War saw struggles between much more powerful dictatorial state apparatuses, but even democracies like Britain built on the experience of the greater state developed in the First World War. The struggle became one to destroy the war-making capacity of the enemy – a tactic not seen much before the American Civil War. Blockades, bombing, movement of population and finally atomic destruction amounted to the greatest total war in history because there could be no real distinction between the fighting fronts and the home fronts any longer.

Refresher questions

Use these questions to remind yourself of the key material covered in this chapter.

1 How important was the increased power of the state to the development of warfare in the Revolutionary Wars?

2 Which was the bigger turning point in the development of total war: the Revolutionary Wars or the American Civil War?

3 Was the greatest change in the history of warfare in this period the development of larger armies?

4 What impact did the Industrial Revolution have on warfare in this period?

5 How important was the establishment of links between industry and the state in the period from 1880 to 1914?

6 Why were urban areas more enthusiastic for war than rural areas in this period?

7 Was the First World War or the Second World War decided more by economic factors?

8 Why did public opinion become more important in war as the nineteenth century progressed?

9 How important were attempts to restrict enemy trade to the outcomes of war in this period?

10 How important was financial strength to warfare?

11 Was the role of the state more important to the outcome of the First or the Second World War?

12 Why did total war come to replace cabinet war after 1792?

13 How far did resources come to be more important than purely military factors after 1850?

14 How far did domestic factors dictate military policy in the Second World War?

15 How far did public opinion lead to both world wars lasting longer than they should have done?

In-depth studies and key debates

The examination requires you to study three topics in depth, and for this unit they are:

- The French Revolutionary Wars 1792–1802
- The American Civil War 1861–5
- The Western Front and the First World War 1914–18.

This section will go into more detail about these periods in relation to these topics, and introduce you to some of the key debates so that you will have enough depth of knowledge to be able to evaluate passages that are set on any of the three studies.

Key debate 1: did the organisation of the state in the French Revolutionary Wars bring about a turning point in the history of warfare?

There has been much debate as to the importance of state organisation in the French Revolutionary War and the degree to which this was a turning point in the history of modern warfare. By the organisation of the state, historians mean the ways that the central government controlled the resources needed to wage war. These included forcing and encouraging its citizens into military service, equipping its forces by using the economic strength of the nation to support war, imposing its power on internal opposition and using propaganda and moral pressure to ensure that the whole nation was committed to the war effort.

The debate among military historians centres on the relative importance of technical developments, particularly in artillery, and these wider developments in the mobilisation of the whole state for war and the use of larger armies and tactics which emerged from the changes brought about by the French Revolution.

The new warfare of the Revolution

The explanation of French success in defending the Revolution, especially in the campaigns of 1793 and 1794, is often made in terms of a new warfare. Rather like the Communist regime in Russia, the political leadership exercised a brutal but effective policy of maintaining control over the generals. Seventeen were executed in 1793 and 67 in 1794. There was a considerable growth in the size of the armies raised by the new French Republic and its minister for war, Carnot, the so-called 'architect of victory'. Revolutionary leaders were able to control and militarise the population far more than the French kings of the old regime.

Some historians see the key to changes in warfare and to French victories in larger and inexperienced forces being prepared to take casualties and having the morale and determination to fight unstintingly for a cause, backed by dictatorial regimes using their power to ensure that they were reinforced and supplied.

Geoffrey Best, in his study *War and Society in Revolutionary Europe 1770–1870* (1982), expresses the view that France took over Prussia's previous position, 'a society organised through and through for war and dependent on war' as a result of the changes made by the Revolutionary Wars and continued by Napoleon. For others, Carnot as minister of war brought a new element of sheer ferocity and supported it by his organisational changes. If men could be conscripted, so also could the resources of the nation to arm, equip, clothe and feed them. A planned war economy was based on fear of the guillotine. This involved requisitioning of crops, the creation of a national loaf and rationing. There was a maximum price, foreign trade was regulated, transport and industrial output were nationalised, and black marketeering was severely punished. Arms, uniforms and equipment were produced on a national scale.

Thus, many military histories see a transition from an age of limited warfare based on dynastic concerns to an age of total and national struggle. The organisation and size of the Revolutionary armies and the whole change in the nature of domestic policy in France in the Revolution brought about a key turning point in the history of warfare.

Change or continuity? The counter-view

However, there are objections. Some have argued that there was no sharp divide between the wars broadly characterised as those of limited war and the Revolutionary total war of the 1790s. There was considerable development in France before the Revolution in terms of military theory and the use of self-sufficient divisions. What the Revolution added was nationalist fervour.

The role of artillery

Some detailed studies of the battles fought by the Revolutionary armies do not always bear out the impact of the new total war. The Battle of Valmy in September 1792 was seen by many as a key turning point. The famous eighteenth-century German writer and philosopher Goethe saw it as such, but the battle was not won by the mass columns of enthusiastic revolutionaries. Specialist studies have pointed out that the key element was an artillery barrage, after which the Prussian armies withdrew. The artillery was the part of the French army least affected by the revolutionary changes, and manned by former royal officers, using professional expertise not relying on mass revolutionary enthusiasm.

The hastily improvised nation in arms and the commandeering of manufactures did not produce the trained artillerymen or the weapons that were instrumental in turning the tide of foreign invasion in 1792. Subsequent battles at Jemappes and Wattignies did use mass columns of untrained men, but it is difficult to assess how important this fervour was. At Valmy, the outnumbered Prussians were unable to overcome the strength of the French position, especially the artillery, which came from the *ancien régime* army, and retreated.

The numbers of men raised look impressive, but by 1797 the Revolutionary army had been reduced from the notional million to under 400,000. The state had faced so much hostility to conscription that it had not called up as many as it was entitled to. Desertion rates were also high. Even after the *Loi Jourdan* (see page 149) had forbidden it, there were still many substitutions, so that many places were in fact filled by those serving for money, not revolutionary zeal. Napoleonic forces were raised by much hiring of foreign troops, and also by compelling rural areas to comply with quotas by force. It was not unusual to see conscripts roped together to prevent their escape. The intense level of state controls imposed in 1793–4, which anticipated the way the states of the twentieth century waged war, was not maintained.

Was there really total war?

Some argue that the performance of total war did not live up to the concept. After the fall of the extreme Robespierre faction in 1794, the armies were supplied by private enterprise, not state-directed factories and workshops. With the lucrative contracts for war supplies came corruption on a large scale. When inflation and shortages became too much of a problem, the French military machine turned more to loot and plunder to sustain itself. This did not point the way to the all-powerful state of the twentieth century, fighting for national goals and ideologies. Rather than modern total war, elements of the Revolutionary Wars were more like the wars of mercenary forces. The historian Michael Howard (1976) quotes a view that, by the late 1790s, the senior officers had both wealth and glory; the junior officers and men had glory but no wealth, and the war commissaries (who organised contracts and supplies) had wealth but no glory.

Overall assessment

Contemporaries were aware that the Revolutionary War was different in nature from some of the wars between kings in the eighteenth century. However, conflicts between strongly motivated opponents fighting for a cause and professional armies were not new. The war between Britain and the American colonies, for instance, had this strong ideological element. The effect of mass armies on enemy commanders could be an important feature, but the military effects of mass charges and highly motivated forces have probably been exaggerated. Valmy, for instance, was won by artillery and indecisive enemy leadership, not rabid revolutionaries. Also, states of this period could not sustain total war indefinitely and the very intense period of 1793–4 was not typical of the whole length of the Revolutionary War. When professional leadership, larger armies and new tactics were combined later by Napoleon after 1799, then there were very important victories, but these owed much less to ideological fervour, and the impact of 'revolutionary warfare' can be overstated in the hard light of battlefield reality.

Key debate 2: did organisation and economic factors determine victory in the American Civil War?

Explanations of the outcome of the American Civil War have put different stress on purely military factors which determined victory and the importance of organisation and resources.

Resources

The gap between the resources of North and South has often been said to have determined the outcome of the war. The Confederate commander Lee said that the outcome was a result of greater Union resources, and historians have echoed this view, arguing that in view of the disparity of resources, it would have taken a miracle to enable the South to win. The North manufactured 97 per cent of arms and most of the USA's iron. The North had the advantages of greater urban population, more factories, more arable land and more ships.

Leadership

The North also had the supposed advantage of a better political leadership and more control over its resources. President Lincoln has been admired as a leader, while his Southern counterpart Jefferson Davis has been seen as weak and temperamental. Some historians have accepted the contemporary press view of Davis as 'Cold, haughty, peevish, narrow-minded, pig headed … While he lives, there is no hope.' They argue that Southern enthusiasm for war fell away after the winter of 1861–2 and point to the limitations of reluctant Southern attempts to conscript mass armies with excessive exemptions and substitutions, and too many officers. Davis's refusal to resort to martial law was in contrast with Lincoln's bold willingness to use it to restrict opposition and confirm the authority of the state. Davis had authority to suspend *habeas corpus* only for sixteen months of the war.

Finance

The Southern economy suffered from having too much capital tied up in non-liquid forms, land and slaves, and the North's embargo prevented the South cashing in on its assets. It failed to finance the war through enough taxes; it could not raise enough loans and resorted to printing money. The 1.5 billion Confederate dollars printed led to high inflation, amounting to 700 per cent by 1863. It is a common view that because of the pressure from the Union blockade, invasion and a flood of paper money, the South's economy simply could not produce enough 'guns and butter' without shortages and inflation.

This is contrasted with the much more widespread and effective taxation system in the North, with a managed paper currency, resulting in less inflation. The war saw a speeding up in the mechanisation of key industries, not only in arms manufacture but also to improve agriculture and the production of clothes and boots. Farm machinery helped to fill the gap caused by the enlistment of the rural population into the armed forces.

Thus, it has been argued that the North's victory was determined by the 'sinews of war'. However, this view can be challenged.

The counter-view

Lack of progress by 1863

Against this, the South in 1863, after two years of warfare, did not look especially vulnerable. It controlled the key fortress at Vicksburg, and by cutting the Mississippi off from the farmers of the West it was putting a great deal of pressure on the Union to sue for peace. Its forces were not poorly equipped. Military historians point out that when Vicksburg fell in 1863, it was not particularly because of superior weaponry; the Southern troops forces had new, modern Lee-Enfield rifles brought in from Britain by blockade runners, while Grant's men had older and less efficient weapons. The Confederate artillery was strong.

The Union forces had been faced with a very difficult task of subduing each of the Confederate states, and for all the North's supposed industrial power and superior organisation, the Union was not much nearer to victory after McClellan's campaigns, while Lee was able to operate effectively and launch major invasions of Northern territory.

The North's blockade was helped by superior naval power funded by an efficient tax system, but this helped to promote European sympathy for the South, and the blockade was not always effective.

Leadership

It has been argued that Lincoln was more determined and effective, as shown by the suspension of *habeas corpus*. However, this led to criticisms in the North, and the outcome of the 1864 presidential election was by no means assured. Many of the policies were unpopular, and many resented the growth of federal power in aspects which included conscription, greater taxation and paper currency. The idea that all Northerners were consistently inspired by Lincoln's leadership and the emancipation of the slaves is not entirely justified. There was a great deal of opposition by the so-called 'Copperheads', and the extension of emancipation of the slaves to areas not controlled by Union forces was carried only by a great deal of political manoeuvring. The view that popular opinion in the South was faltering from 1862, and that government was unable to maintain support, has been challenged.

Davis had more military experience than Lincoln, and although it is true that he faced opposition from governors who supported states' rights, it would not have been wise of him to overcome this by force, given that the main rallying cry of the South was freedom from excessive federal interference. As some historians have stated, the South successfully maintained a higher proportion of its population in arms (three per cent) than the North. The large numbers of casualties endured by the South (260,000 killed and 200,000 wounded) and the persistent determination shown even in the final campaigns do not indicate a failure of government to inspire dedication. The South did not experience the levels of unrest seen in the North. Southern financial policy was less effective and diplomatic efforts to gain foreign recognition failed, factors which have been seen as indicative of weak government. However, even if that were the case, it still has to be shown that Southern defeat derived mainly from domestic factors and not from the events of the battlefield.

Military factors

The crucial turning points were the defeats at Vicksburg and Gettysburg, events which have been seen as being determined more by purely military factors than long-term organisation or resource issues. At Vicksburg, the Southern resources were enough to see off initial attacks in 1862 and to make it very hard for Grant to take the fortress. At Gettysburg, Lee's invasion of the North had been well supported by Davis and he did not lack resources. His failure was essentially a battlefield failure and was a forerunner of those attacks in the First World War, where frontal assaults like the famous Pickett's charge met withering fire from the Union defence. This was a feature of modern warfare rather than an indication that domestic factors, equipment, civilian leadership or lack of resources were the key elements in the Union victory.

The later stages of the war

After the twin defeats of Vicksburg and Gettysburg in 1863 the war changed because the hopes of foreign recognition or participation were lost to the South. The war became more of a war of attrition, but this had dangers for the North as casualties and war weariness increased. It was not until 1864 that the North decided on a campaign of economic destruction, that is after the decisive victories of 1863, when no foreign help would be forthcoming and there was no need to consider international opinion. The North by the later stages of the war had considerable numerical superiority, and resources began to tell when the supply of imported war materials for the South fell away.

Did resources make Southern defeat inevitable?

There is no doubt that by 1864–5 the sheer weight of numbers and the ability of the North to produce more men and more war material were key to its victory – but the issue is whether better exploitation by Lee of initial victories and poor Union military performance might have led to Southern success. If this is so, then the outcome depended not on resources but on the failure of the South to make the most of a very difficult problem faced by Lincoln.

The rebellion, as he saw it, had to be crushed. The war, however, could not be portrayed as a moral crusade against slavery because four slave states remained in the Union. To occupy the South was also a vast task. Had the South concentrated its resources on defensive campaigns, then the technology of the day – the rifle fire and artillery bombardments that were so devastating when the South attacked at Gettysburg – might have worked to its advantage. A long war of attrition against forces which had not been weakened by attacks against the North might have worn the Union down and the South might have won foreign recognition. In defence of the homeland, as with Russia in 1812 or 1941, and by using men who were skilled horseman and more used to weapons than the Union troops, the South might have been victorious even against an enemy with greater resources. Some historians have even suggested that a guerrilla war like that waged by the Boers against Britain from 1899 to 1902 and by North Vietnam against the USA in the 1960s and 1970s might well have been successful. If the war is seen more like a rebellion or a colonial conflict than a war between sovereign states, then there are plenty of examples of success by rebel forces with higher morale and fewer resources defeating more powerful states.

Overall assessment

Although the outcome was not a foregone conclusion, even with the North's superiority of resources, the American Civil War demonstrates that modern warfare cannot easily be divided into 'military factors' and 'organisation and resources'. The best supplied armies cannot achieve victory simply without strong leadership, and resourceful irregular opposition can often overcome strong conventional forces. Initially, neither side was prepared for the huge losses involved in a total war and both sides hoped for victory through Napoleonic military manoeuvre. When this failed, the only real alternative was a war of attrition, with generals accepting the high casualty rate and destruction that this involved. The Union leadership, political and military, were prepared for this fusion of military strategy and deployment of superior resources and so were successful.

Key debate 3: did Germany lose the First World War because of the home front?

The debate is centred on the claims made after the First World War by nationalists that the war was not a purely military defeat but arose from the loss of morale and support on the home front, which in turn led to a weakening of the will to resist.

There is some evidence to suggest that loss of morale and support on the home front was a key aspect of the outcome of the First World War:

- Germany had been very successful in military terms in Russia
- it very nearly defeated the Allies in the west in 1918
- it had developed new tactics – stormtroops – which depended on personal bravery and high morale

- Germany was not invaded in 1918
- severe shortages reduced civilian morale in a way not so true of Britain
- the spread of political discontent weakened the will to win.

In reasoning that the defeat was due to purely military factors, it could be argued that:

- in military terms, the Allies, with the USA, had more potential manpower
- the Allies had more tanks ands a better combined operations policy of using tanks and aircraft with artillery
- the German commanders lacked the resolution of the Allied commanders
- the big German offensive of 1918 had been a military failure.

Explanations of the German collapse in 1918 based on the industrial strength or martial progress of the Allies are seen as flawed by some modern studies. They see the failure of the German army on the Western Front as best understood as the product of a psychological malaise. This was manifested by desertions and a rapid increase in surrendering to the Allies. Some 385,000 prisoners were taken in the final four months of the war in 1918, about half the total prisoners taken by the Allies in the whole of the war. The despair was also evident on the home front because of shortages of food and clothes and the loss of loved ones.

By November 1918, the commanders in the west reported that morale was too low to continue and there were tens of thousands of factory workers on the streets of Berlin. The government had been dominated by the military leaders since 1916 and had failed to organise enough production to meet the resources of the Allies; their efforts to maintain morale had depended too much on heavy-handed authoritarianism; and despite the victory against Russia, the regime had not managed to channel resources into Germany to meet the needs of a hungry population. Defeatism was rife in the forces and on the home front, despite very gallant efforts earlier in the war.

In contrast, the British war effort on the home front had maintained popular support. There were few signs of mutiny or the desire to give up, even after the terrible losses of 1917. The propaganda efforts of the state had been effective, and there was talk of post-war reconstruction and 'homes fit for heroes' after the war. The civilian population had accepted food rationing, which had been much more efficiently organised than had been the case in Germany. Production of arms meant that by 1918 the Allies fielded 18,500 guns and 4500 aircraft in the west against the German 14,000 and 4500. They also had 1,672,000 infantry as opposed to the German 1,395,000, and had built hundreds of tanks compared to the Germans' meagre total of twenty. The mobilisation of the civilian population for war production was greater in France and Britain than in Germany. Concessions to the unions and higher pay had avoided large-scale industrial unrest such as affected Germany by 1918. Britain had produced a popular and inspiring war leader in Lloyd George, whereas Germany had fallen back on leading generals who tried to hand back power to civilian government when it looked as if the war were lost, and thus lost credibility.

Some military historians offer a view which is much less dependent on the home front and issues of morale deriving from mismanagement by the state. They argue that Germany's forces had been pushed beyond breaking point, its formidable Hindenburg Line had been breached, and its armies slowly but surely driven back towards its own frontiers. On 8 August 1918, the British general Sir Henry Rawlinson broke the German line at Amiens using 600 tanks and considerable air support. The purely military factor of a combined arms operation, skilfully undertaken by a British army whose battle skills had developed considerably since the start of the war, may be more important than problems on the home front. The German army, in any case, did not break down in discipline in a similar way to the Russian army in 1917 and was still able to offer quite determined resistance, which meant that no Allied troops were on German soil by the time Germany accepted the armistice. The tendency to move explanations from the military achievements of the Allies in 1918 to the strengths of their home support and the weakness of the German home front may be to shift the balance too far.

Studies of the British army have argued that it made full use of creeping barrages and tanks. Tank crews had learned to support infantry. Ground troops had strong assistance from aircraft. The air force saw its primary role as assisting the army, regardless of loss. Haig had adapted tactics to allow each division to achieve its targets independently and to focus reinforcements where there was success, not to reinforce failure. Had these developments not taken place, then no amount of success on the home front or corresponding weakness within Germany would have been decisive. For all the supposed limitations at home, Germany won the war against Russia and waged a highly effective attack on the Western Front in March and April 1918. The military failure of this attack to be decisive, and the highly skilled Allied counterattacks, must be seen as the key, with the home front as important, but secondary.

Overall assessment

As with the American Civil War, the First World War saw considerable links between purely military factors and the influence of organisation, morale and the so-called home front. The tactics and strategy of the Allies had developed by 1918 and this is often seen as a transformation which led to victory. However, this is doubtful. The tanks were not wonder weapons and often broke down. The Germans too had developed more flexible tactics and by 1918 were waging war with a very experienced army on one front. The combination of air power and infantry has been exaggerated. The military aircraft of 1918 did not have the technical ability of those of the Second World War in supporting infantry advances. The Germans still had formidable defences; they were not fighting on their own territory yet. The war was probably determined by the potential economic power and manpower and weaponry of the Allies, bolstered by the entry of the USA, which undermined morale at every level of the German forces. However, this does need to be seen in the context of the consequences of military decisions and strategy, which resulted in unprecedented losses over an extended period.

Study skills: thematic essay

How to write a conclusion to a thematic essay

You may have already considered the importance of a conclusion when studying units 1 and 2 of the OCR course. As with those units, a conclusion needs to reach a judgement based on what you have already written and should be briefly supported so that it is not an assertion. It should *not* introduce new ideas – if they were important they should have been in the main body of the essay. It is also important *not* to offer a contrary argument to the one you have pursued throughout the rest of your essay. This possibility will be avoided if you have planned and thought through your essay before you started writing (see pages 54–5 for guidance on planning).

It might be that you are largely restating the view that you offered in the opening paragraph; or, in stronger answers, there might be a slight variation to that judgement so that you confirm your original view, but suggest, with a brief example, that there were occasions when this view was not always correct.

As with unit 1 and 2 answers, if the question has a named factor, then you should give a supported judgement about that factor's relative importance, explaining why it is or is not the most important and the role it played in the events you have discussed. If the question asks you to assess a range of issues, the conclusion should explain which you think was the most important and why, and give some brief support for your claim. Remember, a claim is simply an assertion unless there is some evidence to support it and will therefore not score highly.

Consider the question below and the sample conclusions in Responses A and B which follow. Response A is an example of a weak conclusion and Response B an example of a strong conclusion.

> **Assess the importance of the state's ability to mobilise public opinion for warfare in the period from 1792 to 1945.**

The focus of your answer should have been on the importance of the mobilisation of public opinion. This should be explained and assessed. However, you will have needed to compare this factor with other possible key elements which did not depend on it so heavily. In the main body of the essay you should look to compare these elements and demonstrate any links between the developments so that your evaluation of the factor in the question is comparative.

You may have considered the following issues in your essay:

- The importance of public opinion and whether it was consistent throughout the period.
- The deployment of appeals for Revolutionary unity in 1792 and comparison with opponents whose forces were not so ideologically motivated.
- How far public opinion alone could produce military success in the wars of the mid-nineteenth century.
- The growing ability of states to influence public opinion with the increase in literacy, urbanisation and nationalism in the period after 1870.
- The importance of morale and the home front in the First World War.
- The mobilisation of public opinion to an unprecedented extent in the Second World War.
- How wars became increasingly dependent on mass mobilisation.
- How wars became much harder to limit.
- Whether purely military factors remained more important.
- Whether technology rather than public opinion became more decisive.

Response A

Public opinion was increasingly important in warfare as both the size of populations and the nature of warfare changed. Wars between kings previously had not needed mass popular support as people just had to obey. However, after the French Revolution when armies became larger, it was important that the mass of the people supported wars. Most regimes issued propaganda and popular appeals and this reached its height in the twentieth century, as the dictators who fought it were very expert in propaganda and getting mass support. So public opinion was crucial. However, there were other factors and often wars depended more on military factors like leadership and weapons. Thus, it is not always easy to see how important the state's ability to mobilise public opinion was, but it was a major factor after 1792.

Analysis of Response A

- A clear judgement is reached. It explains why public opinion was important, but does not explain why it was more important than other factors.
- There is some awareness of continuity and change or comparison over the period, which is a strong point.
- The relative importance of the factors is not discussed – there is simply a list with no relative judgement.

Response B

After 1792, when the French Revolution changed the nature of warfare by bringing about mass conscripted armies, often motivated by a desire for political change and the cause of liberty, the manipulation of public opinion by the state became a vital element in the conduct of warfare. However, it was never decisive and purely military factors remained more important. The state needed bigger armies, although the very large forces of the French in 1793–4 were not matched for most of the wars of the nineteenth century. These forces needed effective management and motivation and so propaganda, from the marching songs of 1793 to Napoleon's bulletins, through to the patriotic appeals of Garibaldi and the posters and appeals of the world wars, which extended to new media like film and radio, became increasingly important. When morale broke down, as with Russia in 1917 and Germany in 1918, the results could be devastating. Even the most heart-breaking losses and destruction were not matched by loss of the will to fight in the Second World War until the final hopeless weeks. However, through the period, public opinion could not win wars by itself. Armies are often motivated more by *esprit de corps* and a desire not to let down comrades, or fear of the consequences of failure, than by the support or otherwise of public opinion. There are consistent examples of weaponry or superior tactics being greater factors, from Valmy in 1792 to the dropping of the atomic bomb on Japan in 1945. There have often been links between the way wars have been fought and public opinion, as in the way that enthusiastic mass armies without experience were used in French Revolutionary columns or in mass frontal assaults at the Somme; but the determining factors of war are more to be found in weaponry and tactics.

Analysis of Response B

- A clear judgement is reached that public opinion was not the most important factor and about how it is linked to other factors.
- There are links made between the factors and some support for the claim is made, which supports the judgement.
- There is an awareness of the link between factors and this is explained.

Activity

You should now try and write a conclusion to some of the questions below. Ensure that you reach a clear, supported judgement and that when you have to discuss more than one factor your evaluation of the importance of the factors is comparative.

Essay questions

1 How important a turning point in warfare in the period from 1792 to 1945 was the growth in state control over resources in France in 1792–4?
2 'Warfare in the twentieth century was different from that of the period 1792–1914 because state power made it total war.' How far do you agree with this view of warfare in the period from 1792 to 1945?
3 How important was conscription in determining the outcome of war in the period from 1792 to 1945?

Study skills: depth study interpretations question

How to reach a judgement

This section looks at how to reach a judgement about the two passages. In the first paragraph you will have explained the two interpretations and placed them in the context of the wider historical debate about the issue, and in the second and third paragraphs you will have evaluated the strengths and weaknesses of the two interpretations. However, in order to reach the higher mark bands you must reach a supported judgement as to which passage's view about the issue in the question you think is more convincing.

A good conclusion will:

- reach a clear judgement as to which passage's view about the issue in the question is more convincing
- explain why a particular passage is more convincing and why the other is less convincing
- suggest that there are some parts in both passages which are more or less convincing
- briefly support the judgement so that it is not simply an assertion.

Read the question and Passages A and B below about the Revolutionary Wars and then the example conclusions (Responses A and B) that follow:

Evaluate the interpretations in both of the passages and explain which you think is more convincing as an explanation of the importance of the changes to warfare made during the Revolutionary Wars.

PASSAGE A

From Jeremy Black, *Warfare in the Eighteenth Century*, Cassell, 1999, p. 199.

Thanks to Gribeauval's artillery reforms, revolutionary France had the best artillery in Europe. In several other respects the army of revolutionary France was a product of pre-revolutionary changes. The regular army was disrupted through desertion and by the emigration of officers but played a major role in the successes in and after 1792 because the regulars were better trained than the new levies. Yet the political context of warfare was now very different, not least for providing larger armies. In August 1793 the revolutionary government ordered general conscription. Superiority in numbers was important in battles such as Valmy, Jemappes and Wattignies. At Jemappes, the French were able to advance in columns and get back into line at close range, defeating the slow moving Austrians. The French benefited from young and talented commanders.

PASSAGE B

Adapted from J.F.C. Fuller, *The Conduct of War 1789–1961*, Eyre & Spottiswoode, 1961, pp. 33–4.

The first trial between the two forms of war, the old-fashioned antiquated limited war and the as yet untried unlimited warfare of the armed hordes of the Revolution, took place at Valmy on 20 September 1792. Brunswick skilfully withdrew his army after an exchange of fire. Goethe, the famous German writer, who was with the Prussians, said 'From this day on, there begins a new era in the world's history'. The wars of kings were at an end; the wars of peoples were beginning. The Convention decreed a levy of 500,000 men. This was the first step to Conscription – the move to tribal war. Not only was warfare to become unlimited, but total. One French royalist described the effect: 'fifty thousand savage beasts hurl themselves on soldiers whose courage has not been excited by passion'.

Response A

In conclusion, Passage B offers a more convincing view of the impact of the Revolutionary War, as it looks at the long-term significance and includes an eyewitness quotation. It does have some balance in that it makes the point that the Battle of Valmy was only an exchange of fire, but the retreat of Prussia in the face of the 'armed hordes' did mark a new phase in war and there was much more total war afterwards. Soldiers were more inflamed by passion and this helped later victories in the Revolutionary Wars and also the campaigns of Napoleon in Italy. The conscription eventually led to nearly a million men being raised so the writer is correct in seeing the important long-term consequences of the Revolutionary War. Passage A does not say enough about this.

Response B

Both passages acknowledge that political change was important because it led to larger numbers. Passage A is correct in seeing the role of greater numbers in the victories of 1792 and 1793 and these do confirm that a new era had begun, as described in Passage B. However, the more academic and calmer tone of Passage A is more convincing. Passage B argues for too great a break in the continuity of warfare brought about by mass armies. Valmy was not won by mass attacks. The French Revolutionary forces as well as relying on enthusiasm relied on a nucleus of trained men and strong artillery. Bonaparte himself had been trained under the *ancien régime* and had read the military theories of his day. His leadership did not depend on mass revolutionary hordes as suggested in Passage B. Also Passage B does not give much thought to the purely military weaknesses of the Austrians and Prussians. Brunswick withdrew after a very limited engagement, which he might well have won, at Valmy. It is too much of a generalisation in Passage B to say that a new era of wars between peoples resulted from the events of 1792–3. The Revolutionary Wars were intense in 1793–4, but after that they became less popular and political in nature and were fought for more traditional objectives of power and plunder.

Analysis of Responses A and B

Both conclusions offer a judgement and both support their claims. However, Response B is the stronger conclusion:

- Response A focuses almost exclusively on Passage A, with mention of Passage B only in the final line.
- Response B compares the two interpretations in reaching its judgement and is more balanced.
- Response B, although it argues that Passage B is stronger, does not dismiss the valid points made in Passage A.

Activity

Revisit the questions on the passages in Chapters 1–3 (pages 58–9, 98–9 and 132–3) and write a conclusion for those questions.

Timeline

1792	Start of Revolutionary Wars
1793	First coalition formed against France
1796–7	Napoleon's Italian campaign
1798–1802	Second coalition against France
1799	Bonaparte took power in France
1805	Third coalition
1805–7	War of the Third Coalition
1806	Fourth coalition
1808	Peninsular War
1809	Fifth coalition
1812	Napoleon's invasion of Russia
1813	Sixth coalition
1815	Battle of Waterloo
1841	Prussians accepted Dreyse breech-loading needle gun for service
1845	Breech-loading artillery gun invented
1849	Invention of the Minié bullet
1854–6	Crimean War
1859	War of Italian Unification
1861–5	American Civil War
1866–71	Wars of German Unification
1870–1	Franco-Prussian War
1899–1902	Second Boer War
1904–5	Russo-Japanese War
1905	Schlieffen Plan devised

1912–13	Balkan Wars
1914	Start of First World War
1915	First use of poison gas at second Battle of Ypres
1916	Battle of the Somme
	Battle of Verdun
1917	USA joined the war
	Large-scale use of tanks at Battle of Cambrai
1918	Armistice ended First World War
1937–45	War between China and Japan
1939	Germany invaded Poland. France and Britain declared war on Germany
1940	Fall of France
1941	Japan attacked Pearl Harbor. War between Japan and Britain and the USA. Hitler declared war on the USA
	Germany invaded USSR
1942	British victory at El Alamein
	Japanese attacked US and European colonies in South Asia
1943	Germany defeated at Stalingrad
1944	Invasion of France by Britain and the USA
1945	Two atomic bombs dropped on Japan
	Surrender of Germany and Japan

Glossary of terms

American Civil War   Differences had appeared between the Southern states, which maintained slavery, and the North, which no longer used slave labour. There were disputes about whether slavery should be extended to new lands in the West. Compromises failed and eventually, when a president opposed to the extension of slavery, Abraham Lincoln, was elected in 1860, most of the South broke away to form its own country – the Confederacy. Lincoln saw this as rebellion against the American Union and fought to force the South back. A long war with heavy casualties on both sides resulted.

American Revolution   (American War of Independence.) Britain had colonised the eastern coastal areas of North America since the seventeenth century. By the 1770s, disputes had arisen between the colonists and Britain which led to a declaration of independence. Britain failed to maintain control of the colonies in a war from 1776 to 1783. The rebels received help from Britain's European enemies and set up the United States of America.

Ancien régime   The 'old regime'. Refers to the monarchical and aristocratic political and social system that was established in France from the fifteenth century until the French Revolution in 1789.

Arctic route   The route from Britain, Iceland and North America to the northern ports of the Soviet Union, particularly Archangel and Murmansk. It was used to bring in military supplies to the Russians.

Arms race   Used to describe the rapid build-up of arms and competition between European countries in the period before the First World War. It involved the increase in size of both armies and navies.

Artillery   Heavy guns which are capable of firing large shells, usually over long distances.

Atlantic Charter   A statement of shared beliefs, signed by the British leader Churchill and the US President Roosevelt in a meeting in 1941 before the USA entered the war, which affirmed people's right to be free. It became a statement of war aims, although Britain's continuing desire to hold on to its overseas empire made it seem somewhat hypocritical, as did the Anglo-US alliance with the tyrannical Russian leader Stalin.

Atomic bomb   This was developed in a US-funded project and was based on scientific research into releasing extraordinary power by splitting uranium atoms. Two bombs were dropped on Hiroshima and Nagasaki in Japan in August 1945. It is the only use of atomic weapons to date and it brought the Second World War to an end, initiating a new phase in the history of warfare.

Bank of France   Based on the example of the Bank of England, created in the 1690s. British financial stability was a major element in its military success after 1700 and the national banks controlled money supply and the activities of private banks, reducing inflation and encouraging lending to the state which modern wars required.

Battle of Austerlitz   Fought in December 1805 in what is now the Czech Republic. Facing the larger Russian army on higher ground, Napoleon left his right flank weak to tempt the Russians to attack. He then struck at the Russian centre with the bulk of his forces and was also able to assault the Russians from the rear. This classic action achieved the most complete of all Napoleon's victories. The war of 1805–7 was the high point of Napoleon's success as a general.

Battle of Gettysburg   One of the most important battles of the American Civil War. The defeat of the South, some have argued, made its overall defeat inevitable, but the North was unable to follow up its victory and the South was able to hold North Virginia.

Battle of Tsushima Bay   The major naval encounter of the Russo-Japanese War. The Russian fleet had sailed 18,000 miles from the Baltic but because of its poor condition and lack of speed it was quickly defeated, with nearly the whole Russian fleet lost.

Battle of Waterloo   After defeat by his enemies, Emperor Napoleon had been exiled to the small Mediterranean island of Elba in 1814. In 1815 he returned, gathered support, overthrew the French King Louis XVIII and invaded Belgium, where he was defeated in a hard-fought battle in June 1815 in which the British, under the Duke of Wellington, held off French forces until their Prussian allies arrived. Napoleon was then exiled to the Atlantic island of St Helena, where he died in 1821.

Billets   Soldiers' accommodation.

Bugles and runners   Messages on the battlefield were conveyed by a bugler conveying signals by playing a brass instrument or by soldiers literally running between lines with messages for commanders.

Cabinet warfare   The wars between monarchs in the eighteenth century that had limited aims and were often settled by diplomatic negotiations and relatively small territorial changes. These wars were fought by small professional armies.

Cap and ball rifle   The cap replaced the old flintlock firing mechanism which meant that it was more reliable, particularly in damp weather, and was faster to reload.

Central Powers   The term used to describe Germany, Austria-Hungary and Turkey, who were allies against the Entente Powers of France, Britain and Russia in the First World War.

Chassepot rifle   Adopted by the French army after 1866, the Chassepot rifle was a single-shot bolt-action breech-loading weapon which replaced old-fashioned muzzle-loading rifles. It was efficient and fired more rounds more quickly than the older weapons.

Citizen army   Used to distinguish between volunteers and recruits who serve for a short time and then return to their normal lives and long-term professional soldiers who are dedicated to a military life.

Congreve rockets   Relatively small rockets were developed by the Indian Sultan of Mysore in the 1790s for use against the British and could travel 1000 yards before exploding. Sir William Congreve developed them from 1804 and they could then travel 3000 yards. Not very reliable on the battlefield, they were mainly used by the British navy.

Conscription   The calling up by the state of men to fight in the armed forces. Universal conscription spread after 1792 so that every man had a legal obligation for service.

Continental System   A remarkable attempt at economic warfare to counter the traditional British tactic of a naval blockade to prevent trading with France. Napoleon cut off Europe from British trade in the hope of causing unemployment and unrest in Britain. It led to unrest in Europe and despite causing hardship in Britain, it did not lead to Britain withdrawing from the war.

Creeping barrage   Instead of just bombarding enemy lines with artillery before the infantry advances, the creeping barrage involved the artillery fire moving forward in stages; it was first used at the Battle of the Somme. It required precise timing so that the infantry was not hit by its own artillery.

Crimean War   In 1853, Russia went to war with the Ottoman Empire. A rapid Russian advance into the Balkans worried Britain and France, who sent forces to help the Turks. An invasion was made of the Crimean Peninsula to destroy the Russian naval base of Sebastopol and keep Russia from the eastern Mediterranean. The Allied forces were poorly organised and led, and the neglect of casualties led Florence Nightingale to take nurses to Constantinople to look after the wounded. Sebastopol was eventually taken but the peace terms of 1856 were overturned in 1871.

Cult of the offensive   The belief among military strategists that the advantages of attack so outweigh those of defence that the defender would stand no chance of repelling an attack.

D-Day   The name given to the invasion of mainland Europe, through Normandy, which began on 6 June 1944. It was codenamed Operation Overlord.

Decree of Fraternity   The French Republic offered support to any state wishing to overthrow its rulers and establish a democratic system.

Dreyse needle gun   A breech-loading rifle; the name comes from the needle-like firing pin. It was also the first rifle to use the bolt action. Its rate of fire was ten to twelve rounds a minute.

Dual Alliance   Also known as the Franco-Russian alliance. Germany had allowed its alliance with Russia to lapse and with France wanting support against Germany and Russia against Austria-Hungary the two nations overcame ideological differences to sign the treaty.

Dunkirk   With the rapid advance of German forces, the British and French were driven back to the beaches at Dunkirk. In a remarkable achievement the British navy and a flotilla of small boats rescued some 338,000 troops in the period from 27 May to 4 June 1940.

Eastern Orthodoxy   Refers to the Eastern Orthodox Church, which broke from the Western Church in 1054. It is called 'Eastern' because of the geographical location of most of its members.

El Alamein   Named after an oasis and railway junction in the north African desert. The third Battle of El Alamein in 1942 is sometimes seen as a turning point as it was the first decisive victory since the start of the war.

Embargo   A trade ban.

Entente Cordiale   A series of agreements between Britain and France signed in 1904, which resulted in an improvement in relations between the two countries. It resolved issues of colonial dispute, particularly in Africa, and helped to end years of hostility.

First Balkan War   The war was fought in 1912–13 between the Balkan League, made up of Serbia, Bulgaria, Greece and Montenegro, and Turkey. Turkey suffered defeats but the League squabbled over the division of former Turkish land and this led to a second war between members of the League.

First Battle of Bull Run   Also known as the Battle of First Manassas. Fought in 1861 in Virginia, it was the first major battle of the Civil War. It resulted in victory for the South.

First Coalition   This comprised Britain, the Netherlands, Spain, Piedmont, Naples, Prussia, Russia, Austria and Portugal.

First War of Independence   Sometimes known as the Indian Mutiny. Grievances of Indian troops ('sepoys') were linked to opposition among some Indian princes to British rule and a general dislike of British interference with Indian customs and religion. After initial successes, superior British military power led to the suppression of opposition.

French Revolution   Forced by financial problems to call the equivalent of a parliament in 1789, the French King Louis XVI faced increasing challenges to his authority. These led to the overthrow of the monarchy in 1792 and his execution in 1793. The Revolutionary governments fought wars with other European states from 1792. The revolution culminated in a successful general Napoleon Bonaparte taking power in 1799 and declaring himself emperor in 1804.

German Unification   Germany after 1815 was divided and dominated by Austria. The German state of Prussia, led by the statesman Otto von Bismarck, built up its armies and industries and challenged Austria. A joint Prusso-Austrian War against Denmark led to disputes between the victors, and Prussian armies went on to defeat Austria in 1866. France was resentful about loss of influence, and a subsequent war between France and Prussia led to complete Prussian victory and the establishment of a new Prussian-led German Empire in 1871.

Grand Strategy   An overall plan for winning a war.

Guerrillas   Fighters not in uniform or in a regular army who attack enemy forces, often behind their lines. The word comes from the Spanish for 'warriors' or fighters.

Hindenburg Line   A German defensive position built in 1916–17 to counter expected Anglo-French attacks in 1917.

Home front   The activities of civilians to support fighting troops. The term was not used until 1919 and then to describe the activities of civilians during the First World War, but it is applicable to earlier wars.

Howitzer   An artillery weapon that fires projectiles at a high trajectory which then fall with a steep descent.

Hundred Days   The period from when Napoleon returned from exile on Elba, following his defeat in 1814, to his defeat at the Battle of Waterloo in 1815. During this time he rallied his forces and was able to raise an army and renew the war against the allies.

Imperial destiny   There was a traditional Japanese belief that the emperors were descended from the Sun goddess Amaterasu Ōmikami, and emperor worship was revived in the 1920s as part of the Shinto religion. The emperors were declared to be mortal, rather than gods, after the defeat of the Second World War, something that led some traditionalists to suicide. Given this divinity, many nationalists thought that the empire had a destiny to rule Asia and even beyond.

Income tax   A key element of wartime finance. Before this, taxation had been mainly on property or on sales. Income tax was on all forms of income above a certain amount, so ensured that richer people paid more than the poor. It was unpopular and was removed in 1816 but restored in the 1840s and has remained the main British tax.

Industrial Revolution   Economic developments which started initially in Britain in the eighteenth century but eventually spread across Europe, whereby factories and mass production came to replace small-scale production of goods, often carried out in small workshops.

Industrialisation   The development of large-scale and developed industries which used machines to increase production levels and therefore relied on people working in factories or other large-scale enterprises, rather than at home.

Inflation   This is when prices rise. It was a feature of most of the longer wars of this period, as they created shortages and also increased the amount of money in circulation, as governments spent more and printed more money. More money and fewer goods led to higher prices.

Isandlwana   On 22 January 1879, a British invasion of the independent Zulu kingdom in South Africa from

British-held territory was decisively defeated by a Zulu force. The news shocked Britain and Europe as it had been assumed that European military strength would always be too powerful for native peoples. The Zulu leader Cetawayo was a highly skilled commander but could not hold out against superior firepower brought to bear by Britain in 1880.

Island hopping   The policy pursued by the Americans in the Pacific of their troops seizing islands as they moved across the ocean towards Japan, rather than launching an attack directly on Japan.

Krupp   Major German industrial firm and armaments manufacturer.

Kursk   A major battle on the Eastern Front in July and August 1943, it was one of the largest armoured clashes. It was the first time a German strategic offensive was halted before it could break enemy defences and reach strategic depths. The Russian counteroffensive was their first successful summer offensive of the war.

Living off the land   Armies took what food they could find from farms and villages rather than relying on their own supplies provided by the state.

Ludendorff or Spring Offensive   Launched in the spring of 1918 by General Ludendorff, this was a series of German attacks along the Western Front and saw the greatest advance by either side since 1914. It was the final assault by the Germans and an attempt to achieve victory before US troops arrived in numbers. When it failed to bring victory the German command realised it could not win.

Lusitania   A British ocean liner, torpedoed and sunk on 7 May 1915. It caused the death of 1198 passengers and crew, 128 of whom were American. Germany had breached international laws by firing on a non-military ship. However, the ship was carrying munitions. Its sinking helped to shift public opinion in the USA in favour of joining the war.

Machine gun   A rapid-firing gun – modern weapons can fire 1800 rounds a minute. It was first developed in its modern form in 1861 by an inventor called Richard Gatling but a faster model was developed by Hiram Maxim in 1884. It gave defenders huge advantages and made modern war very deadly and destructive for attacking forces.

Magazine rifle   A rifle is a musket with a groove in the barrel which allows the emerging bullet to spin and to travel further with greater accuracy. Rifles initially remained, like muskets, one-shot weapons requiring

reloading each time they were fired. The first breech-loading rifle dates from 1836 – the Dreyse needle gun. Better developed and engineered repeating rifles were the French Chassepot of 1866 and the Colt from 1855. The later part of the nineteenth century saw rapid developments.

Manhattan Project   The research and development project in the USA to develop the atomic bomb. There were concerns about the German production of such a weapon and there was a race to beat them.

March 1917 Revolution   Sometimes called the February Revolution, depending on which calendar is being used. It resulted in the overthrow of the last Russian tsar, Nicholas II, and his replacement by a Provisional Government. This was overthrown in the October Revolution when it was replaced by the Bolsheviks or Communists.

Marseillaise   Now France's national anthem, it was the marching song of revolutionary troops from the south who marched to the support of the Republic in 1792. It urges the spread of revolution and the destruction of tyranny and calls all French citizens to take up arms. It was less widespread at the time than the *Ça Ira* song.

Martial law   When the normal civilian legal system is replaced by the legal authority of the army, which places civilians under its authority and treats them as though they were military personnel.

Massed volley   A line of soldiers firing their weapons at the same time.

Menin Road   The name, after the place to which it led, of the road leading out of Ypres to the front line, down which many British troops went.

Mexican War   The war followed the US annexation of Texas in 1845 and was won by the USA, whose forces advanced a long way into Mexico. It led to a loss of much northern Mexican territory.

Military–industrial complex   The links between the top military leaders in the USA and the engineering, chemical and military industries. Eisenhower coined the phrase but it was widely used by critics of the Cold War who saw big industrial concerns benefiting from exaggerated defence requirements put forward by the military.

Mitrailleuse   A French gun with a large number of barrels so it could fire either multiple rounds at once or several rounds in rapid succession.

Mustard gas   A gas which causes large blisters on exposed skin and in the lungs.

Nation in arms   A concept found in the work of some military theorists in the eighteenth century, who argued that if the whole nation rallied to a cause then the larger and more committed armies would be greatly superior in moral force to the mercenary, professional armies that were the norm.

Nazi–Soviet pact   An agreement signed between Nazi Germany and Communist Russia in August 1939. It allowed Germany to avoid fighting a war on two fronts and gave Russia short-term security from attack.

Non-commissioned officers   Smaller units (platoons) were commanded by a junior officer equivalent to the rank of lieutenant; but within the unit there were senior soldiers equivalent to the modern ranks of corporals and sergeants who maintained discipline and could take over if the officer was killed or wounded.

Normandy beachheads   Britain and USA launched the biggest amphibious invasion in history on 6 June 1944 to invade German-occupied France at Normandy. Their forces secured the beaches but found it more difficult to break from these positions into open country and to thrust towards Germany.

Operation Barbarossa   The name given to the invasion of the USSR by Germany in 1941. It was the greatest military operation in history, involving 4 million men, 600,000 vehicles and 700,000 horses over a front of 2900 kilometres. Initially successful, its three main thrusts did not achieve their key objectives by the time winter conditions prevented further advance, and neither Moscow nor Leningrad fell.

Pearl Harbor   The US naval base in Hawaii and home to the US Pacific fleet. It was attacked by the Japanese on 7 December 1941 and resulted in the USA joining the Second World War.

Phosgene   A colourless gas, which caused about 85 per cent of the 100,000 deaths due to chemical weapons.

Revolutionary France   In 1789, the French Revolution reduced the power of the monarch Louis XVI, who was eventually executed in 1793. After a period in which the monarch was forced to share power with the elected representatives of the people, a republic, a state without a king, was set up in 1792. In 1799, the Republic was overthrown by a successful general, Napoleon Bonaparte, who became emperor in 1804.

Rommel in north Africa   The German General Erwin Rommel (1891–1944) led a special army in north Africa.

His aim was to drive Britain out of Egypt, secure the oil of the Middle East and link with the German attacks in Russia. From 1941 to 1942 Rommel showed Napoleonic flair and drove the British back, but shortage of fuel and supplies led to his defeat at El Alamein in October 1942 and he was forced out of Africa. He plotted against Hitler in 1944 and was made to take his own life.

Second Boer War of 1899–1902   The original European settlers in South Africa were Dutch colonists. Britain gained the Cape of Good Hope after the Napoleonic Wars. When the British abolished slavery, the Dutch (the Boers or farmers) went inland and set up their own states. The discovery of gold, however, in the Boer state of the Transvaal led to British settlers going inland too. As a result of clashes, a war broke out between the Boers and the British in 1899 and lasted until 1902. Initially, British forces suffered defeats. The Boer troops did not fight in the same way as the more formal British forces, relying on hastily improvised troops of cavalry (commandos), often seen as 'irregular' soldiers akin to guerrilla warriors, and were difficult to defeat. In the end, the British resorted to putting the Boers' families in concentration camps and cutting the fighters off from their homelands.

Second Coalition   This comprised Britain, Russia, Austria, Turkey, Portugal and Naples.

Second Front   The attack on mainland Europe through France, which was finally launched with D-Day in June 1944. The other front was the Eastern Front, where Russian troops were fighting Germany.

Second Manassas   Also known as the second Battle of Bull Run and was the culmination of a major campaign by the Confederate Army under Robert E. Lee. The battle saw heavy casualties, but in the end the Union left flank was crushed and driven back to Bull Run.

Second World War   A war that started in Europe over Germany's revision of the Treaty of Versailles, which had ended the 1914–18 war. Germany had broken the terms of the treaty by invading Poland in 1939, leading to a declaration of war by Britain and France. In Asia, war between Japan and China began in 1937 and was extended by Japanese attacks on US and European colonies to secure raw materials from December 1941, starting with the Japanese bombardment of the US fleet at Pearl Harbor, Hawaii. Germany declared war on the USA after this attack. Hitler had invaded the USSR in June 1941. Thus, the Grand Alliance led by Britain, the USA and the USSR (the 'Allies') fought the so-called 'Axis' powers, Germany, Italy and Japan.

Settlement of the West   The rapid expansion westwards in the USA in the nineteenth century owed a lot to the power of the US government, for example in the Homestead Act of 1862 regulating the allocation of lands to settlers. The Native Americans felt the full power of modern military might.

Shot, grape shot and canister shot   Shot is what was fired from cannons. Round lumps of metal were solid or round shot; pieces of metal were known as grapeshot; and canister shot, consisting of small metal balls packaged in a brass container, was an anti-personnel device similar to grapeshot, but made up of larger pieces of metal.

Shrapnel   A British invention. A spherical case shell contained bullets and a timed fuse. When fired, the explosion broke the case and sent the bullets flying among the enemy. The British commander Wellington used it quite extensively.

Slavs   People from eastern and central Europe, often the Balkans, but also Russia. The Austro-Hungarian Empire contained many Slavs.

Smoothbore musket   The inside of the barrels of smoothbore muskets, as the name suggests, was smooth and this limited their range. They were fired from the shoulder while standing. Muskets would later be replaced by rifles.

Splendid isolation   This term, coined in 1896, refers to a desire not to be allied to other countries, therefore allowing freedom of action. It was called 'splendid' because Britain had made the decision from a position of strength and it allowed it to focus on its empire rather than be dragged into European affairs.

Standing army   The permanent army maintained by a state in peacetime.

Stuka   Also known as the Junkers Ju87, this was a German dive-bomber and ground-attack aircraft, which played a significant role in the early *Blitzkrieg* attacks.

Tactics and strategy   Tactics relate to how a battle is fought, the arrangement of forces, the timing and nature of attacks, and how defence is organised. Strategy is the wider conduct, organisation and planning of campaigns or even whole wars.

Total war   War which involves the whole resources, both economic and human, of the countries involved, often with regime change as an aim rather than merely gaining limited lands.

U-boat   An abbreviation for *Unterseeboot* or submarine. U-boats were a major threat in both world wars to Britain as they hit merchant ships bringing essential raw materials, food and war supplies from North America. The British relied on their surface ships to enforce the blockade of Germany.

V-1 and V-2 rockets   German weapons used towards the end of the war. They had a terrifying impact on London, with the V-1 delivering 1 ton of high explosives. However, it could be shot down by anti-aircraft guns. The V-2 was more devastating as it flew at over 2000 miles per hour and could not be seen, and thus spread considerable fear. They were mostly used against civilian targets.

Verdun   The battle lasted from February to December 1916. The German aim was to inflict heavy casualties on the French so that the French army would collapse. One reason why Britain launched the Somme offensive was to take some pressure off the French. The French line held, but the battle of Verdun resulted in some 700,000 casualties.

War economy   All economic resources are employed for the war and resources are controlled and allocated by the state for the war effort.

War of Italian independence   After 1815, Austria dominated Italy, which was divided into a number of states. Central Italy was ruled by the pope and the south by the King of Naples. The Italian state of Piedmont led a movement for greater unity and obtained French support, leading to French armies fighting Austria in northern Italy in 1859. Fuller unity came when a volunteer force under Garibaldi invaded the south and linked up with Piedmontese forces, leading to the formation of a new Kingdom of Italy in 1861.

Western Front   The name given to fighting along the defensive lines drawn up from November 1914 from the Belgian coast to the Swiss border. The fighting on this front in Belgium and France continued until 1918.

Zeppelin raids   German airships that travelled at about 85 miles per hour and could deliver about two tons of bombs. They were used in raids against British cities.

Further reading

Larry Addington, *The Patterns of War Since the Eighteenth Century*, Indiana University Press, 1994.

Geoffrey Best, *War and Society in Revolutionary Europe*, Fontana, 1982.

Jeremy Black, *Warfare in the Eighteenth Century*, Cassell, 1999.

Brian Bond, *The Pursuit of Victory*, Oxford University Press, 1996.

David Chandler, *Napoleon*, Pen & Sword, 2000.

C.J. Esdaile, *The Wars of Napoleon*, Longman, 1995.

J.F.C. Fuller, *The Conduct of War, 1789–1961*, Da Capo Press, 1992.

Michael Glover, *Waterloo to Mons*, Cassell, 1980.

Robert Harvey, *The War of Wars: The Epic Struggle Between Britain and France: 1789–1815*, Constable, 2007.

Brian Holden Reid, *The American Civil War*, Cassell, 1999.

Robert Johnson, *The Changing Nature of Warfare*, Studymates, 2002.

Michael Howard, *War in European History*, Oxford University Press, 2009.

John Keegan, *The Second World War*, Hutchinson, 1989.

B.H. Liddell-Hart, *History of the First World War*, Pan, 2014.

B.H. Liddell-Hart, *History of the Second World War*, Pan, 2014.

Kenneth Macksey, *Technology in War*, Guild Publishing, 1986.

Kenneth Macksey, *The Penguin Encyclopedia of Weapons and Military Technology*, Penguin, 1995.

William McElwee, *The Art of War: Waterloo to Mons*, Purnell, 1974.

James McPherson, *Battle Cry of Freedom*, Oxford University Press, 1988.

Gary Mead, *The Good Soldier: The Biography of Douglas Haig*, Atlantic Books, 2007.

Andrew Roberts, *The Storm of War: A New History of the Second World War*, Penguin, 2010.

Gunther Rothenberg, *The Art of Warfare in the Age of Napoleon*, Spellmount, 1997.

Gary Sheffield, *The Chief: Douglas Haig and the British Army*, Aurum, 2011.

Neil Stewart, *The Changing Nature of Warfare 1700–1945*, Hodder Education, 2002.

Hew Strachan, *European Armies and the Conduct of War*, Routledge, 1983.

Hew Strachan, *The First World War*, Cassell, 1999.

Alexander Watson, *Ring of Steel*, Penguin, 2014.

Geoffrey Wawro, *Warfare and Society in Europe 1792–1914*, Routledge, 2000.

Index